卞尺丹几乙し丹卞と
Translated Language Learning

The Adventures of Pinocchio

匹诺曹历险记

Carlo Collodi
卡罗·科洛迪

English / **普通**话

Copyright © 2024 Tranzlaty
All rights reserved
Published by Tranzlaty
ISBN: 978-1-83566-706-4
Le Avventure di Pinocchio. Storia di un Burattino
Original text by Carlo Callodi
First published in Italianin 1883
Illustrated By Alice Carsey
www.tranzlaty.com

The Piece of Wood that Laughed and Cried like a Child
像孩子一样欢笑和哭泣的木头

Centuries ago there lived...
几个世纪前,那里住着...
"A king!" my little readers will say immediately
"国王!"
No, children, you are mistaken
不,孩子们,你们弄错了
Once upon a time there was a piece of wood
很久很久以前,有一块木头
the wood was in the shop of an old carpenter
这些木头在一个老木匠的店里
this old carpenter was named Master Antonio
这位老木匠名叫安东尼奥大师
Everybody, however, called him Master. Cherry
然而,每个人都称他为师父。樱桃
they called him Master. Cherry on account of his nose
他们称他为师父。樱桃因为他的鼻子
his nose was always as red and polished as a ripe cherry
他的鼻子总是像成熟的樱桃一样红润亮丽
Master Cherry set eyes upon the piece of wood
Cherry 大师盯上了那块木头
his face beamed with delight when he saw the log
当他看到那根木头时,他的脸上洋溢着喜悦的笑容
he rubbed his hands together with satisfaction
他满意地搓了搓手
and the kind master softly spoke to himself
善良的主人轻声自言自语
"This wood has come to me at the right moment"
"这木头来得正是时候"
"I have been planning to make a new table"

"我一直在计划制作一张新桌子"
"it is perfect for the leg of a little table"
"非常适合放在小桌子的腿上"

He immediately went out to find a sharp axe
他立即出去找了一把锋利的斧头

he was going to remove the bark of the wood first
他要先把木头的树皮去掉

and then he was going to remove any rough surface
然后他要去除任何粗糙的表面

and he was just about to strike the wood with his axe
他正要用斧头敲打木头

but just before he struck the wood he heard something
但就在他敲击木头之前,他听到了什么

"Do not strike me so hard!" a small voice implored
"别这么重打我!"一个小小的声音恳求道

He turned his terrified eyes all around the room
他把恐惧的眼睛转遍了房间

where could the little voice possibly have come from?
那个小声音可能是从哪里传来的呢?

he looked everywhere, but he saw nobody!
他到处找,却什么也没看到!

He looked under the bench, but there was nobody
他看了看长凳下面,但没有人

he looked into a cupboard that was always shut
他看着一个总是关着的橱柜

but there was nobody inside the cupboard either
但橱柜里也没有人

he looked into a basket where he kept sawdust
他看向一个装着锯末的篮子

there was nobody in the basket of sawdust either
锯末篮子里也没有人

at last he even opened the door of the shop
最后,他甚至打开了商店的门

and he glanced up and down the empty street

他上下扫视着空荡荡的街道
But there was no one to be seen in the street either
但街上也没有人
"Who, then, could it be?" he asked himself
"那么,那会是谁呢?"
at last he laughed and scratched his wig
最后,他笑了起来,挠了挠他的假发
"I see how it is," he said to himself, amused
"我明白怎么回事了,"他自言自语道,被逗乐了
"evidently the little voice was all my imagination"
"显然,那个小小的声音就是我的全部想象"
"Let us set to work again," he concluded
"让我们重新开始工作吧,"他总结道
he picked up his axe again and set to work
他再次拿起斧头开始工作
he struck a tremendous blow to the piece of wood
他狠狠地砸在了那块木头上
"Oh! oh! you have hurt me!" cried the little voice
"哦!哦!你伤害了我!"
it was exactly the same voice as it was before
那声音和以前一模一样
This time Master. Cherry was petrified
这次是师父。Cherry 被吓坏了
His eyes popped out of his head with fright
他的眼睛惊恐地从脑袋里冒出来
his mouth remained open and his tongue hung out
他的嘴一直张着,舌头伸出来
his tongue almost came to the end of his chin
他的舌头几乎到了下巴的末端
and he looked just like a face on a fountain
他看起来就像喷泉上的一张脸
Master. Cherry first had to recover from his fright
主人。Cherry 首先必须从他的恐惧中恢复过来
the use of his speech returned to him

他又回到了他面前
and he began to talk in a stutter;
他开始结结巴巴地说话；
"where on earth could that little voice have come from?"
"那个小声音到底是从哪里传来的？"
"could it be that this piece of wood has learned to cry?"
"难道这块木头已经学会了哭泣？"
"I cannot believe it," he said to himself
"我简直不敢相信，"他对自己说
"This piece of wood is nothing but a log for fuel"
"这块木头不过是一根燃料用的原木"
"it is just like all the logs of wood I have"
"它就像我所有的原木一样"
"it would only just suffice to boil a saucepan of beans"
"煮一锅豆子就够了"
"Can anyone be hidden inside this piece of wood?"
"这块木头里藏着人吗？"
"If anyone is inside, so much the worse for him"
"如果有人在里面，对他来说就更糟了"
"I will finish him at once," he threatened the wood
"我马上就干掉他，"他威胁着木头
he seized the poor piece of wood and beat it
他抓住那块可怜的木头，敲打它
he mercilessly hit it against the walls of the room
他无情地将它砸在了房间的墙壁上
Then he stopped to see if he could hear the little voice
然后他停下来，看看他是否能听到那个小小的声音
He waited two minutes, nothing. Five minutes, nothing
他等了两分钟，什么也没等。五分钟，什么都没有
he waited another ten minutes, still nothing!
他又等了十分钟，还是什么都没有！

"I see how it is," he then said to himself
"我明白怎么回事了，"他接着自言自语道
he forced himself to laugh and pushed up his wig
他强迫自己笑起来，把假发推了起来
"evidently the little voice was all my imagination!"
"显然，那个小小的声音完全是我的想象！"
"Let us set to work again," he decided, nervously
"我们再开始工作吧，"他紧张地决定
next he started to polish the bit of wood
接下来，他开始擦亮那块木头
but while polishing he heard the same little voice
但是在擦亮的时候，他听到了同样的小声音
this time the little voice was laughing uncontrollably
这一次，那个小声音控制不住地笑了起来
"Stop! you are tickling me all over!" it said
"住手！你把我浑身挠痒痒！
poor Master. Cherry fell down as if struck by lightning
可怜的师父。Cherry 像被闪电击中一样倒下
sometime later he opened his eyes again
过了一会儿，他又睁开了眼睛
he found himself seated on the floor of his workshop
他发现自己坐在工作室的地板上
His face was very changed from before
他的脸色和以前大不相同
and even the end of his nose had changed
甚至他的鼻子末端也发生了变化
his nose was not its usual bright crimson colour
他的鼻子不是平常明亮的深红色
his nose had become icy blue from the fright
他的鼻子因为惊吓而变得冰蓝色

Master. Cherry Gives the Wood Away
主人。Cherry 放弃了木材

At that moment someone knocked at the door
就在这时,有人敲了敲门
"Come in," said the carpenter to the visitor
"进来吧,"木匠对来访者说
he didn't have the strength to rise to his feet
他没有力气站起来
A lively little old man walked into the shop
一个活泼的小老头走进了商店
this lively little man was called Geppetto
这个活泼的小个子叫 Geppetto
although there was another name he was known by
虽然他有另一个名字
there was a group of naughty neighbourhood boys
有一群顽皮的邻居男孩
when they wished to anger him they called him pudding
当他们想激怒他时,他们就称他为布丁
there is a famous yellow pudding made from Indian corn
有一种著名的用印度玉米制成的黄色布丁
and Geppetto's wig looks just like this famous pudding
而 Geppetto 的假发看起来就像这个著名的布丁
Geppetto was a very fiery little old man
Geppetto 是一个非常火爆的小老头
Woe to him who called him pudding!
那叫他布丁的人有祸了!
when furious there was no holding him back
当他愤怒时,没有什么能阻止他
"Good-day, Master. Antonio," said Geppetto
"你好,师父。安东尼奥,"杰佩托说

"what are you doing there on the floor?"
"你在地板上做什么？"
"I am teaching the alphabet to the ants"
"我在教蚂蚁字母表"
"I can't imagine what good it does to you"
"我无法想象这对你有什么好处"
"What has brought you to me, neighbour Geppetto?"
"你怎么来找我呢，邻居杰佩托？"
"My legs have brought me here to you"
"我的双腿把我带到了你身边"
"But let me tell you the truth, Master. Antonio"
"但让我告诉你实话，主人。安东尼奥"
"the real reason I came is to ask a favour of you"
"我来的真正原因是想请你帮个忙"
"Here I am, ready to serve you," replied the carpenter
"我在这里，准备为你服务，"木匠回答
and he got off the floor and onto his knees
他从地板上站起来，跪在地上
"This morning an idea came into my head"
"今天早上，我脑子里冒出了一个主意"
"Let us hear the idea that you had"
"让我们听听你的想法"
"I thought I would make a beautiful wooden puppet"
"我想我会做一个漂亮的木偶"
"a puppet that could dance and fence"
"会跳舞和击剑的木偶"
"a puppet that can leap like an acrobat"
"一个可以像杂技演员一样跳跃的木偶"
"With this puppet I could travel about the world!"
"有了这个木偶，我可以环游世界！"
"the puppet would let me earn a piece of bread"
"木偶会让我赚一块面包"
"and the puppet would let me earn a glass of wine"

"傀儡会让我赚一杯酒"

"What do you think of my idea, Antonio?"
"你觉得我的想法怎么样,安东尼奥?"

"Bravo, pudding!" exclaimed the little voice
"太棒了,布丁!"

it was impossible to know where the voice had came from
不可能知道声音是从哪里来的

Geppetto didn't like hearing himself called pudding
Geppetto 不喜欢听到自己叫布丁

you can imagine he became as red as a turkey
你可以想象他变得像火鸡一样红

"Why do you insult me?" he asked his friend
他问他的朋友:"你为什么侮辱我?

"Who insults you?" his friend replied
"谁侮辱你?"

"You called me pudding!" Geppetto accused him
"你叫我布丁!"杰佩托指责他

"It was not I!" Antonio honestly said
"不是我!"安东尼奥诚实地说

"Do you think I called myself pudding?"
"你觉得我叫自己布丁吗?"

"It was you, I say!", "No!", "Yes!", "No!"
"是你!","不!","是的!","不!"

becoming more and more angry, they came to blows
他们越来越生气,开始大打出手

they flew at each other and bit and fought and scratched
他们互相飞来飞去,咬人、打架、抓挠

as quickly as it had started the fight was over again
它刚开始,战斗就又结束了

Geppetto had the carpenter's grey wig between his teeth

- 8 -

Geppetto 的牙齿夹着木匠的灰色假发
and Master. Antonio had Geppetto's yellow wig
和大师。安东尼奥戴着 Geppetto 的黄色假发
"Give me back my wig" screamed Master. Antonio
「把我的假发还给我，」师父尖叫着。安东尼奥
"and you give me back my wig" screamed Master. Cherry
"你把我的假发还给我，"师父尖叫道。樱桃
"let us be friends again" they agreed
"让我们再次成为朋友"他们同意
The two old men gave each other their wigs back
两位老人把假发还给了对方
and the old men shook each other's hands
老人们互相握手
they swore that all had been forgiven
他们发誓说，一切都被宽恕了
they would remain friends to the end of their lives
他们将保持朋友关系，直到生命的尽头
"Well, then, neighbour Geppetto" said the carpenter
"那么，邻居杰佩托，"木匠说
he asked "what is the favour that you wish of me?"
他问道："你希望我有什么好处？"
this would prove that peace was made
这将证明和平已经达成
"I want a little wood to make my puppet"
"我想要一点木头来做我的木偶"
"will you give me some wood?"
"你能给我点柴火吗？"
Master. Antonio was delighted to get rid of the wood
主人。安东尼奥很高兴能摆脱这些木头
he immediately went to his work bench
他立即去了他的工作台
and he brought back the piece of wood
他把那块木头带回来了

the piece of wood that had caused him so much fear
那块让他如此恐惧的木头

he was bringing the piece of wood to his friend
他把那块木头拿给他的朋友

but then the piece of wood started to shake!
但随后那块木头开始摇晃!

the piece of wood wriggled violently out of his hands
那块木头猛烈地从他的手中扭动着

this piece of wood knew how to make trouble!
这块木头懂得捣乱!

with all its might it struck against poor Geppetto
它用尽全力打击了可怜的 Geppetto

and it hit him right on his poor dried-up shins
它正好击中了他可怜的干涸的小腿

you can imagine the cry that Geppetto gave
你可以想象 Geppetto 发出的呼喊

"is that the courteous way you make your presents?"
"你是这样送礼物的礼貌吗?"

"You have almost lamed me, Master. Antonio!"
"师父,你差点把我瘸了。安东尼奥!"

"I swear to you that it was not I!"
"我向你发誓,那不是我!"

"Do you think I did this to myself?"
"你觉得我对自己做了这些吗?"

"The wood is entirely to blame!"
"木头完全是罪魁祸首!"

"I know that it was the wood"
"我知道那是木头"

"but it was you that hit my legs with it!"
"可是你用它打了我的腿!"

"I did not hit you with it!"
"我没有用它打你!"

"Liar!" exclaimed Geppetto

"骗子！"
"Geppetto, don't insult me or I will call you Pudding!"
"Geppetto，不要侮辱我，否则我会叫你布丁！"
"Knave!", "Pudding!", "Donkey!"
"Knave！"，"布丁！"，"驴子！"
"Pudding!", "Baboon!", "Pudding!"
"布丁！"，"狒狒！"，"布丁！"
Geppetto was mad with rage all over again
Geppetto 又一次被愤怒冲昏了头脑
he had been called been called pudding three times!
他被叫了三次布丁！
he fell upon the carpenter and they fought desperately
他倒在木匠身上，他们拼命地打架
this battle lasted just as long as the first
这场战斗持续的时间与第一场战斗一样长
Master. Antonio had two more scratches on his nose
主人。安东尼奥的鼻子上又有两处划痕
his adversary had lost two buttons off his waistcoat
他的对手从背心上掉了两颗纽扣
Their accounts being thus squared, they shook hands
他们的账目就这样平淡无奇了，他们握了手言和。
and they swore to remain good friends for the rest of their lives
他们发誓要终生保持好朋友关系
Geppetto carried off his fine piece of wood
Geppetto 带走了他的上好木头
he thanked Master. Antonio and limped back to his house
他感谢师父。安东尼奥一瘸一拐地回到了他的房子

Geppetto Names his Puppet Pinocchio
Geppetto 将他的木偶命名为 Pinocchio

Geppetto lived in a small ground-floor room
Geppetto 住在一楼的一个小房间里

his room was only lighted from the staircase
他的房间只有楼梯上的灯光

The furniture could not have been simpler
家具再简单不过了

a rickety chair, a poor bed, and a broken table
一把摇摇晃晃的椅子、一张简陋的床和一张破桌子

At the end of the room there was a fireplace
房间的尽头有一个壁炉

but the fire was painted, and gave no fire
但火是涂上油漆的,没有起火

and by the painted fire was a painted saucepan
在彩绘的火堆旁是一个彩绘的平底锅

and the painted saucepan was boiling cheerfully
彩绘的平底锅欢快地沸腾着

a cloud of smoke rose exactly like real smoke
一团烟雾升起,就像真正的烟雾一样
Geppetto reached home and took out his tools
Geppetto 回到家并拿出了他的工具
and he immediately set to work on the piece of wood
他立即开始制作那块木头
he was going to cut out and model his puppet
他要剪下来给他的木偶做模型
"What name shall I give him?" he said to himself
"我该给他起什么名字呢?"
"I think I will call him Pinocchio"
"我想我会叫他匹诺曹"
"It is a name that will bring him luck"
"这个名字会给他带来好运"
"I once knew a whole family called Pinocchio"
"我曾经认识一个叫匹诺曹的全家人"
"There was Pinocchio the father and Pinocchio the mother"
"有匹诺曹的父亲和匹诺曹的母亲"
"and there were Pinocchio the children"
"还有匹诺曹的孩子们"
"and all of them did well in life"
"他们都过得很好"
"The richest of them was a beggar"
"他们中最富有的是一个乞丐"
he had found a good name for his puppet
他为他的傀儡找到了一个好名字
so he began to work in good earnest
所以他开始认真地工作
he first made his hair, and then his forehead
他先做了头发,然后做了额头
and then he worked carefully on his eyes
然后他小心翼翼地抚摸着自己的眼睛

Geppetto thought he noticed the strangest thing
Geppetto 认为他注意到了最奇怪的事情

he was sure he saw the eyes move!
他确信他看到了眼睛在移动!

the eyes seemed to look fixedly at him
那双眼睛似乎定定地看着他

Geppetto got angry from being stared at
Geppetto 因被盯着而生气

the wooden eyes wouldn't let him out of their sight
那双木头的眼睛不会让他离开他们的视线

"Wicked wooden eyes, why do you look at me?"
"邪恶的木眼,你为什么看着我?"

but the piece of wood made no answer
但那块木头没有回答

He then proceeded to carve the nose
然后他开始雕刻鼻子

but as soon as he had made the nose it began to grow
可是他一把鼻子弄好了,鼻子就开始长起来了

And the nose grew, and grew, and grew
鼻子长大了,长大了,长大了

in a few minutes it had become an immense nose
几分钟后,它就变成了一个巨大的鼻子

it seemed as if it would never stop growing
它似乎永远不会停止增长

Poor Geppetto tired himself out with cutting it off
可怜的 Geppetto 把它剪掉了,让自己疲惫不堪

but the more he cut, the longer the nose grew!
但是他剪得越多,鼻子就越长!

The mouth was not even completed yet
嘴巴甚至还没有完成

but it already began to laugh and deride him
但它已经开始嘲笑和嘲笑他了

"Stop laughing!" said Geppetto, provoked
"别笑了!"

but he might as well have spoken to the wall
但他还不如对着墙说话
"Stop laughing, I say!" he roared in a threatening tone
"别笑了,我说!"他用威胁的语气吼道
The mouth then ceased laughing
然后嘴巴停止了笑
but the face put out its tongue as far as it would go
但那张脸却把舌头伸得尽可能远
Geppetto did not want to spoil his handiwork
Geppetto 不想破坏他的手艺
so he pretended not to see, and continued his labours
所以他假装没看见,继续他的工作
After the mouth he fashioned the chin
在嘴巴之后,他塑造了下巴

then the throat and then the shoulders
然后是喉咙，然后是肩膀
then he carved the stomach and made the arms hands
然后他切开了肚子，使手臂成为了手
now Geppetto worked on making hands for his puppet
现在 Geppetto 致力于为他的木偶制作手
and in a moment he felt his wig snatched from his head
刹那一刻，他感觉到他的假发从他的头上被抢走了
He turned round, and what did he see?
他转过身来，看到了什么？
He saw his yellow wig in the puppet's hand
他看到木偶手中的黄色假发
"Pinocchio! Give me back my wig instantly!"
"匹诺曹！马上把我的假发还给我！
But Pinocchio did anything but return him his wig
但匹诺曹什么也没做，只是把他的假发还给了他
Pinocchio put the wig on his own head instead!
匹诺曹把假发戴在了自己的头上！
Geppetto didn't like this insolent and derisive behaviour
Geppetto 不喜欢这种无礼和嘲笑的行为
he felt sadder and more melancholy than he had ever felt
他感到比以往任何时候都更悲伤、更忧郁
turning to Pinocchio, he said "You young rascal!"
他转向匹诺曹说："你这个年轻的流氓！
"I have not even completed you yet"
"我甚至还没有完成你"
"and you are already failing to respect to your father!"
"你已经没有尊重你的父亲了！"
"That is bad, my boy, very bad!"
"太糟糕了，我的孩子，非常糟糕！"
And he dried a tear from his cheek

"他擦干了脸颊上的一滴泪水

The legs and the feet remained to be done
腿和脚还有待完成
but he soon regretted giving Pinocchio feet
但他很快就后悔给匹诺曹脚
as thanks he received a kick on the point of his nose
作为感谢,他的鼻尖被踢了一脚
"I deserve it!" he said to himself
"我活该!"
"I should have thought of it sooner!"
"我应该早点想到的!"
"Now it is too late to do anything about it!"
"现在做任何事情都太晚了!"
He then took the puppet under the arms
然后他把木偶夹在腋下
and he placed him on the floor to teach him to walk
就把他放在地上,教他走路
Pinocchio's legs were stiff and he could not move
匹诺曹的双腿僵硬,动弹不得
but Geppetto led him by the hand
但 Geppetto 牵着他的手
and he showed him how to put one foot before the other
他教他怎样把一只脚放在另一只脚前面
eventually Pinocchio's legs became limber
最终,匹诺曹的双腿变得灵活
and soon he began to walk by himself
不久,他开始自己走路了
and he began to run about the room
他开始在房间里跑来跑去
then he got out of the house door
然后他走出了屋门
and he jumped into the street and escaped
他跳到街上逃走了

poor Geppetto rushed after him
可怜的 Geppetto 冲上去追赶他

of course he was not able to overtake him
当然,他没能超过他

because Pinocchio leaped in front of him like a hare
因为匹诺曹像野兔一样跳到他面前

and he knocked his wooden feet against the pavement
他把木脚敲在人行道上

it made as much clatter as twenty pairs of peasants' clogs
它发出的咔哒声相当于二十双农民的木屐

"Stop him! stop him!" shouted Geppetto
"住手他!阻止他!

but the people in the street stood still in astonishment
但街上的人们却惊讶地站着不动

they had never seen a wooden puppet running like a horse
他们从未见过像马一样奔跑的木偶

and they laughed and laughed at Geppetto's misfortune
他们嘲笑杰佩托的不幸

At last, as good luck would have it, a soldier arrived
最后,幸运的是,一名士兵来了

the soldier had heard the uproar
士兵听到了骚动

he imagined that a colt had escaped from his master
他想象着一匹小马驹从他的主人那里逃走了

he planted himself in the middle of the road
他把自己栽在了路中间

he waited with the determined purpose of stopping him
他等待着,决心阻止他

thus he would prevent the chance of worse disasters
这样他就可以防止更糟糕的灾难发生

Pinocchio saw the soldier barricading the whole street
匹诺曹看到那个士兵封锁了整条街
so he endeavoured to take him by surprise
所以他努力让他措手不及
he planned to run between his legs
他打算从他的两腿之间跑来跑去
but the soldier was too clever for Pinocchio
但这个士兵对匹诺曹来说太聪明了
The soldier caught him cleverly by the nose
士兵巧妙地抓住了他的鼻子
and he gave Pinocchio back to Geppetto
他把匹诺曹还给了 Geppetto
Wishing to punish him, Geppetto intended to pull his ears
为了惩罚他，Geppetto 打算揪他的耳朵
But he could not find Pinocchio's ears!
但他找不到匹诺曹的耳朵！
And do you know the reason why?
你知道为什么吗？
he had forgotten to make him any ears
他忘了给他做任何耳朵
so then he took him by the collar
于是他就抓住了他的衣领
"We will go home at once," he threatened him
"我们马上回家，"他威胁他
"as soon as we arrive we will settle our accounts"
"我们一到就算账"
At this information Pinocchio threw himself on the ground
听到这个消息，匹诺曹扑倒在地上
he refused to go another step
他拒绝再向前迈进
a crowd of inquisitive people began to assemble
一群好奇的人开始聚集

they made a ring around them
他们在他们周围做了一个环
Some of them said one thing, some another
他们中的一些人说了一件事，有些人说了另一件事
"Poor puppet!" said several of the onlookers
"可怜的傀儡！"
"he is right not to wish to return home!"
"他不想回家是对的！"
"Who knows how Geppetto will beat him!"
"谁知道 Geppetto 会怎么打败他！"
"Geppetto seems a good man!"
"Geppetto 看起来是个好人！"
"but with boys he is a regular tyrant!"
"可是，在男孩子们面前，他就是个普通的暴君！"
"don't leave that poor puppet in his hands"
"不要把那个可怜的傀儡留在他手里"
"he is quite capable of tearing him to pieces!"
"他完全有能力把他撕成碎片！"
from what was said the soldier had to step in again
从他们所说的话来看，士兵不得不再次介入
the soldier gave Pinocchio his freedom
士兵给了匹诺曹自由
and the soldier led Geppetto to prison
士兵把 Geppetto 带到了监狱
The poor man was not ready to defend himself with words
这个可怜的人不准备用言语为自己辩护
he cried like a calf "Wretched boy!"
他像小牛一样喊道："可怜的孩子！
"to think how I laboured to make him a good puppet!"
"想想我怎么费力才把他变成个好木偶！"
"But all I have done serves me right!"
"可是我所做的一切都对我有益！"

"I should have thought of it sooner!"
"我应该早点想到的！"

The Talking Little Cricket Scolds Pinocchio
会说话的小蟋蟀责骂匹诺曹

poor Geppetto was being taken to prison
可怜的 Geppetto 被关进监狱
all of this was not his fault, of course
当然，这一切都不是他的错
he had not done anything wrong at all
他根本没有做错任何事情
and that little imp Pinocchio found himself free
那个小鬼匹诺曹发现自己自由了
he had escaped from the clutches of the soldier
他从士兵的魔掌中逃脱了
and he ran off as fast as his legs could carry him
他用双腿能载着他跑得最快的速度
he wanted to reach home as quickly as possible
他想尽快回家
therefore he rushed across the fields
因此他冲过田野
in his mad hurry he jumped over thorny hedges
在他疯狂的匆忙中，他跳过了荆棘丛生的树篱
and he jumped across ditches full of water
他跳过了满是水的沟渠
Arriving at the house, he found the door ajar
到了房子里，他发现门半开着
He pushed it open, went in, and fastened the latch
他推开门，走进去，把门闩锁上
he threw himself on the floor of his house
他扑倒在自己家的地板上
and he gave a great sigh of satisfaction

他满意地长舒了一口气

But soon he heard someone in the room
但很快他就听到房间里有人

something was making a sound like "Cri-cri-cri!"
有什么东西发出了"吵-吵-吵"的声音。

"Who calls me?" said Pinocchio in a fright
"谁叫我？"匹诺曹惊恐地说

"It is I!" answered a voice
"是我！"

Pinocchio turned round and saw a little cricket
匹诺曹转过身来，看到了一只小蟋蟀

the cricket was crawling slowly up the wall
蟋蟀慢慢地爬上了墙

"Tell me, little cricket, who may you be?"
"告诉我，小蟋蟀，你是谁？"

"who I am is the talking cricket"
"我是谁就是会说话的蟋蟀"

"and I have lived in this room a hundred years or more"
"我已经在这个房间里住了一百年或更长时间"

"Now, however, this room is mine," said the puppet
"可是，现在这个房间是我的了，"木偶说

"if you would do me the pleasure, go away at once"
"如果你愿意，就马上走吧。"

"and when you're gone, please never come back"
"当你走了，请永远不要回来"

"I will not go until I have told you a great truth"
"除非我告诉你一个伟大的真理，否则我不会去"

"Tell it me, then, and be quick about it"
"那么，告诉我，快点"

"Woe to those boys who rebel against their parents"
"那些悖逆父母的男孩有祸了"

"and woe to boys who run away from home"

"离家出走的男孩有祸了"
"They will never come to any good in the world"
"他们永远不会在世界上得到任何好处"
"and sooner or later they will repent bitterly"
"他们迟早会痛悔"
"Sing all you want you little cricket"
"唱你想唱的一切,你这只小蟋蟀"
"and feel free to sing as long as you please"
"只要你愿意,就可以随意唱歌"
"For me, I have made up my mind to run away"
"对我来说,我已经下定决心要逃跑了"
"tomorrow at daybreak I will run away for good"
"明天黎明时分,我将永远逃跑"
"if I remain I shall not escape my fate"
"如果我留下来,我就逃脱不了了我的命运"
"it is the same fate as all other boys"
"这和其他男孩的命运是一样的。"
"if I stay I shall be sent to school"
"如果我留下来,我就会被送去上学"
"and I shall be made to study by love or by force"
"我将因爱或被迫学习"
"I tell you in confidence, I have no wish to learn"
"我私信地告诉你,我不想学习"
"it is much more amusing to run after butterflies"
"追逐蝴蝶更有趣"
"I prefer climbing trees with my time"
"我更喜欢利用时间爬树"
"and I like taking young birds out of their nests"
"我喜欢把幼鸟从巢里带出来"
"Poor little goose" interjected the talking cricket
"可怜的小鹅,"会说话的蟋蟀插嘴说
"don't you know you will grow up a perfect donkey?"
"你不知道你会长成一头完美的驴吗?"

"and every one will make fun of you"
"每个人都会取笑你"
Pinocchio was not pleased with what he heard
匹诺曹对他所听到的并不满意
"Hold your tongue, you wicked, ill-omened croaker!"
"住嘴,你这个邪恶的、不祥的黄花鱼!"
But the little cricket was patient and philosophical
但小蟋蟀很有耐心,也很有哲理
he didn't become angry at this impertinence
他并没有因为这种无礼而生气
he continued in the same tone as he had before
他继续用和刚才一样的语气
"perhaps you really do not wish to go to school"
"也许你真的不想去上学"
"so why not at least learn a trade?"
"那么为什么不至少学一门手艺呢?"
"a job will enable you to earn a piece of bread!"
"一份工作就能让你赚到一块面包!"
"What do you want me to tell you?" replied Pinocchio
"你要我告诉你什么?"
he was beginning to lose patience with the little cricket
他开始对这只小蟋蟀失去耐心
"there are many trades in the world I could do"
"世界上有很多行业我可以做"
"but only one calling really takes my fancy"
"但只有一个召唤真正让我心动"
"And what calling is it that takes your fancy?"
"那么,你喜欢什么召唤呢?"
"to eat, and to drink, and to sleep"
"吃、喝、睡"
"I am called to amuse myself all day"
"我被召唤整天自娱自乐"
"to lead a vagabond life from morning to night"

"从早到晚过流浪生活"
the talking little cricket had a reply for this
会说话的小蟋蟀对此有个回答
"most who follow that trade end in hospital or prison"
"大多数从事这种交易的人都在医院或监狱里"
"Take care, you wicked, ill-omened croaker"
"小心点,你这个邪恶的、不祥的黄花鱼"
"Woe to you if I fly into a passion!"
"如果我飞起来激动起来,你就有祸了!"
"Poor Pinocchio I really pity you!"
"可怜的匹诺曹,我真的很可怜你!"
"Why do you pity me?"
"你为什么可怜我?"
"I pity you because you are a puppet"
"我可怜你,因为你是个傀儡"
"and I pity you because you have a wooden head"
"我可怜你,因为你有个木头"
At these last words Pinocchio jumped up in a rage
听到这最后几个字,匹诺曹气得跳了起来
he snatched a wooden hammer from the bench
他从长凳上抓起一把木锤

and he threw the hammer at the talking cricket
他把锤子扔向那只会说话的蟋蟀

Perhaps he never meant to hit him
也许他从来没有打算打他

but unfortunately it struck him exactly on the head
但不幸的是,它正好击中了他的头

the poor Cricket had scarcely breath to cry "Cri-cri-cri!"
可怜的蟋蟀几乎喘不过气来喊道:"吵-吵-吵!

he remained dried up and flattened against the wall
他仍然干涸,平靠在墙上

The Flying Egg
飞蛋

The night was quickly catching up with Pinocchio
夜晚很快就赶上了匹诺曹

he remembered that he had eaten nothing all day
他记得自己一整天都没吃东西

he began to feel a gnawing in his stomach
他开始感到肚子在啃咬

the gnawing very much resembled appetite
啃咬很像食欲

After a few minutes his appetite had become hunger
几分钟后,他的胃口变得饥饿

and in little time his hunger became ravenous
不一会儿,他的饥饿就变得贪婪

Poor Pinocchio ran quickly to the fireplace
可怜的匹诺曹飞快地跑到壁炉前。

the fireplace where a saucepan was boiling
炖锅正在沸腾的壁炉

he was going to take off the lid
他要把盖子取下来

then he could see what was in it
然后他可以看到里面有什么
but the saucepan was only painted on the wall
但平底锅只画在墙上
You can imagine his feelings when he discovered this
你可以想象他发现这个时的感受
His nose, which was already long, became even longer
他的鼻子本来就很长,现在变得更长了
it must have grown by at least three inches
它必须至少长了3英寸
He then began to run about the room
然后他开始在房间里跑来跑去
he searched in the drawers and every imaginable place
他在抽屉里和所有能想象到的地方都找来找
he hoped to find a bit of bread or crust
他希望能找到一点面包或面包皮
perhaps he could find a bone left by a dog
也许他能找到狗留下的骨头
a little moldy pudding of Indian corn
一点发霉的印度玉米布丁
somewhere someone might have left a fish bone
某人可能留下了鱼骨头的地方
even a cherry stone would be enough
即使是一颗樱桃石也足够了
if only there was something that he could gnaw
要是有他能啃的东西就好了
But he could find nothing to get his teeth into
但他找不到任何可以咬牙切齿的东西
And in the meanwhile his hunger grew and grew
与此同时,他的饥饿感越来越大
Poor Pinocchio had no other relief than yawning
可怜的匹诺曹除了打哈欠之外没有其他的解脱
his yawns were so big his mouth almost reached his ears

他的哈欠太大了，嘴巴几乎要到了耳朵
and felt as if he were going to faint
他觉得自己好像要晕倒了
Then he began to cry desperately
然后他开始绝望地哭泣
"The talking little cricket was right"
"会说话的小蟋蟀是对的"
"I did wrong to rebel against my papa"
"我反抗我爸爸是错的"
"I should not have ran away from home"
"我不应该离家出走"
"If my papa were here I wouldn't be dying of yawning!"
"如果我爸爸在这里，我就不会打哈欠死了！"
"Oh! what a dreadful illness hunger is!"
"哦！饥饿是一种多么可怕的疾病啊！"
Just then he thought he saw something in the dust-heap
就在这时，他觉得自己在尘土堆里看到了什么
something round and white that looked like a hen's egg
看起来像鸡蛋的圆白色东西
he sprung up to his feet and seized hold of the egg
他跳起来，抓住了鸡蛋
It was indeed a hen's egg, as he thought
正如他所想的那样，这确实是一个母鸡的蛋
Pinocchio's joy was beyond description
匹诺曹的喜悦是无法形容的
he had to make sure that he wasn't just dreaming
他必须确保他不仅仅是在做梦
so he kept turning the egg over in his hands
所以他不停地把蛋在手里翻来覆去
he felt and kissed the egg
他摸到并亲吻了那个蛋

"And now, how shall I cook it?"
"那么,我该怎么煮呢?"
"Shall I make an omelet?"
"我做个煎蛋卷好吗?"
"it would be better to cook it in a saucer!"
"最好在碟子里煮!"
"Or would it not be more savory to fry it?"
"或者油炸不是更美味吗?"
"Or shall I simply boil the egg?"
"还是我干脆把鸡蛋煮熟?"
"No, the quickest way is to cook it in a saucer"
"不,最快的方法是在碟子里煮"
"I am in such a hurry to eat it!"
"我真急吃!"

Without loss of time he got an earthenware saucer
他没有浪费时间,得到了一个陶碟

he placed the saucer on a brazier full of red-hot embers
他把碟子放在一个装满炽热余烬的火盆上

he didn't have any oil or butter to use
他没有任何油或黄油可以使用。

so he poured a little water into the saucer
于是他往碟子里倒了一点水

and when the water began to smoke, crack!
当水开始冒烟时,噼里啪啦!

he broke the egg-shell over the saucer
他打破了碟子上的蛋壳

and he let the contents of the egg drop into the saucer
他让鸡蛋里的东西掉进碟子里

but the egg was not full of white and yolk
但鸡蛋里没有装满蛋白和蛋黄

instead, a little chicken popped out the egg
相反,一只小鸡从鸡蛋里弹出来

it was a very gay and polite little chicken
那是一只非常同性恋和有礼貌的小鸡
the little chicken made a beautiful courtesy
小鸡做了一个漂亮的礼节
"A thousand thanks, Master. Pinocchio"
「千谢万谢，师父。匹诺曹"
"you have saved me the trouble of breaking the shell"
"你省去了我破壳的麻烦"
"Adieu, until we meet again" the chicken said
"再见了，直到我们再次见面"鸡说
"Keep well, and my best compliments to all at home!"
"祝你身体健康，我向家里的所有人致以最诚挚的赞美！"
the little chicken spread its little wings
小鸡张开了它的小翅膀
and the little chicken darted through the open window
小鸡从敞开的窗户里飞奔而来

and then the little chicken flew out of sight
然后小鸡就飞出了视线
The poor puppet stood as if he had been bewitched
这个可怜的木偶站着，仿佛被施了魔法
his eyes were fixed, and his mouth was open
他的眼睛定着，嘴巴张着
and he still had the egg-shell in his hand
他手里还拿着蛋壳
slowly he Recovered from his stupefaction
他慢慢地从昏迷中恢复过来
and then he began to cry and scream
然后他开始哭泣和尖叫
he stamped his feet on the floor in desperation
他绝望地跺着脚跺着地板
amidst his sobs he gathered his thoughts
在他的啜泣中，他整理了自己的思绪
"Ah, indeed, the talking little cricket was right"
"啊，确实，那只会说话的小蟋蟀是对的"
"I should not have run away from home"
"我不应该离家出走"
"then I would not now be dying of hunger!"
"那我现在就不会饿死了！"
"and if my papa were here he would feed me"
"如果我爸爸在这里，他会喂我吃的"
"Oh! what a dreadful illness hunger is!"
"哦！饥饿是一种多么可怕的疾病啊！"
his stomach cried out more than ever
他的肚子比以往任何时候都更加呐喊
and he did not know how to quiet his hunger
他不知道如何平息他的饥饿
he thought about leaving the house
他想离开房子
perhaps he could make an excursion in the neighborhood

也许他可以在附近短途旅行
he hoped to find some charitable person
他希望找到一些慈善人士
maybe they would give him a piece of bread
也许他们会给他一块面包

Pinocchio's Feet Burn to Cinders
匹诺曹的脚烧成灰烬

It was an especially wild and stormy night
那是一个特别狂野和暴风雨的夜晚
The thunder was tremendously loud and fearful
雷声非常响亮和可怕
the lightning was so vivid that the sky seemed on fire
闪电是如此鲜艳，以至于天空似乎着火了
Pinocchio had a great fear of thunder
匹诺曹非常害怕打雷
but hunger can be stronger than fear
但饥饿可能比恐惧更强大
so he closed the door of the house
于是他关上了房子的门
and he made a desperate rush for the village
他拼命地冲向村子
he reached the village in a hundred bounds
他在一百个边界内到达了村庄
his tongue was hanging out of his mouth
他的舌头从嘴里伸出来
and he was panting for breath like a dog
他像条狗一样喘着粗气
But he found the village all dark and deserted
但他发现这个村庄一片漆黑，空无一人
The shops were closed and the windows were shut
商店关门了，窗户也关上了

and there was not so much as a dog in the street
街上连一条狗都没有

It seemed like he had arrived in the land of the dead
他似乎已经来到了死亡之地

Pinocchio was urged on by desperation and hunger
匹诺曹被绝望和饥饿催促着

he took hold of the bell of a house
他抓住了房子的钟声

and he began to ring the bell with all his might
他开始用尽全力敲响钟声

"That will bring somebody," he said to himself
"那会带人来的,"他对自己说

And it did bring somebody!
它确实带来了一些人!

A little old man appeared at a window
一个小老人出现在窗户前

the little old man still had a night-cap on his head
小老头头上还戴着一顶睡帽

he called to him angrily
他生气地叫他

"What do you want at such an hour?"
"你在这种时候想要什么?"

"Would you be kind enough to give me a little bread?"
"你能不能给我一点面包?"

the little old man was very obliging
小老头非常热心

"Wait there, I will be back directly"
"在那儿等着,我马上回来"

he thought it was one of the local rascals
他以为那是当地的一个流氓

they amuse themselves by ringing the house-bells at night
他们在晚上敲响门铃来自娱自乐

After half a minute the window opened again

半分钟后，窗户再次打开
the voice of the same little old man shouted to Pinocchio
同一个小老头的声音对匹诺曹喊道
"Come underneath and hold out your cap"
"到下面来，拿出你的帽子"
Pinocchio pulled off his cap and held it out
匹诺曹摘下帽子，伸出手来
but Pinocchio's cap was not filled with bread or food
但匹诺曹的帽子里没有装满面包或食物
an enormous basin of water was poured down on him
一大盆水倒在他身上
the water soaked him from head to foot
水从头到脚都浸湿了他
as if he had been a pot of dried-up geraniums
仿佛他是一罐干涸的天竺葵
He returned home like a wet chicken
他像一只湿鸡一样回到家
he was quite exhausted with fatigue and hunger
他因疲劳和饥饿而筋疲力尽
he no longer had the strength to stand
他再也没有力气站起来了
so he sat down and rested his damp and muddy feet
于是他坐下来，让湿漉漉的泥泞的脚休息一下
he put his feet on a brazier full of burning embers
他把脚放在一个装满燃烧余烬的火盆上
and then he fell asleep, exhausted from the day
然后他睡着了，一天累得精疲力尽
we all know that Pinocchio has wooden feet
我们都知道匹诺曹有木脚
and we know what happens to wood on burning embers
我们知道燃烧的余烬上会有什么变化
little by little his feet burnt away and became cinders

他的脚一点一点地烧掉,变成灰烬

Pinocchio continued to sleep and snore
匹诺曹继续睡觉和打鼾

his feet might as well have belonged to someone else
他的脚也可能属于别人

At last he awoke because someone was knocking at the door
最后,他醒来了,因为有人在敲门

"Who is there?" he asked, yawning and rubbing his eyes
"谁在那儿?"他问道,一边打哈欠,一边揉揉眼睛

"It is I!" answered a voice
"是我!"

And Pinocchio recognized Geppetto's voice
匹诺曹认出了 Geppetto 的声音

Geppetto Gives his own Breakfast to Pinocchio
Geppetto 将自己的早餐送给匹诺曹

Poor Pinocchio's eyes were still half shut from sleep
可怜的匹诺曹的眼睛仍然半闭着

he had not yet discovered what had happened
他还没有发现发生了什么

his feet had were completely burnt off
他的脚已经完全烧掉了

he heard the voice of his father at the door
他听到了他父亲在门口的声音

and he jumped off the chair he had slept on
他从他睡过的椅子上跳了下来

he wanted to run to the door and open it
他想跑到门前打开门

but he stumbled around and fell on the floor
但他跌跌撞撞地倒在了地板上

imagine having a sack of wooden ladles
想象一下有一袋木勺

imagine throwing the sack off the balcony
想象一下把麻袋从阳台上扔下来

that is was the sound of Pinocchio falling to the floor
那是匹诺曹倒在地板上的声音

"Open the door!" shouted Geppetto from the street
"开门！"

"Dear papa, I cannot," answered the puppet
"亲爱的爸爸，我不能，"木偶回答

and he cried and rolled about on the ground
他哭着在地上滚来滚去

"Why can't you open the door?"
"你怎么开不开门？"

"Because my feet have been eaten"
"因为我的脚被吃了"

"And who has eaten your feet?"
"谁吃了你的脚？"

Pinocchio looked around for something to blame
匹诺曹环顾四周，寻找可以责怪的东西

eventually he answered "the cat ate my feet"
"最后他回答说："猫吃了我的脚"

"Open the door, I tell you!" repeated Geppetto
"开门，我告诉你！"

"If you don't open it, you shall have the cat from me!"
"如果你不打开它，你就可以从我这里得到那只猫！"

"I cannot stand up, believe me"
"我站不起来，相信我"

"Oh, poor me!" lamented Pinocchio
"哦，可怜的我！"

"I shall have to walk on my knees for the rest of my life!"
"我得跪着走一辈子！"

Geppetto thought this was another one of the puppet's tricks
Geppetto 认为这是木偶的另一个伎俩

he thought of a means of putting an end to his tricks
他想到了一个办法来结束他的伎俩

he climbed up the wall and got in through the window
他爬上墙,从窗户进去

He was very angry when he first saw Pinocchio
当他第一次看到匹诺曹时,他非常生气

and he did nothing but scold the poor puppet
他什么也没做,只是骂了这个可怜的傀儡

but then he saw Pinocchio really was without feet
但随后他看到匹诺曹真的没有脚

and he was quite overcome with sympathy again
他又一次被同情所征服

Geppetto took his puppet in his arms
Geppetto 把他的木偶抱在怀里

and he began to kiss and caress him
他开始亲吻和爱抚他
he said a thousand endearing things to him
他对他说了一千句可爱的话
big tears ran down his rosy cheeks
大颗的泪水顺着他红润的脸颊流下
"My little Pinocchio!" he comforted him
"我的小匹诺曹！"
"how did you manage to burn your feet?"
"你是怎么烧伤脚的？"
"I don't know how I did it, papa"
"我不知道我是怎么做到的，爸爸"
"but it has been such a dreadful night"
"但这是一个如此可怕的夜晚"
"I shall remember it as long as I live"
"只要我活着，我就会记住它"
"there was thunder and lightning all night"
"整晚雷电相传"
"and I was very hungry all night"
"我整晚都非常饿"
"and then the talking cricket scolded me"
"然后那只会说话的蟋蟀骂了我"
"the talking cricket said 'it serves you right'"
"会说话的蟋蟀说'它对你有用'"
"he said; 'you have been wicked and deserve it'"
"他说;'你是邪恶的，活该'"
"and I said to him: 'Take care, little Cricket!'"
"我对他说：'小心点，小蟋蟀！'"
"and he said; 'You are a puppet'"
"他说;'你是个傀儡'"
"and he said; 'you have a wooden head'"
"他说;'你有个木头'"
"and I threw the handle of a hammer at him"

"我把锤柄扔向他"
"and then the talking little cricket died"
"然后那只会说话的小蟋蟀死了"
"but it was his fault that he died"
"但他死了是他的错"
"because I didn't wish to kill him"
"因为我不想杀他"
"and I have proof that I didn't mean to"
"而且我有证据证明我不是故意的"
"I had put an earthenware saucer on burning embers"
"我在燃烧的余烬上放了一个陶碟"
"but a chicken flew out of the egg"
"但一只鸡从蛋里飞出来了"
"the chicken said; 'Adieu, until we meet again'"
"鸡说;'再见,直到我们再次见面'"
'send my compliments to all at home'
"向家里的所有人致以赞美"
"and then I got even more hungry"
"然后我就更饿了"
"then there was that little old man in a night-cap"
"然后是那个戴着睡帽的小老头"
"he opened the window up above me"
"他打开了我上方的窗户"
"and he told me to hold out my hat"
"他叫我把帽子拿出来"
"and he poured a basinful of water on me"
"他把一盆水倒在我身上"
"asking for a little bread isn't a disgrace, is it?"
"要一点面包不是丢脸吧?"
"and then I returned home at once"
"然后我立刻回家了"
"I was hungry and cold and tired"
"我又饿又冷又累"

"and I put my feet on the brazier to dry them"
"我把脚放在火盆上擦干"
"and then you returned in the morning"
"然后你早上回来了"
"and I found my feet were burnt off"
"我发现我的脚被烧掉了"
"and I am still hungry"
"我还是饿着"
"but I no longer have any feet!"
"可是我已经没有脚了！"
And poor Pinocchio began to cry and roar
可怜的匹诺曹开始哭泣和咆哮
he cried so loudly that he was heard five miles off
他哭得如此之大，以至于在五英里外都能听到他的声音
Geppetto, only understood one thing from all this
Geppetto，从这一切中只明白了一件事
he understood that the puppet was dying of hunger
他明白这个傀儡快饿死了
so he drew from his pocket three pears
于是他从口袋里掏出三个梨子
and he gave the pears to Pinocchio
他把梨子给了匹诺曹
"These three pears were intended for my breakfast"
"这三个梨是给我做早餐的"
"but I will give you my pears willingly"
"但我愿意把我的梨给你"
"Eat them, and I hope they will do you good"
"吃掉它们，我希望它们对你有好处"
Pinocchio looked at the pears distrustfully
匹诺曹不信任地看着梨子
"but you can't expect me to eat them like that"
"但你不能指望我会那样吃它们"
"be kind enough to peel them for me"

"请好心帮我剥皮"
"Peel them?" said Geppetto, astonished
"剥皮吗？" Geppetto 惊讶地说
"I didn't know you were so dainty and fastidious"
"我不知道你这么娇小又挑剔"
"These are bad habits to have, my boy!"
"这些都是坏习惯，我的孩子！"
"we must accustom ourselves to like and to eat everything"
"我们必须习惯于喜欢和吃一切"
"there is no knowing to what we may be brought"
"我们不知道会带来什么"
"There are so many chances!"
"机会太多了！"
"You are no doubt right," interrupted Pinocchio
"你无疑是对的，" 匹诺曹打断了他
"but I will never eat fruit that has not been peeled"
"但我绝不吃未剥皮的果"
"I cannot bear the taste of rind"
"我受不了外皮的味道"
So good Geppetto peeled the three pears
太好了 Geppetto 剥了三个梨
and he put the pear's rinds on a corner of the table
他把梨的外皮放在桌子的一角
Pinocchio had eaten the first pear
匹诺曹吃了第一个梨
he was about to throw away the pear's core
他正要扔掉梨子的核
but Geppetto caught hold of his arm
但 Geppetto 抓住了他的手臂
"Do not throw the core of the pear away"
"不要把梨核扔掉"
"in this world everything may be of use"

"在这个世界上，一切都可能是有用的"
But Pinocchio refused to see the sense in it
但匹诺曹拒绝看到其中的意义
"I am determined I will not eat the core of the pear"
"我决心不吃梨核"
and Pinocchio turned upon him like a viper
匹诺曹像毒蛇一样转向他
"Who knows!" repeated Geppetto
"谁知道呢！"
"there are so many chances," he said
"机会太多了，"他说
and Geppetto never lost his temper even once
而 Geppetto 从来没有发过脾气
And so the three pear cores were not thrown out
因此，三个梨核没有被扔掉
they were placed on the corner of the table with the rinds
它们被放在桌子的角落里，有外皮
after his small feast Pinocchio yawned tremendously
在他的小宴席之后，匹诺曹打了个大大的哈欠
and he spoke again in a fretful tone
他又用一种烦躁的语气说
"I am as hungry as ever!"
"我和以前一样饿！"
"But, my boy, I have nothing more to give you!"
"可是，我的孩子，我没有什么可给你的了！"
"You have nothing? Really? Nothing?"
"你什么都没有？真？什么都没有？
"I have only the rind and the cores of the pears"
"我只有梨的外皮和核"
"One must have patience!" said Pinocchio
"人必须要有耐心！"
"if there is nothing else I will eat the pear's rind"

"如果没有别的，我就吃梨皮"
And he began to chew the rind of the pear
他开始咀嚼梨的外皮
At first he made a wry face
起初，他做了一个苦笑的表情
but then, one after the other, he quickly ate them
但随后，他一个接一个地迅速地吃掉了它们
and after the pear's rinds he even ate the cores
在梨的外皮之后，他甚至吃掉了梨核
when he had eaten everything he rubbed his belly
当他吃完所有东西后，他揉了揉自己的肚子
"Ah! now I feel comfortable again"
"啊！现在我又感觉舒服了"
"Now you see I was right," smiled Gepetto
"现在你明白我是对的，"Gepetto 笑着说
"it's not good to accustom ourselves to our tastes"
"习惯自己的口味不好"
"We can never know, my dear boy, what may happen to us"
"我们永远无法知道，我亲爱的孩子，我们会发生什么事"
"There are so many chances!"
"机会太多了！"

Geppetto Makes Pinocchio New Feet
Geppetto 让 Pinocchio 焕然一新

the puppet had satisfied his hunger
木偶满足了他的饥饿感
but he began to cry and grumble again
但他又开始哭泣和抱怨
he remembered he wanted a pair of new feet
他记得他想要一双新脚
But Geppetto punished him for his naughtiness

但 Geppetto 因为他的顽皮而惩罚了他
he allowed him to cry and to despair a little
他允许他哭泣，让他有点绝望
Pinocchio had to accept his fate for half the day
匹诺曹不得不接受半天的命运
at the end of the day he said to him:
最后，他对他说：
"Why should I make you new feet?"
"我为什么要给你做新的脚？"
"To enable you to escape again from home?"
"为了让你能再次逃离家乡？"
Pinocchio sobbed at his situation
匹诺曹对他的处境啜泣
"I promise you that for the future I will be good"
"我向你保证，未来我会好起来的"
but Geppetto knew Pinocchio's tricks by now
但 Geppetto 现在已经知道匹诺曹的把戏了
"All boys who want something say the same thing"
"所有想要什么的男孩都说同样的事情"
"I promise you that I will go to school"
"我答应你，我会去上学"
"and I will study and bring home a good report"
"我要研究，带一份好报告回家"
"All boys who want something repeat the same story"
"所有想要什么的男孩都重复同样的故事"
"But I am not like other boys!" Pinocchio objected
"可是我跟别的男孩子不一样！"匹诺曹反对
"I am better than all of them," he added
"我比他们所有人都好，"他补充道
"and I always speak the truth," he lied
"我总是说真话，"他撒谎
"I promise you, papa, that I will learn a trade"
"我答应你，爸爸，我会学一门手艺"

"I promise that I will be the consolation of your old age"
"我保证,我会成为你晚年的安慰"
Geppetto's eyes filled with tears on hearing this
听到这话,Geppetto 的眼睛里充满了泪水
his heart was sad at seeing his son like this
看到儿子这样,他的心里很伤心
Pinocchio was in such a pitiable state
匹诺曹处于如此可怜的状态
He did not say another word to Pinocchio
他没有对匹诺曹再说一句话
he got his tools and two small pieces of seasoned wood
他拿到了工具和两小块陈年木头
he set to work with great diligence
他开始非常勤奋地工作
In less than an hour the feet were finished
在不到一个小时的时间里,脚就完成了
They might have been modelled by an artist of genius
他们可能是由一位天才艺术家塑造的
Geppetto then spoke to the puppet
Geppetto 然后与木偶交谈
"Shut your eyes and go to sleep!"
"闭上眼睛睡觉吧!"
And Pinocchio shut his eyes and pretended to sleep
匹诺曹闭上眼睛,假装睡着了
Geppetto got an egg-shell and melted some glue in it
Geppetto 找了一个蛋壳,在里面融化了一些胶水
and he fastened Pinocchio's feet in their place
他把匹诺曹的脚固定在他们的位置上
it was masterfully done by Geppetto
这是由 Geppetto 巧妙完成的
not a trace could be seen of where the feet were joined
看不到脚趾连接处的痕迹
Pinocchio soon realized that he had feet again

匹诺曹很快意识到他又长了脚

and then he jumped down from the table
然后他从桌子上跳了下来

he jumped around the room with energy and joy
他充满活力和喜悦地在房间里跳来跳去

he danced as if he had gone mad with his delight
他跳舞,仿佛他被他的喜悦发疯了

"thank you for all you have done for me"
"感谢你为我所做的一切"

"I will go to school at once," Pinocchio promised
"我马上去上学,"匹诺曹承诺

"but to go to school I shall need some clothes"
"但要去上学,我需要一些衣服"

by now you know that Geppetto was a poor man
现在你知道 Geppetto 是个穷人了

he had not so much as a penny in his pocket
他口袋里连一分钱都没有

so he made him a little dress of flowered paper
所以他用花纸做了一件小衣服给他

a pair of shoes from the bark of a tree
一双来自树皮的鞋子

and he made a hat out of the bread
他用饼做了一顶帽子

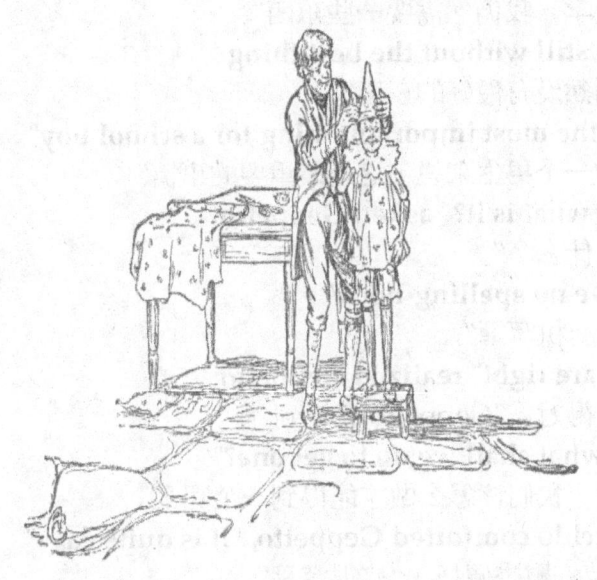

Pinocchio ran to look at himself in a crock of water
匹诺曹跑去看自己在一缸水里
he was ever so pleased with his appearance
他对自己的外表一直很满意
and he strutted about the room like a peacock
他像孔雀一样在房间里昂首阔步
"I look quite like a gentleman!"
"我看起来挺像个绅士！"
"Yes, indeed," answered Geppetto
"是的，确实如此，"杰佩托回答
"it is not fine clothes that make the gentleman"
"造就绅士的不是漂亮的衣服"
"rather, it is clean clothes that make a gentleman"
"相反，干净的衣服才是绅士"
"By the way," added the puppet
"对了，"木偶补充道
"to go to school there's still something I need"

"要上学,我仍然需要一些东西"
"I am still without the best thing"
"我仍然没有最好的东西"
"it is the most important thing for a school boy"
"对于一个男生来说,这是最重要的事情"
"And what is it?" asked Geppetto
"那是什么?"
"I have no spelling-book"
"我没有拼写簿"
"You are right" realized Geppetto
"你说得对,"Geppetto 意识到
"but what shall we do to get one?"
"可是,我们该怎么做才能得到一个呢?"
Pinocchio comforted Geppetto, "It is quite easy"
匹诺曹安慰杰佩托,"这很容易"
"all we have to do is go to the bookseller's"
"我们所要做的就是去书店"
"all I have to do is buy from them"
"我所要做的就是从他们那里购买"
"but how do we buy it without money?"
"但是,没有钱我们怎么买呢?"
"I have got no money," said Pinocchio
"我没有钱,"匹诺曹说
"Neither have I," added the good old man, very sadly
"我也没有,"这位善良的老人非常伤心地补充道
although he was a very merry boy, Pinocchio became sad
虽然他是一个非常快乐的男孩,但匹诺曹变得悲伤起来
poverty, when it is real, is understood by everybody
贫穷,当它是真实的时,每个人都能理解
"Well, patience!" exclaimed Geppetto, rising to his feet
"嗯,耐心点!" Geppetto 惊呼道,站了起来
and he put on his old corduroy jacket

他穿上了他的旧灯芯绒夹克
and he ran out of the house into the snow
他就跑出屋子，跑进雪地里
He returned back to the house soon after
不久之后，他回到了房子里
in his hand he held a spelling-book for Pinocchio
他手里拿着一本给匹诺曹写的拼字簿
but the old jacket he had left with was gone
但他留下的旧夹克已经不见了
The poor man was in his shirt-sleeves
那个穷人穿着衬衫袖子
and outdoors it was cold and snowing
而外面又冷又下雪
"And your jacket, papa?" asked Pinocchio
"爸爸，你的夹克呢？"
"I have sold it," confirmed old Geppetto
"我已经卖掉了，"老 Geppetto 确认道
"Why did you sell it?" asked Pinocchio
"你为什么卖掉它？"
"Because I found my jacket was too hot"
"因为我发现我的夹克太热了"
Pinocchio understood this answer in an instant
匹诺曹瞬间明白了这个答案
Pinocchio was unable to restrain the impulse of his heart
匹诺曹无法抑制自己心中的冲动
Because Pinocchio did have a good heart after all
因为匹诺曹毕竟有一颗善良的心
he sprang up and threw his arms around Geppetto's neck
他跳起来，用双臂搂住了 Geppetto 的脖子
and he kissed him again and again a thousand times
他一遍又一千次地亲吻他

Pinocchio Goes to See a Puppet Show
匹诺曹去看木偶戏

eventually it stopped snowing outside
最终,外面的雪停了
and Pinocchio set out to go to school
和匹诺曹开始上学
and he had his fine spelling-book under his arm
他的胳膊下夹着他那本精美的拼写本
he walked along with a thousand ideas in his head
他带着一千个想法走着
his little brain thought of all the possibilities
他的小脑袋想到了所有的可能性
and he built a thousand castles in the air
他在空中建造了一千座城堡
each castle was more beautiful than the other
每座城堡都比另一座更美丽
And, talking to himself, he said;
"然后,他自言自语地说;
"Today at school I will learn to read at once"
"今天在学校,我马上就学会读书"
"then tomorrow I will begin to write"
"那么明天我就开始写"
"and the day after tomorrow I will learn the numbers"
"后天我会知道这些数字"
"all of these things will prove very useful"
"所有这些都将被证明非常有用"
"and then I will earn a great deal of money"
"然后我会赚很多钱"
"I already know what I will do with the first money"
"我已经知道我该用第一笔钱做什么了"
"I will immediately buy a beautiful new cloth coat"
"我马上买一件漂亮的新布大衣"

"my papa will not have to be cold anymore"
"我爸爸不必再冷了"
"But what am I saying?" he realized
"但我在说什么？"
"It shall be all made of gold and silver"
"都要用金银做"
"and it shall have diamond buttons"
"它应该有菱形纽扣"
"That poor man really deserves it"
"那个可怜的人真的活该"
"he bought me books and is having me taught"
"他给我买了书，还教我"
"and to do so he has remained in a shirt"
"为了做到这一点，他一直穿着衬衫"
"he has done all this for me in such cold weather"
"他在这么冷的天气里为我做了这一切"
"only papas are capable of such sacrifices!"
"只有爸爸才能做出这样的牺牲！"
he said all this to himself with great emotion
他对自己说了这一切，心情激动
but in the distance he thought he heard music
但在远处，他以为自己听到了音乐
it sounded like pipes and the beating of a big drum
听起来像风笛和大鼓的敲击声
He stopped and listened to hear what it could be
他停下来听听那会是什么
The sounds came from the end of a street
声音从街道的尽头传来
and the street led to a little village on the seashore
街道通向海边的一个小村庄
"What can that music be?" he wondered
"那音乐会是什么？"
"What a pity that I have to go to school"

"我得去上学真可惜"
"if only I didn't have to go to school..."
"如果我不必去上学就好了……"
And he remained irresolute
他仍然不坚定
It was, however, necessary to come to a decision
然而,有必要做出决定
"Should I go to school?" he asked himself
他问自己:"我应该去上学吗?"
"or should I go after the music?"
"还是我应该去追音乐呢?"
"Today I will go and hear the music" he decided
"今天我要去听音乐,"他决定
"and tomorrow I will go to school"
"明天我就去上学"
the young scapegrace of a boy had decided
一个男孩的年轻替罪羊已经决定了
and he shrugged his shoulders at his choice
他对自己的选择耸了耸肩
The more he ran the nearer came the sounds of the music
他跑得越多,音乐声就越近
and the beating of the big drum became louder and louder
大鼓的敲击声越来越响亮
At last he found himself in the middle of a town square
最后,他发现自己在一个城镇广场的中央
the square was quite full of people
广场上挤满了人
all the people were all crowded round a building
所有的人都挤在一栋建筑周围
and the building was made of wood and canvas
这座建筑是用木头和帆布建造的

and the building was painted a thousand colours
这座建筑被涂上了一千种颜色
"What is that building?" asked Pinocchio
"那是什么建筑？"
and he turned to a little boy
他转向一个小男孩
"Read the placard," the boy told him
"读标语牌，"男孩告诉他
"it is all written there," he added
"一切都写在那里，"他补充说
"read it and and then you will know"
"读一读，你就会知道"
"I would read it willingly," said Pinocchio
"我愿意读它，"匹诺曹说
"but it so happens that today I don't know how to read"
"但碰巧今天我不知道怎么读书"
"Bravo, blockhead! Then I will read it to you"
"太棒了，笨蛋！然后我会读给你听。
"you see those words as red as fire?"
"你觉得那些字像火一样红吗？"
"The Great Puppet Theatre," he read to him
"伟大的木偶剧院，"他读给他听
"Has the play already begun?"
"戏剧已经开始了吗？"
"It is beginning now," confirmed the boy
"现在开始了，"男孩确认道
"How much does it cost to go in?"
"进去要花多少钱？"
"A dime is what it costs you"
"一毛钱就是你的成本"
Pinocchio was in a fever of curiosity
匹诺曹好奇心极强
full of excitement he lost all control of himself

他兴奋不已，完全失去了对自己的控制
and Pinocchio lost all sense of shame
匹诺曹失去了所有的羞耻感
"Would you lend me a dime until tomorrow?"
"你能借我一毛钱到明天吗？"
"I would lend it to you willingly," said the boy
"我愿意借给你，"男孩说
"but unfortunately today I cannot give it to you"
"但不幸的是，今天我不能给你"
Pinocchio had another idea to get the money
匹诺曹有另一个获得这笔钱的想法
"I will sell you my jacket for a dime"
"我会以一毛钱的价格把我的夹克卖给你"
"but your jacket is made of flowered paper"
"可是你的外套是花纸做的"
"what use could I have for such a jacket?"
"我这件夹克有什么用呢？"
"imagine it rained and the jacket got wet"
"想象一下下雨了，夹克湿了"
"it would be impossible to get it off my back"
"不可能把它从我的背上取下来"
"Will you buy my shoes?" tried Pinocchio
"你愿意买我的鞋子吗？"
"They would only be of use to light the fire"
"他们只会用来点火"
"How much will you give me for my cap?"
"你愿意给我多少钱买我的帽子？"
"That would be a wonderful acquisition indeed!"
"那确实是一次很棒的收购！"
"A cap made of bread crumb!" joked the boy
"一顶面包屑做的帽子！"
"There would be a risk of the mice coming to eat it"
"老鼠有吃它的风险"

"they might eat it whilst it was still on my head!"
"他们可能会趁它还在我头上的时候吃掉它!"

Pinocchio was on thorns about his predicament
匹诺曹对他的困境感到困惑

He was on the point of making another offer
他正准备再提出一个报价

but he had not the courage to ask him
但他没有勇气问他

He hesitated, felt irresolute and remorseful
他犹豫了,感到不坚决和懊悔

At last he raised the courage to ask
最后,他鼓起勇气问道

"Will you give me a dime for this new spelling-book?"
"你能给我一毛钱买这本新的拼写书吗?"

but the boy declined this offer too
但男孩也拒绝了这个提议

"I am a boy and I don't buy from boys"
"我是男孩,我不从男孩那里买东西"

a hawker of old clothes had overheard them
一个穿旧衣服的小贩偷听了他们

"I will buy the spelling-book for a dime"
"我花一毛钱买下这本拼写书"

And the book was sold there and then
这本书就在那里卖掉了

poor Geppetto had remained at home trembling with cold
可怜的 Geppetto 一直呆在家里,冻得发抖

in order that his son could have a spelling-book
这样他的儿子就可以有一本拼写簿

The Puppets Recognize their Brother Pinocchio
木偶认出了他们的兄弟匹诺曹

Pinocchio was in the little puppet theatre
匹诺曹在小木偶剧院里

an incident occurred that almost produced a revolution
发生了一个几乎引发革命的事件

The curtain had gone up and the play had already begun
帷幕已经拉开，戏剧已经开始

Harlequin and Punch were quarrelling with each other
Harlequin 和 Punch 互相争吵

every moment they were threatening to come to blows
他们每时每刻都在威胁要来打击

All at once Harlequin stopped and turned to the public
突然，Harlequin 停了下来，转向公众

he pointed with his hand to someone far down in the pit
他用手指着坑里远处的某个人

and he exclaimed in a dramatic tone
他用一种戏剧性的语气喊道

"Gods of the firmament!"
"苍穹之神！"

"Do I dream or am I awake?"
"我是在做梦还是醒着？"

"But, surely that is Pinocchio!"
"但是，那肯定是匹诺曹！"

"It is indeed Pinocchio!" cried Punch
"确实是匹诺曹！"

And Rose peeped out from behind the scenes
罗斯从幕后了出来

"It is indeed himself!" screamed Rose
"确实是他自己！"

and all the puppets shouted in chorus

所有的木偶都齐声喊叫
"It is Pinocchio! it is Pinocchio!"
"是匹诺曹！是匹诺曹！"
and they leapt from all sides onto the stage
他们从四面八方跳上舞台
"It is Pinocchio!" all the puppets exclaimed
"是匹诺曹！"
"It is our brother Pinocchio!"
"是我们的兄弟匹诺曹！"
"Long live Pinocchio!" they cheered together
"匹诺曹万岁！"
"Pinocchio, come up here to me," cried Harlequin
"匹诺曹，到我这儿来，"丑角喊道
"throw yourself into the arms of your wooden brothers!"
"投身于你们的木头兄弟的怀抱！"
Pinocchio couldn't decline this affectionate invitation
匹诺曹无法拒绝这个深情的邀请
he leaped from the end of the pit into the reserved seats
他从坑的尽头跳进了预留座位
another leap landed him on the head of the drummer
另一次跳跃使他落在了鼓手的头上
and he then sprang upon the stage
然后他跳上了舞台
The embraces and the friendly pinches
拥抱和友好的捏捏
and the demonstrations of warm brotherly affection
以及热情的兄弟之情
Pinocchio reception from the puppets was beyond description
木偶对匹诺曹的接受程度无法形容
The sight was doubtless a moving one
这景象无疑是令人感动的

but the public in the pit had become impatient
但坑里的公众已经变得不耐烦了
they began to shout, "we came to watch a play"
他们开始大喊:"我们是来看戏的"
"go on with the play!" they demanded
"继续这出戏!"
but the puppets didn't continue the recital
但木偶们没有继续独奏
the puppets doubled their noise and outcries
木偶们把他们的噪音和哭声加倍了
they put Pinocchio on their shoulders
他们把匹诺曹放在肩上
and they carried him in triumph before the footlights
他们凯旋地把他带到了脚灯前。
At that moment the ringmaster came out
就在这时,马戏团团长出来了
He was a big and ugly man
他是个又大又丑的男人
the sight of him was enough to frighten anyone
看到他就足以吓到任何人
His beard was as black as ink and long
他的胡子像墨水一样黑,而且很长
and his beard reached from his chin to the ground
他的胡须从下巴一直到地上
and he trod upon his beard when he walked
走路时踩着自己的胡须
His mouth was as big as an oven
他的嘴巴像烤箱一样大
and his eyes were like two lanterns of burning red glass
他的眼睛像两盏燃烧的红玻璃灯笼
He carried a large whip of twisted snakes and foxes' tails
他拿着一根由扭曲的蛇和狐狸尾巴组成的大鞭子

and he cracked his whip constantly
他不停地抽打他的鞭子
At his unexpected appearance there was a profound silence
当他出乎意料地出现时，一片深深的寂静
no one dared to even breathe
甚至没有人敢呼吸
A fly could have been heard in the stillness
在寂静中可以听到一只苍蝇的声音
The poor puppets of both sexes trembled like leaves
两性的可怜傀儡都像树叶一样颤抖着
"have you come to raise a disturbance in my theatre?"
"你来我的剧院闹事了吗？"
he had the gruff voice of a goblin
他有个妖精的粗哑嗓音
a goblin suffering from a severe cold
一个患有严重感冒的哥布林
"Believe me, honoured sir, it it not my fault!"
"相信我，尊敬的先生，这不是我的错！"
"That is enough from you!" he blared
"你说够了！"
"Tonight we will settle our accounts"
"今晚我们算账"
soon the play was over and the guests left
很快，戏剧结束了，客人们离开了
the ringmaster went into the kitchen
马戏团团长走进厨房
a fine sheep was being prepared for his supper
一只漂亮的羊正在为他的晚餐做准备
it was turning slowly on the fire
它正在慢慢地点燃火
there was not enough wood to finish roasting the lamb
没有足够的木材来完成烤羊肉
so he called for Harlequin and Punch

所以他叫来了 Harlequin 和 Punch

"Bring that puppet here," he ordered them
"把那个木偶带到这里来，"他命令他们

"you will find him hanging on a nail"
"你会发现他挂在钉子上"

"It seems to me that he is made of very dry wood"
"在我看来，他是由非常干燥的木头制成的"

"I am sure he would make a beautiful blaze"
"我相信他会做出美丽的火焰"

At first Harlequin and Punch hesitated
起初，Harlequin 和 Punch 犹豫不决

but they were appalled by a severe glance from their master
但他们被主人严厉的目光吓了一跳

and they had no choice but to obey his wishes
他们别无选择，只能服从他的愿望

In a short time they returned to the kitchen
不一会儿，他们又回到了厨房

this time they were carrying poor Pinocchio
这次他们带着可怜的匹诺曹

he was wriggling like an eel out of water
他像一条离开水的鳗鱼一样蠕动着

and he was screaming desperately
他拼命地尖叫

"Papa! papa! save me! I will not die!"
"爸爸！爸爸！救我！我不会死的！"

The Fire-Eater Sneezes and Pardons Pinocchio
食火者打喷嚏并原谅匹诺曹

The ringmaster looked like a wicked man
马戏团团长看起来像个恶人
and he was known by all as Fire-eater
他被大家称为 Fire-eater
his black beard covered his chest and legs
他的黑胡子遮住了胸口和腿
it was like he was wearing an apron
就像他穿着围裙一样
and this made him look especially wicked
这使他看起来特别邪恶
On the whole, however, he did not have a bad heart
然而，总的来说，他并没有坏心
he saw poor Pinocchio brought before him
他看到可怜的匹诺曹被带到他面前
he saw the puppet struggling and screaming
他看到木偶在挣扎和尖叫
"I will not die, I will not die!"
"我不会死，我不会死！"
and he was quite moved by what he saw
他被他所看到的深深打动了
he felt very sorry for the helpless puppet
他为这个无助的傀儡感到非常遗憾
he tried to hold his sympathies within himself
他试图把自己的同情心藏在心里
but after a little they all came out
但过了一会儿，他们都出来了
he could contain his sympathy no longer
他再也抑制不住自己的同情了
and he let out an enormous violent sneeze
他猛地打了个喷嚏
up until that moment Harlequin had been worried

直到那一刻，Harlequin 一直很担心

he had been bowing down like a weeping willow
他像垂柳一样低头

but when he heard the sneeze he became cheerful
但当他听到喷嚏声时，他变得高兴起来

he leaned towards Pinocchio and whispered;
他靠向匹诺曹，低声说；

"Good news, brother, the ringmaster has sneezed"
"好消息，兄弟，马戏团团长打了个喷嚏"

"that is a sign that he pities you"
"那是他怜悯你的信号"

"and if he pities you, then you are saved"
"他若怜悯你，你就得救了"

most men weep when they feel compassion
大多数男人在感到同情时都会哭泣

or at least they pretend to dry their eyes
或者至少他们假装擦干眼睛

Fire-Eater, however, had a different habit
然而，Fire-Eater 有一个不同的习惯

when moved by emotion his nose would tickle him
当他被情感所感动时，他的鼻子会让他痒痒的。

the ringmaster didn't stop acting the ruffian
马戏团团长并没有停止扮演痞子

"are you quite done with all your crying?"
"你哭得够呛吗？"

"my stomach hurts from your lamentations"
"你的哀歌让我的肚子痛"

"I feel a spasm that almost..."
"我感到痉挛，几乎……"

and the ringmaster let out another loud sneeze
马戏团团长又打了个大声的喷嚏

"Bless you!" said Pinocchio, quite cheerfully
"保佑你！"

"Thank you! And your papa and your mamma?"
"谢谢你！那你爸爸和妈呢？

"are they still alive?" asked Fire-Eater
"他们还活着吗？"

"My papa is still alive and well," said Pinocchio
"我爸爸还活着，而且很好，"匹诺曹说

"but my mamma I have never known," he added
"可是我的妈妈我从来不认识，"他又说

"good thing I did not have you thrown on the fire"
"还好我没有把你扔进火里"

"your father would have lost all who he still had"
"你爸爸会失去他所拥有的一切"

"Poor old man! I pity him!"
"可怜的老头子！我可怜他！"

"Etchoo! etchoo! etchoo!" Fire-eater sneezed
"Etchoo！Etchoo！etchoo！噬火者打喷嚏

and he sneezed again three times
他又打了三个喷嚏

"Bless you," said Pinocchio each time
"保佑你，"匹诺曹每次都说

"Thank you! Some compassion is due to me"
"谢谢你！一些同情心是我应该的。

"as you can see I have no more wood"
"正如你所看到的，我没有更多的木头了"

"so I will struggle to finish roasting my mutton"
"所以我会很难烤完我的羊肉"

"you would have been of great use to me!"
"你对我真是大用处啊！"

"However, I have had pity on you"
"不过，我很可怜你"

"so I must have patience with you"
"所以我必须对你有耐心"

"Instead of you I will burn another puppet"

"我要烧掉另一个傀儡"

At this call two wooden gendarmes immediately appeared
这叫声响起，两个木制宪兵立刻出现了

They were very long and very thin puppets
他们是很长很细的木偶

and they had wonky hats on their heads
他们头上戴着一顶摇摇欲坠的帽子

and they held unsheathed swords in their hands
他们手里拿着未出鞘的剑

The ringmaster said to them in a hoarse voice:
马戏团团长用嘶哑的声音对他们说：

"Take Harlequin and bind him securely"
"抓住丑角，把他牢牢地绑起来"

"and then throw him on the fire to burn"
"然后把他扔在火上烧"

"I am determined that my mutton shall be well roasted"
"我决心让我的羊肉烤好"

imagine how poor Harlequin must have felt!
想象一下 Harlequin 的感受一定是多么可怜！

His terror was so great that his legs bent under him
他的恐惧是如此之大，以至于他的双腿在他下面弯曲

and he fell with his face on the ground
他就脸朝地上倒下

Pinocchio was agonized by what he was seeing
匹诺曹对他所看到的感到痛苦

he threw himself at the ringmaster's feet
他扑倒在马戏团团长的脚下

he bathed his long beard with his tears
他用泪水沐浴着长长的胡须

and he tried to beg for Harlequin's life
他试图乞求 Harlequin 的性命

"Have pity, Sir Fire-Eater!" Pinocchio begged

"可怜吧，食火者先生！"匹诺曹恳求道
"Here there are no sirs," the ringmaster answered severely
"这里没有先生，"马戏团团长严肃地回答
"Have pity, Sir Knight!" Pinocchio tried
"可怜吧，骑士爵士！"匹诺曹尝试过
"Here there are no knights!" the ringmaster answered
"这里没有骑士！"
"Have pity, Commander!" Pinocchio tried
"可怜吧，指挥官！"匹诺曹尝试过
"Here there are no commanders!"
"这里没有指挥官！"
"Have pity, Excellence!" Pinocchio pleaded
"可怜吧，卓越！"匹诺曹恳求道
Fire-eater quite liked what he had just heard
Fire-eater 很喜欢他刚才听到的
Excellence was something he did aspire to
卓越是他所渴望的
and the ringmaster began to smile again
马戏团团长又开始微笑了
and he became at once kinder and more tractable
他立刻变得更善良，更容易相处
Turning to Pinocchio, he asked:
他转向匹诺曹问道：
"Well, what do you want from me?"
"嗯，你想从我这里得到什么？"
"I implore you to pardon poor Harlequin"
"我恳求你原谅可怜的丑角"
"For him there can be no pardon"
"对他来说，不能得到赦免"
"I have spared you, if you remember"
"如果你还记得的话，我饶过你"
"so he must be put on the fire"

"所以他必须被放在火上"

"I am determined that my mutton shall be well roasted"

"我决心让我的羊肉烤好"

Pinocchio stood up proudly to the ringmaster

匹诺曹自豪地站起来向马戏团团长站起来

and he threw away his cap of bread crumb

他扔掉了他的面包屑帽

"In that case I know my duty"

"既然如此，我知道我的责任"

"Come on, gendarmes!" he called the soldiers

"来吧，宪兵们！"

"Bind me and throw me amongst the flames"

"把我捆起来，扔在火焰里"

"it would not be just for Harlequin to die for me!"

"不仅仅是让 Harlequin 为我而死！"

"he has been a true friend to me"

"他一直是我真正的朋友"

Pinocchio had spoken in a loud, heroic voice

匹诺曹用响亮而英勇的声音说话

and his heroic actions made all the puppets cry

他的英姿飒爽，让所有的傀儡都哭了

Even though the gendarmes were made of wood

尽管宪兵是用木头做的

they wept like two newly born lambs

他们哭泣，像两只刚出生的羔羊

Fire-eater at first remained as hard and unmoved as ice

起初，噬火者仍然像冰一样坚硬，一动不动

but little by little he began to melt and sneeze

但渐渐地，他开始融化和打喷嚏

he sneezed again four or five times

他又打了四五个喷嚏

and he opened his arms affectionately

他深情地张开双臂

"You are a good and brave boy!" he praised Pinocchio
"你是个好孩子，勇敢无畏！"
"Come here and give me a kiss"
"过来给我一个吻"
Pinocchio ran to the ringmaster at once
匹诺曹立刻跑向马戏团团长
he climbed up the ringmaster's beard like a squirrel
他像松鼠一样爬上了马戏团团长的胡须
and he deposited a hearty kiss on the point of his nose
"他在他的鼻尖上亲了一下
"Then the pardon is granted?" asked poor Harlequin
"那么赦免了？"
in a faint voice that was scarcely audible
用一种几乎听不见的微弱声音
"The pardon is granted!" answered Fire-Eater
"赦免了！"
he then added, sighing and shaking his head:
然后他又说，叹了口气，摇了摇头：
"I must have patience with my puppets!"
"我得对我的木偶有耐心！"
"Tonight I shall have to eat the mutton half raw;"
"今晚我得吃羊肉半生吃。"
"but another time, woe to him who displeases me!"
"但又一次，使我不高兴的人有祸了！"
At the news of the pardon the puppets all ran to the stage
听到赦免的消息，木偶们都跑上了舞台
they lit all the lamps and chandeliers of the show
他们点亮了演出的所有灯具和枝形吊灯
it was as if there was a full-dress performance
就好像有一场盛装表演
they began to leap and to dance merrily
他们开始欢快地跳跃和跳舞

when dawn had come they were still dancing
黎明时分，他们仍然在跳舞

Pinocchio Receives Five Gold Pieces
匹诺曹获得五枚金币

The following day Fire-eater called Pinocchio over
第二天，噬火者打电话给匹诺曹过来
"What is your father's name?" he asked Pinocchio
"你爸爸叫什么名字？"
"My father is called Geppetto," Pinocchio answered
"我爸爸叫 Geppetto，"匹诺曹回答
"And what trade does he follow?" asked Fire-eater
"他从事什么行业呢？"
"He has no trade, he is a beggar"
"他没有生意，他是个乞丐"
"Does he earn much?" asked Fire-eater
"他赚多少钱吗？"

"No, he has never a penny in his pocket"
"不，他的口袋里从来没有一分钱"
"once he bought me a spelling-book"
"有一次他给我买了一本拼写书"
"but he had to sell the only jacket he had"
"但他不得不卖掉他唯一的夹克"
"Poor devil! I feel almost sorry for him!"
"可怜的魔鬼！我几乎为他感到难过！"
"Here are five gold pieces for him"
"这里有五块金币给他"
"Go at once and take the gold to him"
"你快去把金子拿给他。"
Pinocchio was overjoyed by the present
匹诺曹对现在感到欣喜若狂
he thanked the ringmaster a thousand times
他感谢了一千次马戏团团长
He embraced all the puppets of the company
他接受了公司的所有傀儡
he even embraced the troop of gendarmes
他甚至拥抱了宪兵部队
and then he set out to return straight home
然后他就踏上了回家的路
But Pinocchio didn't get very far
但匹诺曹并没有走得很远
on the road he met a Fox with a lame foot
在路上，他遇到了一只脚瘸了的狐狸
and he met a Cat blind in both eyes
他遇到了一只两只眼睛都瞎了的猫
they were going along helping each other
他们一起互相帮助
they were good companions in their misfortune
他们是不幸的好伙伴
The Fox, who was lame, walked leaning on the Cat
狐狸瘸了，靠在猫上走路

and the Cat, who was blind, was guided by the Fox
而那只瞎眼的猫则由狐狸引导
the Fox greeted Pinocchio very politely
狐狸非常有礼貌地向匹诺曹打招呼
"Good-day, Pinocchio," said the Fox
"你好，匹诺曹，"狐狸说
"How do you come to know my name?" asked the puppet
"你是怎么知道我的名字的？"
"I know your father well," said the fox
"我很了解你爸爸，"狐狸说
"Where did you see him?" asked Pinocchio
"你在哪里看到他？"
"I saw him yesterday, at the door of his house"
"我昨天在他家门口看到他了"
"And what was he doing?" asked Pinocchio
"他在做什么？"
"He was in his shirt and shivering with cold"
"他穿着衬衫，冻得发抖"
"Poor papa! But his suffering is over now"
"可怜的爸爸！但他的痛苦现在已经结束了。
"in the future he shall shiver no more!"
"将来他不会再发抖了！"
"Why will he shiver no more?" asked the fox
"他为什么不再发抖了呢？"
"Because I have become a gentleman" replied Pinocchio
"因为我已经成为一个绅士了，"匹诺曹回答
"A gentleman—you!" said the Fox
"一位绅士——你！"
and he began to laugh rudely and scornfully
他开始粗鲁地、轻蔑地笑起来
The Cat also began to laugh with the fox

猫也开始和狐狸一起笑
but she did better at concealing her laughter
但她更善于掩饰自己的笑声
and she combed her whiskers with her forepaws
她用前爪梳理着胡须
"There is little to laugh at," cried Pinocchio angrily
"没什么好笑的,"匹诺曹生气地叫道
"I am really sorry to make your mouth water"
"我真的很抱歉让你垂涎三尺"
"if you know anything then you know what these are"
"如果你知道什么,那么你就知道这些是什么"
"you can see that they are five pieces of gold"
"你看得出来,他们是五块金子"
And he pulled out the money that Fire-eater had given him
"说着,他掏出了噬火者给他的钱
for a moment the fox and the cat did a strange thing
有那么一会儿,狐狸和猫做了一件奇怪的事情
the jingling of the money really got their attention
钱的叮当声真的引起了他们的注意
the Fox stretched out the paw that seemed crippled
狐狸伸出那只看起来残废的爪子
and the Cat opened wide her two eyes
猫睁大了她的两只眼睛
her eyes looked like two green lanterns
她的眼睛看起来像两盏绿灯笼

it is true that she shut her eyes again
她确实又闭上了眼睛

she was so quick that Pinocchio didn't notice
她跑得太快了,匹诺曹没注意到

the Fox was very curious about what he had seen
狐狸对他所看到的东西非常好奇

"what are you going to do with all that money?"
"你打算用这些钱做什么?"

Pinocchio was all too proud to tell them his plans
匹诺曹太骄傲了,不敢告诉他们他的计划

"First of all, I intend to buy a new jacket for my papa"
"首先,我打算给我爸爸买一件新夹克"

"the jacket will be made of gold and silver"
"夹克将由金和银制成"

"and the coat will come with diamond buttons"
"外套将带有钻石纽扣"

"and then I will buy a spelling-book for myself"

"然后我就为自己买一本拼写书"
"You will buy a spelling book for yourself?"
"你会自己买一本拼写书吗?"
"Yes indeed, for I wish to study in earnest"
"确实是的,因为我想认真学习"
"Look at me!" said the Fox
"狐狸说:"瞧瞧我!""
"Through my foolish passion for study I have lost a leg"
"由于我对学习的愚蠢热情,我失去了一条腿"
"Look at me!" said the Cat
"看着我!"
"Through my foolish passion for study I have lost my eyes"
"由于我对学习的愚蠢热情,我失去了我的眼睛"
At that moment a white Blackbird began his usual song
就在这时,一只白色的黑鸟开始了他往常的歌声
"Pinocchio, don't listen to the advice of bad companions"
"匹诺曹,别听坏伙伴的劝告"
"if you listen to their advice you will repent it!"
"如果你听他们的建议,你就会后悔的!"
Poor Blackbird! If only he had not spoken!
可怜的黑鸟!要是他没说话就好了!
The Cat, with a great leap, sprang upon him
猫猛地一跃,扑向他
she didn't even give him time to say "Oh!"
她甚至没有给他说"哦!
she ate him in one mouthful, feathers and all
她一口气吃掉了他,包括羽毛和所有的东西
Having eaten him, she cleaned her mouth
吃了他之后,她擦了擦嘴

and then she shut her eyes again
然后她又闭上了眼睛
and she feigned blindness just as before
她像以前一样假装失明
"Poor Blackbird!" said Pinocchio to the Cat
"可怜的黑鸟!"
"why did you treat him so badly?"
"你为什么对他这么差?"
"I did it to give him a lesson"
"我这样做是为了给他一个教训"
"He will learn not to meddle in other people's affairs"
"他会学会不插手别人的事情"
by now they had gone almost half-way home
这时,他们几乎已经走了一半的路
the Fox, halted suddenly, and spoke to the puppet
狐狸突然停了下来,对木偶说了一句话
"Would you like to double your money?"
"你想把你的钱翻倍吗?"
"In what way could I double my money?"
"我怎样才能把钱翻倍呢?"
"Would you like to multiply your five miserable coins?"
"你愿意把你的五枚可怜的硬币加倍吗?"
"I would like that very much! but how?"
"我非常喜欢那个!但是怎么做呢?
"The way to do it is easy enough"
"方法很简单"
"Instead of returning home you must go with us"
"与其回家,不如跟我们走"
"And where do you wish to take me?"
"那你想带我去哪里?"
"We will take you to the land of the Owls"
"我们将带您前往猫头鹰之地"

Pinocchio reflected a moment to think
匹诺曹沉思了一会儿
and then he said resolutely "No, I will not go"
然后他坚决地说:"不,我不去。
"I am already close to the house"
"我已经离房子很近了"
"and I will return home to my papa"
"我要回家去找我爸爸"
"he has been waiting for me in the cold"
"他一直在寒冷中等我"
"all day yesterday I did not come back to him"
"昨天一整天我都没有回到他身边"
"Who can tell how many times he sighed!"
"谁能说得清他叹了多少次!"
"I have indeed been a bad son"
"我确实是个坏儿子"
"and the talking little cricket was right"
"会说话的小蟋蟀是对的"
"Disobedient boys never come to any good"
"不听话的男孩永远不会有任何好处"
"what the talking little cricket said is true"
"会说话的小蟋蟀说的是真的"
"many misfortunes have happened to me"
"我遭遇了许多不幸"
"Even yesterday in fire-eater's house I took a risk"
"甚至昨天在噬火者的房子里,我也冒了个险"
"Oh! it makes me shudder to think of it!"
"哦!想想就让我不寒而栗!"
"Well, then," said the Fox, "you've decided to go home?"
"那么,"狐狸说,"你决定回家了吗?
"Go, then, and so much the worse for you"
"那么,走吧,对你来说就更糟了"

"So much the worse for you!" repeated the Cat
"对你来说，情况更糟了！"
"Think well of it, Pinocchio," they advised him
"好好想想，匹诺曹，"他们劝他
"because you are giving a kick to fortune"
"因为你正在给财富带来刺激"
"a kick to fortune!" repeated the Cat
"真是太幸运了！"
"all it would have taken would have been a day"
"只需要一天"
"by tomorrow your five coins could have multiplied"
"到明天，你的五个硬币可能会成倍增加"
"your five coins could have become two thousand"
"你的五枚硬币本来可以变成两千枚"
"Two thousand sovereigns!" repeated the Cat
"两千索维林！"
"But how is it possible?" asked Pinocchio
"但怎么可能呢？"
and he remained with his mouth open from astonishment
他惊讶地张大了嘴巴
"I will explain it to you at once," said the Fox
"我马上就给你解释一下，"狐狸说
"in the land of the Owls there is a sacred field"
"在猫头鹰的土地上有一片圣地"
"everybody calls it the field of miracles"
"大家都称它为奇迹之地"
"In this field you must dig a little hole"
"在这块地里，你必须挖一个小坑"
"and you must put a gold coin into the hole"
"你得把金币放进洞里"
"then you cover up the hole with a little earth"
"那你就用一点泥土把洞盖起来"

"you must get water from the fountain nearby"
"你得从附近的喷泉取水"
"you must water they hole with two pails of water"
"你得用两桶水浇灌他们洞"
"then sprinkle the hole with two pinches of salt"
"然后在洞里撒上两撮盐"
"and when night comes you can go quietly to bed"
"当夜幕降临时，你可以安静地上床睡觉"
"during the night the miracle will happen"
"在夜间，奇迹将发生"
"the gold pieces you planted will grow and flower"
"你种下的金子必长大开花"
"and what do you think you will find in the morning?"
"那你觉得早上会找到什么呢？"
"You will find a beautiful tree where you planted it"
"你会在你种的地方找到一棵美丽的树"
"they tree will be laden with gold coins"
"树上必满是金币"
Pinocchio grew more and more bewildered
匹诺曹越来越困惑
"let's suppose I bury my five coins in that field"
"假设我把我的五枚硬币埋在那块地里"
"how many coins might I find the following morning?"
"第二天早上我能找到多少枚硬币？"
"That is an exceedingly easy calculation," replied the Fox
"那可是个极其容易的计算，"狐狸回答
"a calculation you can make with your hands"
"你可以用双手进行的计算"
"Every coin will give you an increase of five-hundred"
"每枚硬币都会给你增加五百"
"multiply five hundred by five and you have your answer"

"将 500 乘以 5，你就有答案了"
"you will find two-thousand-five-hundred shining gold pieces"
"你会找到两千五百块闪闪发光的金币"
"Oh! how delightful!" cried Pinocchio, dancing for joy
"哦！多么令人愉快啊！"匹诺曹叫道，高兴得手舞足蹈
"I will keep two thousand for myself"
"我自己留两千"
"and the other five hundred I will give you two"
"另外五百块我给你两块"
"A present to us?" cried the Fox with indignation
"给我们的礼物吗？"
and he almost appeared offended at the offer
他几乎对这个提议感到被冒犯
"What are you dreaming of?" asked the Fox
"你在梦什么？"
"What are you dreaming of?" repeated the Cat
"你在梦什么？"
"We do not work to accumulate interest"
"我们工作不是为了积累利息"
"we work solely to enrich others"
"我们的工作只是为了让他人富裕"
"to enrich others!" repeated the Cat
"为了丰富别人！"
"What good people!" thought Pinocchio to himself
"多么好的人啊！"
and he forgot all about his papa and the new jacket
他把他爸爸和那件新夹克忘得一干二净
and he forgot about the spelling-book
他忘记了那本拼写簿
and he forgot all of his good resolutions
他忘记了他所有的好决心
"Let us be off at once" he suggested

"我们马上走吧,"他建议道
"I will go with you two to the field of Owls"
"我和你们两个一起去猫头鹰的田野"

The Inn of the Red Craw-Fish
红小龙虾旅馆

They walked, and walked, and walked
他们走着,走着,走着
all tired out, they finally arrived at an inn
他们都累得精疲力尽,终于来到了一家旅馆
The Inn of The Red Craw-Fish
The Inn of The Red Craw-Fish
"Let us stop here a little," said the Fox
"我们在这里停一会儿,"狐狸说
"we should have something to eat," he added
"我们应该吃点东西,"他补充道
"we need to rest ourselves for an hour or two"
"我们需要休息一两个小时"
"and then we will start again at midnight"
"然后我们将在午夜再次出发"
"we'll arrive at the Field of Miracles in the morning"
"我们早上到达奇迹之地"
Pinocchio was also tired from all the walking
匹诺曹也因为走路而疲惫不堪
so he was easily convinced to go into the inn
所以他很容易就被说服进了客栈
all three of them sat down at a table
他们三个人都在一张桌子旁坐下
but none of them really had any appetite
但他们都没有真正的胃口

The Cat was suffering from indigestion
猫患有消化不良
and she was feeling seriously indisposed
她感到非常不舒服
she could only eat thirty-five fish with tomato sauce
她只能吃三十五条番茄酱鱼
and she had just four portions of noodles with Parmesan
她只吃了四份帕尔马干酪面条
but she thought the noodles weres not seasoned enough
但她认为面条不够调味
so she asked three times for the butter and grated cheese!
所以她要了三次黄油和磨碎的奶酪！
The Fox could also have gone without eating
狐狸也可能不吃东西就走了
but his doctor had ordered him a strict diet
但他的医生要求他严格饮食

so he was forced to content himself simply with a hare
所以他只好用一只野兔来满足自己

the hare was dressed with a sweet and sour sauce
野兔涂上了酸甜的酱汁

it was garnished lightly with fat chickens
它轻轻地用肥鸡装饰

then he ordered a dish of partridges and rabbits
然后他点了一盘鹧鸪和兔子

and he also ate some frogs, lizards and other delicacies
他还吃了一些青蛙、蜥蜴和其他美味佳肴

he really could not eat anything else
他真的不能吃其他任何东西

He cared very little for food, he said
他说，他对食物非常不关心

and he said he struggled to put it to his lips
他说他努力把它放到嘴里

The one who ate the least was Pinocchio
吃得最少的是匹诺曹

He asked for some walnuts and a hunch of bread
他要了一些核桃和一大块面包

and he left everything on his plate
他把一切都留在了盘子里

The poor boy's thoughts were not with the food
这个可怜的男孩心思不在食物上

he continually fixed his thoughts on the Field of Miracles
他不断地把自己的思想集中在奇迹的原野上

When they had supped, the Fox spoke to the host
他们吃完饭后，狐狸对主人说话

"Give us two good rooms, dear inn-keeper"
"给我们两个好房间，亲爱的客栈老板"

"please provide us one room for Mr. Pinocchio"
"请为我们提供一个房间给匹诺曹先生"

"and I will share the other room with my companion"

"我要和我的同伴同住另一个房间。"
"We will snatch a little sleep before we leave"
"我们走之前会睡一会儿"
"Remember, however, that we wish to leave at midnight"
"不过,请记住,我们希望在午夜出发"
"so please call us, to continue our journey"
"所以请打电话给我们,继续我们的旅程"
"Yes, gentlemen," answered the host
"是的,先生们,"主人回答
and he winked at the Fox and the Cat
他对狐狸和猫眨了眨眼
it was as if he said "I know what you are up to"
就好像他说"我知道你在做什么"
the wink seemed to say, "we understand one another!"
眨眼似乎在说:"我们彼此理解!
Pinocchio was very tired from the day
匹诺曹从那天开始就非常疲惫
he fell asleep as soon as he got into his bed
他一上床就睡着了
and as soon as he started sleeping he started to dream
他一开始睡觉就开始做梦
he dreamed that he was in the middle of a field
他梦见自己在田野中央
the field was full of shrubs as far as the eye could see
目之所及,田野上长满了灌木
the shrubs were covered with clusters of gold coins
灌木上覆盖着一簇簇金币
the gold coins swung in the wind and rattled
金币在风中摇晃,嘎嘎作响
and they made a sound like, "tzinn, tzinn, tzinn"
他们发出声音,像"tzinn, tzinn, tzinn"
they sounded as if they were speaking to Pinocchio
他们听起来像是在对匹诺曹说话

"Let who whoever wants to come and take us"
"谁想来带我们走"
Pinocchio was just about to stretch out his hand
匹诺曹正要伸出手
he was going to pick handfuls of those beautiful gold pieces
他要挑选一把那些美丽的金币
and he almost was able to put them in his pocket
他差点就把它们装进了口袋里
but he was suddenly awakened by three knocks on the door
但他突然被三声敲门声吵醒了
It was the host who had come to wake him up
是来叫醒他的主人
"I have come to let you know it's midnight"
"我来是想让你知道现在是午夜"
"Are my companions ready?" asked the puppet
"我的同伴们准备好了吗？"
"Ready! Why, they left two hours ago"
"准备好了！哎呀，他们两个小时前就走了"
"Why were they in such a hurry?"
"他们为什么这么着急？"
"Because the Cat had received a message"
"因为猫收到了一条信息"
"she got news that her eldest kitten was ill"
"她得到消息，说她最大的小猫生病了"
"Did they pay for the supper?"
"他们付了晚饭费吗？"
"What are you thinking of?"
"你在想什么？"
"They are too well educated to dream of insulting you"
"他们受过良好的教育，做梦也想侮辱你"
"a gentleman like you would not let his friends pay"

"像你这样的绅士不会让他的朋友付钱的"
"What a pity!" thought Pinocchio
"真可惜！"
"such an insult would have given me much pleasure!"
"这样的侮辱会给我带来很大的乐趣！"
"And where did my friends say they would wait for me?"
"我的朋友说他们会在哪里等我？"
"At the Field of Miracles, tomorrow morning at daybreak"
"在奇迹之地，明天早晨黎明"
Pinocchio paid a coin for the supper of his companions
匹诺曹为他的同伴们支付了一枚硬币
and then he left for the field of Miracles
然后他就去了奇迹的田野
Outside the inn it was almost pitch black
客栈外面几乎是一片漆黑
Pinocchio could only make progress by groping his way
匹诺曹只能摸索着前进
it was impossible to see his hand's in front of him
不可能看到他的手在他面前
Some night-birds flew across the road
一些夜鸟飞过马路
they brushed Pinocchio's nose with their wings
他们用翅膀擦过匹诺曹的鼻子
it caused him a terrible fright
这让他受到了可怕的恐惧
springing back, he shouted: "who goes there?"
他跳起来，喊道："谁去那里？
and the echo in the hills repeated in the distance
山丘上的回声在远处重复
"Who goes there?" - "Who goes there?" - "Who goes there?"

"谁去那里？" - "谁去那里？" - "谁去那里？"
on the trunk of the tree he saw a little light
在树干上，他看到一点光亮
it was a little insect he saw shining dimly
那是一只小虫子，他看到它微弱地闪耀着光芒
like a night-light in a lamp of transparent china
就像透明中国灯中的夜灯
"Who are you?" asked Pinocchio
"你是谁？"
the insect answered in a low voice;
虫子低声回答；
"I am the ghost of the talking little cricket"
"我是会说话的小蟋蟀的幽灵"
the voice was fainter than can be described
声音微弱得无法形容
the voice seemed to come from the other world
声音似乎来自另一个世界
"What do you want with me?" said the puppet
"你想找我干什么？"
"I want to give you some advice"
"我想给你一些建议"
"Go back and take the four coins that you have left"
"回去拿你剩下的四枚硬币"
"take your coins to your poor father"
"把你的硬币给你可怜的爸爸"
"he is weeping and in despair at home"
"他在家里哭泣和绝望"
"because you have not returned to him"
"因为你还没有回到他那里"
but Pinocchio had already thought of this
但匹诺曹已经想到了这一点
"By tomorrow my papa will be a gentleman"
"到明天，我爸爸就会成为一位绅士了"

"these four coins will become two thousand"
"这四枚硬币将变成两千"
"Don't trust those who promise to make you rich in a day"
"不要相信那些承诺让你一天变得富有的人"
"Usually they are either mad or rogues!"
"通常他们要么是疯子,要么是流氓!"
"Give ear to me, and go back, my boy"
"听我的话,回吧,我的孩子"
"On the contrary, I am determined to go on"
"相反,我决心继续"
"The hour is late!" said the cricket
"时间很晚了!"
"I am determined to go on"
"我决心继续"
"The night is dark!" said the cricket
"夜很黑!"
"I am determined to go on"
"我决心继续"
"The road is dangerous!" said the cricket
"这条路很危险!"
"I am determined to go on"
"我决心继续"
"boys are bent on following their wishes"
"男孩们一心要追随自己的愿望"
"but remember, sooner or later they repent it"
"但要记住,他们迟早会悔改的"
"Always the same stories. Good-night, little cricket"
"总是相同的故事。晚安,小蟋蟀"
The Cricket wished Pinocchio a good night too
蟋蟀也祝匹诺曹晚安
"may Heaven preserve you from dangers and assassins"

"愿天堂保护你免受危险和刺客的伤害"
then the talking little cricket vanished suddenly
然后,那只会说话的小蟋蟀突然消失了
like a light that has been blown out
就像一盏被吹灭的光
and the road became darker than ever
路面变得比以往任何时候都更黑暗

Pinocchio Falls into the Hands of the Assassins
匹诺曹落入刺客之手

Pinocchio resumed his journey and spoke to himself
匹诺曹继续他的旅程,自言自语
"how unfortunate we poor boys are"
"我们这些可怜的男孩多么不幸"
"Everybody scolds us and gives us good advice"
"每个人都责骂我们,给我们很好的建议"
"but I don't choose to listen to that tiresome little cricket"
"但我不选择听那只令人厌烦的小蟋蟀的话"
"who knows how many misfortunes are to happen to me!"
"谁知道我身上会遭遇多少不幸呢!"
"I haven't even met any assassins yet!"
"我甚至还没见过任何刺客!"
"That is, however, of little consequence"
"不过,这无关紧要"
"for I don't believe in assassins"
"因为我不相信刺客"
"I have never believed in assassins"
"我从来不相信刺客"
"I think that assassins have been invented purposely"

"我认为刺客是故意发明的"
"papas use them to frighten little boys"
"爸爸用它们来吓唬小男孩"
"and then little boys are scared of going out at night"
"然后小男孩们就害怕晚上出门"
"Anyway, let's suppose I was to come across assassins"
"不管怎样,假设我遇到了刺客"
"do you imagine they would frighten me?"
"你觉得他们会吓到我吗?"
"they would not frighten me in the least"
"他们丝毫不会吓到我"
"I will go to meet them and call to them"
"我去迎接他们,呼唤他们"
'Gentlemen assassins, what do you want with me?'
"绅士们,刺客们,你们想找我干什么?"
'Remember that with me there is no joking'
"记住,我不能开玩笑"
'Therefore, go about your business and be quiet!'
"所以,去做你的事吧,安静点!"
"At this speech they would run away like the wind"
"听到这番话,他们就会像风一样逃跑"
"it could be that they are badly educated assassins"
"可能是他们是受过不良教育的刺客"
"then the assassins might not run away"
"这样刺客就不会逃跑了"
"but even that isn't a great problem"
"但即使这样也不是什么大问题"
"then I would just run away myself"
"那我就自己逃跑"
"and that would be the end of that"
"那就结束吧"
But Pinocchio had no time to finish his reasoning
但匹诺曹没有时间完成他的推理

he thought that he heard a slight rustle of leaves
他以为他听到了树叶的轻微沙沙声
He turned to look where the noise had come from
他转过身去看声音的来源
and he saw in the gloom two evil-looking black figures
他在黑暗中看到了两个看起来邪恶的黑色人影
they were completely enveloped in charcoal sacks
他们完全被木炭袋包裹着
They were running after him on their tiptoes
他们踮着脚尖追着他跑
and they were making great leaps like two phantoms
他们像两个幽灵一样飞跃着
"Here they are in reality!" he said to himself
"他们在现实中就在这里！"
he didn't have anywhere to hide his gold pieces
他没有地方可以藏他的金币
so he put them in his mouth, under his tongue
"就把它们放在嘴里，放在他的舌头下
Then he turned his attention to escaping
然后他把注意力转向逃跑
But he did not manage to get very far
但他没能走得很远
he felt himself seized by the arm
他感到自己被那只胳膊抓住了

and he heard two horrid voices threatening him
他听到两个可怕的声音威胁他
"Your money or your life!" they threatened
他们威胁说:"要么你的钱,要么你的命!
Pinocchio was not able to answer in words
匹诺曹无法用语言回答
because he had put his money in his mouth
因为他把钱放在嘴里
so he made a thousand low bows
于是他低低地鞠了一千个鞠躬
and he offered a thousand pantomimes
他提供了一千个哑剧
He tried to make the two figures understand
他试图让这两个人明白
he was just a poor puppet without any money
他只是一个没有任何钱的穷人
he had not as much as a nickel in his pocket
他口袋里连一分钱都没有

but the two robbers were not convinced
但两个劫匪并不相信

"Less nonsense and out with the money!"
"少废话，带着钱出去！"

And the puppet made a gesture with his hands
然后木偶用手做了一个手势

he pretended to turn his pockets inside out
他假装把口袋里里外外翻过来

Of course Pinocchio didn't have any pockets
当然，匹诺曹没有任何口袋

but he was trying to signify, "I have no money"
但他试图表示，"我没有钱"

slowly the robbers were losing their patience
慢慢地，强盗们失去了耐心

"Deliver up your money or you are dead," said the taller one
"交出你的钱，不然你就死定了，"高个子说

"Dead!" repeated the smaller one
"死了！"

"And then we will also kill your father!"
"然后我们也要杀了你的爸爸！"

"Also your father!" repeated the smaller one again
"还有你的爸爸！"

"No, no, no, not my poor papa!" cried Pinocchio in despair
"不，不，不，不是我可怜的爸爸！"

and as he said it the coins clinked in his mouth
"说着，硬币在他的嘴里叮叮当当

"Ah! you rascal!" realized the robbers
"啊！你这个流氓！"

"you have hidden your money under your tongue!"
"你把钱藏在嘴里了！"

"Spit it out at once!" he ordered him

"马上吐出来！"
"spit it out," repeated the smaller one
"吐出来，"小个子重复道
Pinocchio was obstinate to their commands
匹诺曹固执地服从他们的命令
"Ah! you pretend to be deaf, do you?"
"啊！你装聋，是吗？"
"leave it to us to find a means"
"让我们自己想办法"
"we will find a way to make you give up your money"
"我们会想办法让你放弃你的钱"
"We will find a way," repeated the smaller one
"我们会找到办法的，"小个子重复道
And one of them seized the puppet by his nose
其中一个人抓住了木偶的鼻子
and the other took him by the chin
另一个人抓住了他的下巴
and they began to pull brutally
他们开始残忍地拉扯
one pulled up and the other pulled down
一个拉起，另一个拉下
they tried to force him to open his mouth
他们试图强迫他张开嘴
But it was all to no purpose
但这一切都是徒劳的
Pinocchio's mouth seemed to be nailed together
匹诺曹的嘴巴似乎被钉在一起了
Then the shorter assassin drew out an ugly knife
然后，矮个子刺客掏出了一把丑陋的刀
and he tried to put it between his lips
他试图把它放在嘴里
But Pinocchio, as quick as lightning, caught his hand
但匹诺曹像闪电一样迅速抓住了他的手
and he bit him with his teeth

他就用牙齿咬他
and with one bite he bit the hand clean off
他一口咬住了那只手
but it wasn't a hand that he spat out
但他吐出的不是一只手
it was hairier than a hand, and had claws
它比手还多毛，还有爪子
imagine Pinocchio's astonishment when saw a cat's paw
想象一下匹诺曹看到猫的爪子时的惊讶
or at least that's what he thought he saw
或者至少他认为自己看到了
Pinocchio was encouraged by this first victory
匹诺曹对这首场胜利感到鼓舞
now he used his fingernails to break free
现在他用指甲挣脱了
he succeeded in liberating himself from his assailants
他成功地将自己从袭击者手中解放出来
he jumped over the hedge by the roadside
他跳过了路边的树篱
and began to run across the fields
开始在田野上奔跑
The assassins ran after him like two dogs chasing a hare
刺客们像两只狗追赶兔子一样追着他跑
and the one who had lost a paw ran on one leg
失去一只爪子的那只用一条腿跑
and no one ever knew how he managed it
没有人知道他是怎么做到的
After a race of some miles Pinocchio could run no more
跑了几英里后，匹诺曹再也跑不动了
he thought his situation was lost
他认为他的处境已经迷失了
he climbed the trunk of a very high pine tree

他爬上了一棵非常高的松树的树干
and he seated himself in the topmost branches
他坐在最上面的树枝上
The assassins attempted to climb after him
刺客们试图追赶他
when they reached half-way up the tree they slid down again
当他们爬到树的一半时,他们又滑了下来
and they arrived on the ground with their skin grazed
他们来到地上,皮肤被擦伤了
But they didn't give up so easily
但他们并没有那么轻易放弃
they piled up some dry wood beneath the pine
他们在松树下堆了一些干木头
and then they set fire to the wood
然后他们放火烧了木头
very quickly the pine began to burn higher
很快,松树开始燃烧得更高
like a candle blown by the wind
就像被风吹动的蜡烛
Pinocchio saw the flames rising higher and higher
匹诺曹看到火焰越来越高
he did not wish to end his life like a roasted pigeon
他不想像一只烤鸽子一样结束自己的生命
so he made a stupendous leap from the top of the tree
于是他从树顶上跳了下来
and he ran across the fields and vineyards
他跑过田野和葡萄园
The assassins followed him again
刺客们又跟着他
and they kept behind him without giving up
他们一直跟在他身后,没有放弃
The day began to break and they were still pursuing him

天亮了,他们仍然在追赶他
Suddenly Pinocchio found his way barred by a ditch
突然,匹诺曹发现他的路被一条沟挡住了
it was full of stagnant water the colour of coffee
里面到处都是死水,是咖啡的颜色
What was our Pinocchio to do now?
我们的匹诺曹现在该怎么办?
"One! two! three!" cried the puppet
"一!二!三个!
making a rush, he sprang to the other side
他冲向另一边
The assassins also tried to jump over the ditch
刺客们也试图跳过壕沟
but they had not measured the distance
但他们没有测量距离
splish splash! they fell into the middle of the ditch
啪啪啪!他们掉进了沟里

Pinocchio heard the plunge and the splashing
匹诺曹听到了坠落和水花的声音
"A fine bath to you, gentleman assassins"
"给你们洗个好澡，绅士们"
And he felt convinced that they were drowned
他确信他们已经被淹死了
but it's good that Pinocchio did look behind him
但匹诺曹确实看了看他的身后，这很好
because his two assassins had not drowned
因为他的两个刺客没有淹死
the two assassins had got out the water again
两名刺客又从水里出来了
and they were both still running after him
他们俩都还在追他
they were still enveloped in their sacks
他们仍然被包裹在他们的袋子里
and the water was dripping from them
水从他们身上滴落
as if they had been two hollow baskets
仿佛它们是两个空心的篮子

The Assassins Hang Pinocchio to the Big Oak Tree
刺客将匹诺曹吊在大橡树上

At this sight, the puppet's courage failed him
看到这一幕，木偶的勇气让他失望了
he was on the point of throwing himself on the ground
他几乎要把自己扔在地上
and he wanted to give himself over for lost
他想为了失去而放弃自己
he turned his eyes in every direction
他把目光转向四面八方

he saw a small house as white as snow
他看到一座像雪一样洁白的小房子
"If only I had breath to reach that house"
"如果我还有一口气能到达那所房子就好了"
"perhaps then I might be saved"
"也许那时我就可以得救了"
without delaying an instant he recommenced running
他毫不迟疑地重新开始奔跑
poor little Pinocchio was running for his life
可怜的小匹诺曹正在逃命
he ran through the wood with the assassins after him
他穿过树林，刺客们跟在他后面
there was a desperate race of nearly two hours
这是一场近两个小时的绝望比赛
and finally he arrived quite breathless at the door
最后，他气喘吁吁地来到门口
he desperately knocked on the door of the house
他拼命地敲门
but no one answered Pinocchio's knock
但没有人回应匹诺曹的敲门声
He knocked at the door again with great violence
他又猛烈地敲了敲门
because he heard the sound of steps approaching him
因为他听到了脚步声向他走来
and he heard the the heavy panting of his persecutors
他听到了迫害他的人沉重的喘息
there was the same silence as before
一如既往的寂静
he saw that knocking was useless
他看到敲门没用
so he began in desperation to kick and pommel the door
所以他开始绝望地踢门和敲门
The window next to the door then opened

然后门旁边的窗户打开了
and a beautiful Child appeared at the window
一个漂亮的孩子出现在窗前
the beautiful child had blue hair
这个漂亮的孩子有一头蓝头发
and her face was as white as a waxen image
她的脸白得像蜡像
her eyes were closed as if she was asleep
她闭着眼睛,仿佛睡着了
and her hands were crossed on her breast
她的双手交叉在胸前
Without moving her lips in the least, she spoke
她没有动动嘴唇,开口了
"In this house there is no one, they are all dead"
"这房子里没有人,他们都死了"
and her voice seemed to come from the other world
她的声音似乎来自另一个世界
but Pinocchio shouted and cried and implored
但匹诺曹大喊大叫,哭泣,恳求
"Then at least open the door for me"
"那么至少为我开门"
"I am also dead," said the waxen image
"我也死了,"蜡像说
"Then what are you doing there at the window?"
"那你在窗边做什么?"
"I am waiting to be taken away"
"我在等着被带走"
Having said this she immediately disappeared
说完这句话,她立刻消失了
and the window was closed again without the slightest noise
窗户又关上了,没有丝毫声音
"Oh! beautiful Child with blue hair," cried Pinocchio"
"哦!美丽的蓝头发孩子,"匹诺曹叫道。

"open the door, for pity's sake!"
"开门吧,看在可怜的份上!"

"Have compassion on a poor boy pursued..."
"怜悯被追捕的穷男孩……"

But he could not finish the sentence
但他没能把这句话说完

because he felt himself seized by the collar
因为他觉得自己被项圈抓住了

the same two horrible voices said to him threateningly:
同样的两个可怕的声音威胁地对他说:

"You shall not escape from us again!"
"你不能再离开我们了!"

"You shall not escape," panted the little assassin
"你逃不掉,"小刺客气喘吁吁地说

The puppet saw death was staring him in the face
木偶看到死神正盯着他的脸

he was taken with a violent fit of trembling
他被吓得浑身发抖

the joints of his wooden legs began to creak
他的木腿关节开始吱吱作响

and the coins hidden under his tongue began to clink
藏在他舌头下的硬币开始叮当作响

"will you open your mouth—yes or no?" demanded the assassins
"你会张开你的嘴——是还是不是?"

"Ah! no answer? Leave it to us"
"啊!没有回答?交给我们吧"

"this time we will force you to open it!"
"这次我们就逼你打开它!"

"we will force you," repeated the second assassin
"我们会强迫你,"第二个刺客重复道

And they drew out two long, horrid knives
他们拔出两把可怕的长刀

and the knifes were as sharp as razors
刀子像剃刀一样锋利
they attempted to stab him twice
他们试图刺伤他两次
but the puppet was lucky in one regard
但这个傀儡在一个方面是幸运的
he had been made from very hard wood
他是用非常坚硬的木头制成的
the knives broke into a thousand pieces
刀子碎成一千块
and the assassins were left with just the handles
而刺客们只剩下了把手
for a moment they could only stare at each other
有那么一刻，他们只能互相凝视着
"I see what we must do," said one of them
"我知道我们必须做什么，"其中一人说
"He must be hung! Let us hang him!"
"他必须被绞死！让我们把他吊死吧！
"Let us hang him!" repeated the other
"让我们把他吊死吧！"
Without loss of time they tied his arms behind him
他们毫不犹豫地将他的手臂绑在身后
and they passed a running noose round his throat
他们把一个套索套在他的喉咙上
and they hung him to the branch of the Big Oak
他们把他挂在大橡树的树枝上
They then sat down on the grass watching Pinocchio
然后他们坐在草地上看着匹诺曹
and they waited for his struggle to end
他们等待他的挣扎结束
but three hours had already passed
但三个小时已经过去了
the puppet's eyes were still open
木偶的眼睛还睁着

his mouth was closed just as before
他的嘴巴和以前一样闭着
and he was kicking more than ever
他踢得比以往任何时候都多
they had finally lost their patience with him
他们终于对他失去了耐心
they turned to Pinocchio and spoke in a bantering tone
他们转向匹诺曹，用戏谑的语气说话
"Good-bye Pinocchio, see you again tomorrow"
"再见，匹诺曹，明天再见"
"hopefully you'll be kind enough to be dead"
"希望你能好心地死去"
"and hopefully you will have your mouth wide open"
"希望你能张大嘴巴"
And they walked off in a different direction
他们朝着不同的方向走去
In the meantime a northerly wind began to blow and roar
与此同时，北风开始吹来咆哮
and the wind beat the poor puppet from side to side
风把这个可怜的木偶左右打着

the wind made him swing about violently
风使他猛烈地摆动
like the clatter of a bell ringing for a wedding
就像婚礼的钟声
And the swinging gave him atrocious spasms
摆动使他剧烈痉挛
and the noose became tighter and tighter around his throat
绞索在他的喉咙上越来越紧
and finally it took away his breath
最后,它使他喘不过气来
Little by little his eyes began to grow dim
渐渐地,他的眼睛开始变得暗淡

he felt that death was near
他觉得死亡近在咫尺
but Pinocchio never gave up hope
但匹诺曹从未放弃希望
"perhaps some charitable person will come to my assistance"
"也许会有慈善人士来帮我"
But he waited and waited and waited
但他等啊等啊等
and in the end no one came, absolutely no one
最后没有人来，绝对没有人
then he remembered his poor father
然后他想起了他可怜的父亲
thinking he was dying, he stammered out
他以为自己快死了，结结巴巴地说
"Oh, papa! papa! if only you were here!"
"噢，爸爸！爸爸！要是你在这儿就好了！"
His breath failed him and he could say no more
他喘不过气来，不能再说什么了
He shut his eyes and opened his mouth
他闭上眼睛，张开嘴巴
and he stretched out his arms and legs
他伸出胳膊和腿
he gave one final long shudder
他最后一次长长地颤抖了一下
and then he hung stiff and insensible
然后他僵硬地挂着

The Beautiful Child Rescues the Puppet
美丽的孩子拯救了木偶

poor Pinocchio was still suspended from the Big Oak tree
可怜的匹诺曹仍然被吊在大橡树上

but apparently Pinocchio was more dead than alive
但显然匹诺曹死得比活着的要多

the beautiful Child with blue hair came to the window again
美丽的蓝发孩子又来到了窗前

she saw the unhappy puppet hanging by his throat
她看到那个不快乐的木偶挂在他的喉咙上

she saw him dancing up and down in the gusts of the wind
她看到他在阵风中起起伏伏

and she was moved by compassion for him
她因对他的怜悯而感动

the beautiful child struck her hands together
美丽的孩子用手拍打着

and she gave three little claps
她轻轻地拍了三下掌

there came a sound of wings flying rapidly
传来了翅膀飞快的声音

a large Falcon flew on to the window-sill
一只大猎鹰飞到了窗台上

"What are your orders, gracious Fairy?" he asked
"你有什么命令,亲切的仙女?"
and he inclined his beak in sign of reverence
他歪着喙,表示崇敬
"Do you see that puppet dangling from the Big Oak tree?"
"你看到那个挂在大橡树上的木偶了吗?"
"I see him," confirmed the falcon
"我看到他了,"猎鹰确认道
"Fly over to him at once," she ordered him
"马上飞到他身边,"她命令他
"use your strong beak to break the knot"
"用你强壮的喙打破这个结"
"lay him gently on the grass at the foot of the tree"
"轻轻地把他放在树脚下的草地上"
The Falcon flew away to carry out his orders
猎鹰飞走执行他的命令
and after two minutes he returned to the child

两分钟后，他又回到了孩子身边
"I have done as you commanded"
"我照你的吩咐做了"
"And how did you find him?"
"你是怎么找到他的？"
"when I first saw him he appeared dead"
"我第一次看到他时，他似乎已经死了"
"but he couldn't really have been entirely dead"
"但他不可能真的完全死了"
"I loosened the noose around his throat"
"我松开了他喉咙上的绞索"
"and then he gave soft a sigh"
"然后他向 Soft 叹了口气"
"he muttered to me in a faint voice"
"他用微弱的声音对我喃喃自语"
"'Now I feel better!' he said"
"'现在我感觉好多了！'

The Fairy then struck her hands together twice
然后仙女双手合拢了两次

as soon as she did this a magnificent Poodle appeared
她一这样做，一只华丽的贵宾犬就出现了

the poodle walked upright on his hind legs
贵宾犬用后腿直立行走

it was exactly as if he had been a man
就好像他曾经是个男人一样

He was in the full-dress livery of a coachman
他穿着马车夫的正装制服

On his head he had a three-cornered cap braided with gold
他头上戴着一顶镶金子的三角帽

his curly white wig came down on to his shoulders
他卷曲的白色假发垂到肩上

he had a chocolate-collared waistcoat with diamond

buttons
他有一件巧克力领的马甲，上面有钻石纽扣
and he had two large pockets to contain bones
他有两个大口袋，用来装骨头
the bones that his mistress gave him at dinner
他的情妇在晚餐时送给他的骨头
he also had a pair of short crimson velvet breeches
他还有一条深红色天鹅绒短裤
and he wore some silk stockings
他穿着一些丝袜
and he wore smart Italian leather shoes
他穿着时髦的意大利皮鞋
hanging behind him was a species of umbrella case
他身后挂着一种伞盒
the umbrella case was made of blue satin
伞套由蓝色缎面制成
he put his tail into it when the weather was rainy
他趁着下雨的时候把尾巴伸进去
"Be quick, Medoro, like a good dog!"
"快点，Medoro，像条好狗一样！"
and the fairy gave her poodle the commands
仙女就向她的贵宾犬发出了命令
"get the most beautiful carriage harnessed"
"驾驭最漂亮的马车"
"and have the carriage waiting in my coach-house"
"让马车在我的马车房里等着。"
"and go along the road to the forest"
"沿着通往森林的路走"
"When you come to the Big Oak tree you will find a poor puppet"
"当你来到大橡树时，你会发现一个可怜的木偶"
"he will be stretched on the grass half dead"
"他将被拉在草地上，半死不活"
"you will have to pick him up gently"

"你得轻轻地把他抱起来"
"lay him flat on the cushions of the carriage"
"把他平放在马车的垫子上"
"when you have done this bring him here to me"
"当你做完这些之后，把他带到我这里来。"
"Do you understand?" she asked one last time
"你明白吗？"
The Poodle showed that he had understood
贵宾犬表明他已经明白了
he shook the case of blue satin three or four times
他摇晃了蓝色缎面的盒子三四次
and then he ran off like a race-horse
然后他像赛马一样跑开了
soon a beautiful carriage came out of the coach-house
不久，一辆漂亮的马车从马车房里出来
The cushions were stuffed with canary feathers
靠垫上塞满了金丝雀的羽毛
the carriage was lined on the inside with whipped cream
马车内部衬有生奶油
and custard and vanilla wafers made the seating
蛋奶冻和香草威化饼占据了座位
The little carriage was drawn by a hundred white mice
小马车上拉着一百只白老鼠
and the Poodle was seated on the coach-box
贵宾犬坐在马车车厢上
he cracked his whip from side to side
他把鞭子左右抽打
like a driver when he is afraid that he is behind time
就像一个司机，当他害怕自己落后于时间时
less than a quarter of an hour passed
不到一刻钟就过去了
and the carriage returned to the house
马车回到了房子里

The Fairy was waiting at the door of the house
仙女在房子门口等着
she took the poor puppet in her arms
她把这个可怜的木偶抱在怀里
and she carried him into a little room
她把他抱进了一个小房间
the room was wainscoted with mother-of-pearl
房间用珍珠母装饰着护墙板
she called for the most famous doctors in the neighbourhood
她召集了附近最著名的医生
They came immediately, one after the other
他们马上一个接一个地来了
a Crow, an Owl, and a talking little cricket
一只乌鸦、一只猫头鹰和一只会说话的小蟋蟀
"I wish to know something from you, gentlemen," said the Fairy
"我想从你们那里知道些什么,先生们,"仙女说
"is this unfortunate puppet alive or dead?"
"这个不幸的木偶是活着还是死了?"
the Crow started by feeling Pinocchio's pulse
乌鸦从摸匹诺曹的脉搏开始
he then felt his nose and his little toe
然后他摸了摸自己的鼻子和小脚趾
he carefully made his diagnosis of the puppet
他仔细地对这个木偶进行了诊断
and then he solemnly pronounced the following words:
然后他郑重地念出以下几句话:
"To my belief the puppet is already dead"
"我相信这个傀儡已经死了"
"but there is always the chance he's still alive"
"但他总有机会还活着"
"I regret," said the Owl, "to contradict the Crow"

"我很遗憾，"猫头鹰说，"反驳乌鸦"
"my illustrious friend and colleague"
"我杰出的朋友和同事"
"in my opinion the puppet is still alive"
"在我看来，木偶还活着"
"but there's always a chance he's already dead"
"但他总有可能已经死了"
lastly the Fairy asked the talking little Cricket
最后，仙女问会说话的小蟋蟀
"And you, have you nothing to say?"
"那你呢，你没什么要说的吗？"
"doctors are not always called upon to speak"
"医生并不总是被要求发言"
"sometimes the wisest thing is to be silent"
"有时最明智的做法是保持沉默"
"but let me tell you what I know"
"但让我告诉你我所知道的"
"that puppet has a face that is not new to me"
"那个木偶的脸对我来说并不陌生"
"I have known him for some time!"
"我认识他有一段时间了！"
Pinocchio had lain immovable up to that moment
匹诺曹一直躺着一动不动
he was just like a real piece of wood
他就像一块真正的木头
but then he was seized with a fit of convulsive trembling
但随后他就被一阵抽搐的颤抖抓住了
and the whole bed shook from his shaking
整张床都因他的摇晃而颤抖
the talking little Cricket continued talking
会说话的小蟋蟀继续说话
"That puppet there is a confirmed rogue"

- 110 -

"那个傀儡,那里有个已确认的流氓"
Pinocchio opened his eyes, but shut them again immediately
匹诺曹睁开了眼睛,但又立即闭上了
"He is a good for nothing ragamuffin vagabond"
"他是个一无是处的流浪汉"
Pinocchio hid his face beneath the clothes
匹诺曹把脸藏在衣服下面
"That puppet there is a disobedient son"
"那个傀儡那里有一个不听话的儿子"
"he will make his poor father die of a broken heart!"
"他会让他可怜的父亲死于心碎!"
At that instant everyone could hear something
在那一刻,每个人都能听到什么
suffocated sound of sobs and crying was heard
听到令人窒息的啜泣和哭泣声
the doctors raised the sheets a little
医生们把床单稍微抬高了一点
Imagine their astonishment when they saw Pinocchio
想象一下他们看到匹诺曹时的惊讶
the crow was the first to give his medical opinion
乌鸦是第一个给出他的医学意见的人
"When a dead person cries he's on the road to recovery"
"当一个死者哭泣时,他就走在康复的路上"
but the owl was of a different medical opinion
但猫头鹰的医学观点不同
"I grieve to contradict my illustrious friend"
"我为反驳我杰出的朋友而感到悲痛"
"when the dead person cries it means he's is sorry to die"
"当死者哭泣时,意味着他对死感到遗憾"

Pinocchio Refuses to Take his Medicine
匹诺曹拒绝吃药

The doctors had done all that they could
医生们已经尽了他们所能
so they left Pinocchio with the fairy
所以他们把匹诺曹留给了仙女
the Fairy touched Pinocchio's forehead
仙子摸了摸匹诺曹的额头
she could tell that he had a high fever
她看得出来他发了高烧
the Fairy knew exactly what to give Pinocchio
仙子很清楚该给匹诺曹什么
she dissolved a white powder in some water
她把一种白色的粉末溶在一些水中
and she offered Pinocchio the tumbler of water
她把那杯水递给匹诺曹
and she reassured him that everything would fine
她向他保证，一切都会好起来的
"Drink it and in a few days you will be cured"
"喝了它，几天后你就会痊愈"
Pinocchio looked at the tumbler of medicine
匹诺曹看着那杯药
and he made a wry face at the medicine
他对着药做了一个苦笑的表情
"Is it sweet or bitter?" he asked plaintively
"是甜的还是苦的？"
"It is bitter, but it will do you good"
"这很苦，但对你有好处"
"If it is bitter, I will not drink it"
"如果它是苦的，我就不喝"
"Listen to me," said the Fairy, "drink it"
"听我说，"仙女说，"喝吧"
"I don't like anything bitter," he objected

"我不喜欢任何苦涩的东西，"他反对道
"I will give you a lump of sugar"
"我给你一块糖"
"it will take away the bitter taste"
"它会带走苦味"
"but first you have to drink your medicine"
"但首先你得喝你的药"
"Where is the lump of sugar?" asked Pinocchio
"那块糖在哪儿？"
"Here is the lump of sugar," said the Fairy
"这是那块糖，"仙女说
and she took out a piece from a gold sugar-basin
她从金糖盆里拿出一块
"please give me the lump of sugar first"
"请先给我那块糖"
"and then I will drink that bad bitter water"
"然后我就喝那恶水"
"Do you promise me?" she asked Pinocchio
"你答应我吗？"她问匹诺曹
"Yes, I promise," answered Pinocchio
"是的，我保证，"匹诺曹回答
so the Fairy gave Pinocchio the piece of sugar
于是仙女把那块糖给了匹诺曹
and Pinocchio crunched up the sugar and swallowed it
匹诺曹把糖嘎吱嘎吱地吞了下去
he licked his lips and enjoyed the taste
他舔了舔嘴唇，享受着那种味道
"It would be a fine thing if sugar were medicine!"
"如果糖是药就好了！"
"then I would take medicine every day"
"那我就每天吃药"
the Fairy had not forgotten Pinocchio's promise
仙子没有忘记匹诺曹的承诺

"keep your promise and drink this medicine"
"信守诺言,喝这药"
"it will restore you back to health"
"它会让你恢复健康"
Pinocchio took the tumbler unwillingly
匹诺曹不情愿地接过了玻璃杯
he put the point of his nose to the tumbler
他把鼻子的尖端放在不倒翁上
and he lowered the tumbler to his lips
他把玻璃杯放到嘴边
and then again he put his nose to it
然后他又把鼻子凑了起来
and at last he said, "It is too bitter!"
最后他说:"这太苦了!
"I cannot drink anything so bitter"
"我不能喝这么苦的东西"
"you don't know yet if you can't," said the Fairy
"如果你不能,你还不知道,"仙女说
"you have not even tasted it yet"
"你还没尝过"
"I can imagine how it's going to taste!"
"我可以想象它会是什么味道!"
"I know it from the smell," objected Pinocchio
"我从气味中知道,"匹诺曹反对道
"first I want another lump of sugar please"
"请先我想要另一块糖"
"and then I promise that will drink it!"
"然后我保证它会喝掉它!"
The Fairy had all the patience of a good mamma
仙女拥有好妈妈的所有耐心
and she put another lump of sugar in his mouth
她又把一块糖放进他的嘴里
and again, she presented the tumbler to him

她又把玻璃杯递给他
"I still cannot drink it!" said the puppet
"我还是不能喝它!"
and Pinocchio made a thousand grimaced faces
匹诺曹做了一千个鬼脸
"Why can't you drink it?" asked the fairy
"你为什么不能喝呢?"
"Because that pillow on my feet bothers me"
"因为我脚上的那个枕头让我很困扰"
The Fairy removed the pillow from his feet
仙女把枕头从脚上拿下来
Pinocchio excused himself again
匹诺曹又为自己找了个借口
"I've tried my best but it doesn't help me"
"我已经尽力了,但对我没有帮助"
"Even without the pillow I cannot drink it"
"即使没有枕头,我也喝不下它"
"What is the matter now?" asked the fairy
"现在怎么了?"仙女问道
"The door of the room is half open"
"房间的门半开着"
"it bothers me when doors are half open"
"当门半开时,我感到很困扰"
The Fairy went and closed the door for Pinocchio
仙女去为匹诺曹关上了门
but this didn't help, and he burst into tears
但这无济于事,他泪流满面
"I will not drink that bitter water—no, no, no!"
"我不喝那苦水——不,不,不!"
"My boy, you will repent it if you don't"
"我的孩子,如果你不这样做,你会后悔的"
"I don't care if I will repent it," he replied
"我不在乎我是否会后悔,"他回答

"Your illness is serious," warned the Fairy
"你的病很严重，"仙女警告道
"I don't care if my illness is serious"
"我不在乎我的病是不是严重"
"The fever will carry you into the other world"
"发烧会带你进入另一个世界"
"then let the fever carry me into the other world"
"那就让发烧带我去另一个世界吧"
"Are you not afraid of death?"
"你不怕死吗？"
"I am not in the least afraid of death!"
"我一点也不怕死！"
"I would rather die than drink bitter medicine"
"我宁死也不喝苦药"
At that moment the door of the room flew open
就在这时，房间的门飞开了
four rabbits as black as ink entered the room
四只黑得像墨水一样的兔子走进了房间
on their shoulders they carried a little bier
他们的肩膀上扛着一个小棺材

"What do you want with me?" cried Pinocchio
"你想找我干什么？"

and he sat up in bed in a great fright
他惊恐地从床上坐了起来

"We have come to take you," said the biggest rabbit
"我们是来带你来的，"最大的兔子说

"you cannot take me yet; I am not dead"
"你还不能带我走;我没死"

"where are you planning to take me to?"
"你打算带我去哪里？"

"No, you are not dead yet," confirmed the rabbit
"不，你还没死呢，"兔子确认道

"but you have only a few minutes left to live"
"但你只剩下几分钟的生命了"

"because you refused the bitter medicine"
"因为你拒绝了苦药"

"the bitter medicine would have cured your fever"
"苦药本来可以治好你的发烧的"

"Oh, Fairy, Fairy!" the puppet began to scream
"哦，仙女，仙女！"木偶开始尖叫

"give me the tumbler at once," he begged
"马上把不倒翁给我，"他恳求道

"be quick, for pity's sake, I do not want die"
"快点，看在可怜的份上，我不想死"

"no, I will not die today"
"不，我今天不会死"

Pinocchio took the tumbler with both hands
匹诺曹双手接过玻璃杯

and he emptied the water one one big gulp
他一大口地倒空了水
"We must have patience!" said the rabbits
"我们得有耐心！"
"this time we have made our journey in vain"
"这一次，我们的旅程是徒劳的"
they took the little bier on their shoulders again
他们又把小棺材扛在肩上
and they left the room back to where they came from
他们离开了房间，回到了他们来的地方
and they grumbled and murmured between their teeth
他们咕哝着，咬牙切齿地喃喃自语
Pinocchio's recovery did not take long at all
匹诺曹的康复并没有花很长时间
a few minutes later he jumped down from the bed
几分钟后，他从床上跳了下来
wooden puppets have a special privilege

木制木偶有特殊特权
they seldom get seriously ill like us
他们很少像我们一样病得很重
and they are lucky to be cured very quickly
他们很幸运能很快被治愈
"has my medicine done you good?" asked the fairy
"我的药对你有用吗？"
"your medicine has done me more than good"
"你的药对我有好处"
"your medicine has saved my life"
"你的药救了我的命"
"why didn't you take your medicine sooner?"
"你为什么不早点吃药？"
"Well, Fairy, we boys are all like that!"
"嗯，仙女，我们男孩子都是这样的！"
"We are more afraid of medicine than of the illness"
"我们更害怕药物而不是疾病"
"Disgraceful!" cried the fairy in indignation
"可耻！"仙女愤慨地喊道
"Boys ought to know the power of medicine"
"男孩应该知道医学的力量"
"a good remedy may save them from a serious illness"
"好的补救措施可以使他们免于重病"
"and perhaps it even saves you from death"
"也许它甚至可以让你免于死亡"
"next time I shall not require so much persuasion"
"下次我就不需要那么多劝说了"
"I shall remember those black rabbits"
"我会记住那些黑兔子"
"and I shall remember the bier on their shoulders"
"我会记住他们肩上的棺材"
"and then I shall immediately take the tumbler"
"然后我马上拿走那杯酒"

"and I will drink all the medicine in one go!"
"我要一口气把药都喝光！"
The Fairy was happy with Pinocchio's words
仙子对匹诺曹的话很满意
"Now, come here to me and sit on my lap"
"现在，到我这里来，坐在我的腿上"
"and tell me all about the assassins"
"告诉我关于刺客的一切"
"how did you end up hanging from the big Oak tree?"
"你是怎么挂在那棵大橡树上的？"
And Pinocchio ordered all the events that happened
匹诺曹下令将发生的所有事件都安排了下来
"You see, there was a ringmaster; Fire-eater"
"你看，有个马戏团团长;噬火者"
"Fire-eater gave me some gold pieces"
"噬火者给了我一些金币"
"he told me to take the gold to my father"
"他让我把金子拿给我爸爸"
"but I didn't take the gold straight to my father"
"但我没有直接把金子拿给我爸爸"
"on the way home I met a Fox and a Cat"
"在回家的路上，我遇到了一只狐狸和一只猫"
"they made me an offer I couldn't refuse"
"他们给了我一个我无法拒绝的提议"
'Would you like those pieces of gold to multiply?'
"你想让那些金子成倍增加吗？"
"'Come with us and,' they said"
"'跟我们来吧，'他们说。"
'we will take you to the Field of Miracles'
"我们将带您前往奇迹之地"
"and I said, 'Let's go to the Field of Miracles'"
"我说，'我们去奇迹之地吧'"
"And they said, 'Let us stop at this inn'"

"and we stopped at the Red Craw-Fish in"
"他们说,'让我们在这家客栈停下来吧'"
"all of us went to sleep after our food"
"我们在红小龙虾停了下来"
"all of us went to sleep after our food"
"我们所有人吃完饭都睡着了"
"when I awoke they were no longer there"
"当我醒来时,他们已经不在那里了"
"because they had to leave before me"
"因为他们必须在我之前离开"
"Then I began to travel by night"
"然后我开始在夜间旅行"
"you cannot imagine how dark it was"
"你无法想象它有多黑"
"that's when I met the two assassins"
"就在那时,我遇到了那两个刺客"
"and they were wearing charcoal sacks"
"他们穿着木炭袋"
"they said to me: 'Out with your money'"
"他们对我说:'把你的钱拿出来'"
"and I said to them, 'I have no money'"
"我对他们说:'我没有钱。'"
"because I had hidden the four gold pieces"
"因为我把那四块金子藏起来了"
"I had put the money in my mouth"
"我把钱放进了嘴里"
"one tried to put his hand in my mouth"
"一个人试图把手伸进我的嘴里"
"and I bit his hand off and spat it out"
"我咬掉了他的手,把它吐了出来"
"but instead of a hand it was a cat's paw"
"但不是一只手,而是一只猫的爪子"
"and then the assassins ran after me"
"然后刺客们就追着我跑"

"and I ran and ran as fast as I could"
"我跑了,跑得尽可能快"
"but in the end they caught me anyway"
"但最后他们还是抓住了我"
"and they tied a noose around my neck"
"他们在我的脖子上绑了一根绞索"
"and they hung me from the Big Oak tree"
"他们把我吊在大橡树上"
"they waited for me to stop moving"
"他们等我停下来"
"but I never stopped moving at all"
"但我从未停止过移动"
"and then they called up to me"
"然后他们打电话给我"
'Tomorrow we shall return here'
"明天我们再来"
'then you will be dead with your mouth open'
"那你就会张着嘴死去"
'and we will have the gold under your tongue'
"我们会把金子藏在你的舌头下"
the Fairy was interested in the story
仙子对这个故事很感兴趣
"And where have you put the pieces of gold now?"
"那你现在把金子放哪儿了?"
"I have lost them!" said Pinocchio, dishonestly
"我把他们弄丢了!"
he had the pieces of gold in his pocket
他的口袋里有金子
as you know Pinocchio already had a long nose
如你所知,匹诺曹已经有一个长鼻子了
but lying made his nose grow even longer
但撒谎使他的鼻子变得更长
and his nose grew another two inches

他的鼻子又长了两英寸
"And where did you lose the gold?"
"那你把金子丢在哪儿了？"
"I lost it in the woods," he lied again
"我在树林里丢了，"他又撒了谎
and his nose also grew at his second lie
他的鼻子也在他的第二个谎言中长大了
"worry not about the gold," said the fairy
"不用担心金子，"仙女说
"we will go to the woods and find your gold"
"我们去树林找你的金子"
"all that is lost in those woods is always found"
"在那些树林中丢失的一切总能找到"
Pinocchio got quite confused about his situation
匹诺曹对自己的处境感到非常困惑
"Ah! now I remember all about it," he replied
"啊！现在我记得这一切，"他回答说
"I didn't lose the four gold pieces at all"
"我根本没有丢失那四块金币"
"I just swallowed your medicine, didn't I?"
"我刚刚吞下了你的药，不是吗？"
"I swallowed the coins with the medicine"
"我把硬币和药一起吞了下去"
at this daring lie his nose grew even longer
听到这个大胆的谎言，他的鼻子变得更长了
now Pinocchio could not move in any direction
现在匹诺曹无法向任何方向移动
he tried to turn to his left side
他试着转向他的左侧
but his nose struck the bed and window-panes
可是他的鼻子撞到了床和窗玻璃上
he tried to turn to the right side
他试图转向右侧

but now his nose struck against the walls
但现在他的鼻子撞到了墙壁上
and he could not raise his head either
他也抬不起头来
because his nose was long and pointy
因为他的鼻子又长又尖
and his nose could have poke the Fairy in the eye
他的鼻子可以戳到仙女的眼睛
the Fairy looked at him and laughed
仙子看着他，笑了起来
Pinocchio was very confused about his situation
匹诺曹对自己的处境感到非常困惑
he did not know why his nose had grown
他不知道自己的鼻子为什么长大了
"What are you laughing at?" asked the puppet
"你在笑什么？"
"I am laughing at the lies you've told me"
"我在嘲笑你对我说的谎言"
"how can you know that I have told lies?"
"你怎么知道我说了谎？"
"Lies, my dear boy, are found out immediately"
"谎言，我亲爱的孩子，马上就被发现了"
"in this world there are two sorts of lies"
"这个世界上有两种谎言"
"There are lies that have short legs"
"有短腿的谎言"
"and there are lies that have long noses"
"还有长鼻子的谎言"
"Your lie is one of those that has a long nose"
"你的谎言是长鼻子的谎言之一"
Pinocchio did not know where to hide himself
匹诺曹不知道该往哪里躲
he was ashamed of his lies being discovered
他为自己的谎言被发现而感到羞愧

he tried to run out of the room
他试图跑出房间
but he did not succeed at escaping
但他没有成功逃脱
his nose had gotten too long to escape
他的鼻子已经长得太长了,无法逃脱
and he could no longer pass through the door
他再也进不了门

Pinocchio Meets the Fox and the Cat Again
匹诺曹再次遇见狐狸和猫

the Fairy understood the importance of the lesson
仙女明白这节课的重要性
she let the puppet to cry for a good half-hour
她让木偶哭了足足半个小时
his nose could no longer pass through the door
他的鼻子再也进不来了
telling lies is the worst thing a boy can do
说谎是男孩能做的最糟糕的事情
and she wanted him to learn from his mistakes
她希望他从错误中吸取教训
but she could not bear to see him weeping
但她不忍心看到他哭泣
she felt full of compassion for the puppet
她对这个木偶充满了同情心
so she clapped her hands together again
于是她又拍了拍手
a thousand large Woodpeckers flew in from the window
一千只大啄木鸟从窗户飞进来
The woodpeckers immediately perched on Pinocchio's nose

啄木鸟立即栖息在匹诺曹的鼻子上
and they began to peck at his nose with great zeal
他们开始非常热情地啄他的鼻子
you can imagine the speed of a thousand woodpeckers
你可以想象一千只啄木鸟的速度
within no time at all Pinocchio's nose was normal
很快,匹诺曹的鼻子就恢复了正常
of course you remember he always had a big nose
你当然记得他总是个大鼻子
"What a good Fairy you are," said the puppet
"你真是个好仙女,"木偶说
and Pinocchio dried his tearful eyes
匹诺曹擦干了他泪流满面的眼睛
"and how much I love you!" he added
"我多么爱你啊!"
"I love you also," answered the Fairy
"我也爱你,"仙女回答
"if you remain with me you shall be my little brother"
"如果你留在我身边,你就是我的弟弟"
"and I will be your good little sister"
"我将成为你的好妹妹"
"I would like to remain very much," said Pinocchio
"我非常想留下来,"匹诺曹说
"but I have to go back to my poor papa"
"但我必须回到我可怜的爸爸那里去"
"I have thought of everything," said the fairy
"我什么都想过了,"仙女说
"I have already let your father know"
"我已经让你爸爸知道了"
"and he will come here tonight"
"他今晚会来的"
"Really?" shouted Pinocchio, jumping for joy
"真的吗?"匹诺曹喊道,高兴得跳了起来

"Then, little Fairy, I have a wish"
"那么,小仙女,我有一个愿望"
"I would very much like to go and meet him"
"我非常想去见他"
"I want to give a kiss to that poor old man"
"我想给那个可怜的老人一个吻"
"he has suffered so much on my account"
"他为我受了这么多苦"
"Go, but be careful not to lose your way"
"去吧,但要小心,不要迷路"
"Take the road that goes through the woods"
"走穿过树林的路"
"I am sure that you will meet him there"
"我相信你会在那里见到他"
Pinocchio set out to go through the woods
匹诺曹出发穿过树林
once in the woods he began to run like a kid
一进树林,他就开始像个孩子一样奔跑
But then he had reached a certain spot in the woods
但后来他已经到了树林里的某个地方
he was almost in front of the Big Oak tree
他几乎在大橡树前面
he thought he heard people amongst the bushes
他以为他在灌木丛中听到了人的声音
In fact, two persons came out on to the road
事实上,有两个人走上了路
Can you guess who they were?
你能猜出他们是谁吗?
they were his two travelling companions
他们是他的两个旅伴
in front of him was the Fox and the Cat
在他面前的是狐狸和猫
his companions who had taken him to the inn
带他去客栈的同伴

"Why, here is our dear Pinocchio!" cried the Fox
"哎呀，我们亲爱的匹诺曹在这里！"
and he kissed and embraced his old friend
他亲吻并拥抱了他的老朋友
"How came you to be here?" asked the fox
"你怎么会在这里？"
"How come you to be here?" repeated the Cat
"你怎么会在这里？"
"It is a long story," answered the puppet
"说来话长，"木偶回答
"I will tell you the story when I have time"
"有空的时候我会告诉你这个故事"
"but I must tell you what happened to me"
"但我必须告诉你，我发生了什么事。"
"do you know that the other night I met with assassins?"

- 128 -

"你知道那天晚上我遇到了刺客吗?"
"Assassins! Oh, poor Pinocchio!" worried the Fox
"刺客们!哦,可怜的匹诺曹!"
"And what did they want?" he asked
"他们想要什么?"
"They wanted to rob me of my gold pieces"
"他们想抢我的金币"
"Villains!" said the Fox
"恶棍!"
"Infamous villains!" repeated the Cat
"臭名昭著的恶棍!"
"But I ran away from them," continued the puppet
"但我从他们身边逃走了,"木偶继续说
"they did their best to catch me"
"他们尽了最大的努力来抓住我"
"and after a long chase they did catch me"
"经过长时间的追逐,他们终于抓住了我"
"they hung me from a branch of that oak tree"
"他们把我吊在那棵橡树的树枝上"
And Pinocchio pointed to the Big Oak tree
匹诺曹指着那棵大橡树
the Fox was appalled by what he had heard
狐狸对他所听到的一切感到震惊
"Is it possible to hear of anything more dreadful?"
"还能听到比这更可怕的事吗?"
"In what a world we are condemned to live!"
"我们注定要生活在一个多么美好的世界里!"
"Where can respectable people like us find a safe refuge?"
"像我们这样受人尊敬的人在哪里可以找到安全的避难所?"
the conversation went on this way for some time
谈话就这样持续了一段时间

in this time Pinocchio observed something about the Cat
在这段时间里,匹诺曹观察到了关于猫的一些事情
the Cat was lame of her front right leg
猫的右前腿瘸了
in fact, she had lost her paw and all its claws
事实上,她已经失去了她的爪子和所有的爪子
Pinocchio wanted to know what had happened
匹诺曹想知道发生了什么
"What have you done with your paw?"
"你用你的爪子干了什么?"
The Cat tried to answer, but became confused
猫试图回答,但变得困惑
the Fox jumped in to explain what had happened
福克斯跳进来解释了发生了什么
"you must know that my friend is too modest"
"你要知道,我的朋友太谦虚了"
"her modesty is why she doesn't usually speak"
"她的谦虚是她通常不说话的原因"
"so let me tell the story for her"
"那么,让我替她讲讲这个故事吧"
"an hour ago we met an old wolf on the road"
"一个小时前,我们在路上遇到了一只老狼"
"he was almost fainting from want of food"
"他几乎要因为缺乏食物而昏倒"
"and he asked alms of us"
"他向我们请求施舍"
"we had not so much as a fish-bone to give him"
"我们连一根鱼骨头都没给他。"
"but what did my friend do?"
"可是我的朋友是怎么做的呢?"
"well, she really has the heart of a César"
"嗯,她真的有一颗凯撒的心"

"She bit off one of her fore paws"
"她咬掉了一只前爪"
"and the threw her paw to the poor beast"
"然后把她的爪子扔给那只可怜的野兽"
"so that he might appease his hunger"
"这样他就可以解饥了"
And the Fox was brought to tears by his story
狐狸被他的故事感动得流泪
Pinocchio was also touched by the story
匹诺曹也被这个故事所感动
approaching the Cat, he whispered into her ear
走近猫,他在她耳边低语
"If all cats resembled you, how fortunate the mice would be!"
"如果所有的猫都像你,老鼠该多幸运啊!"
"And now, what are you doing here?" asked the Fox
"那么,你在这里做什么?"
"I am waiting for my papa," answered the puppet
"我在等我爸爸,"木偶回答
"I am expecting him to arrive at any moment now"
"我期待他现在随时到来"
"And what about your pieces of gold?"
"那你的金子呢?"
"I have got them in my pocket," confirmed Pinocchio
"我把它们放在口袋里了,"匹诺曹确认道
although he had to explain that he had spent one coin
虽然他不得不解释说他花了一枚硬币
the cost of their meal had come to one piece of gold
他们的餐费已经降到了一块金子
but he told them not to worry about that
但他告诉他们不要担心
but the Fox and the Cat did worry about it
但狐狸和猫确实担心它

"Why do you not listen to our advice?"
"你为什么不听我们的劝告呢？"
"by tomorrow you could have one or two thousand!"
"到明天，你可能会有一两千个！"
"Why don't you bury them in the Field of Miracles?"
"你为什么不把他们埋在奇迹之地？"
"Today it is impossible," objected Pinocchio
"今天这是不可能的，"匹诺曹反对道
"but don't worry, I will go another day"
"不过别担心，我改天再去"
"Another day it will be too late!" said the Fox
"改天再晚！"
"Why would it be too late?" asked Pinocchio
"为什么太晚了？"
"Because the field has been bought by a gentleman"
"因为这块地已经被一位绅士买下了"
"after tomorrow no one will be allowed to bury money there"
"明天之后，任何人都不允许在那里埋钱"
"How far off is the Field of Miracles?"
"奇迹之地有多远？"
"It is less than two miles from here"
"离这里不到两英里"
"Will you come with us?" asked the Fox
"你愿意跟我们一起去吗？"
"In half an hour we can be there"
"半小时后我们就可以到"
"You can bury your money straight away"
"你可以马上把钱埋起来"
"and in a few minutes you will collect two thousand coins"
"几分钟后，你将收集到两千个硬币"
"and this evening you will return with your pockets

full"
"今天晚上你会带着满满的口袋回来"
"Will you come with us?" the Fox asked again
"你愿意跟我们一起去吗？"
Pinocchio thought of the good Fairy
匹诺曹想起了善良的仙女
and Pinocchio thought of old Geppetto
匹诺曹想起了老杰佩托
and he remembered the warnings of the talking little cricket
他想起了那只会说话的小蟋蟀的警告
and he hesitated a little before answering
他犹豫了一会儿才回答
by now you know what kind of boy Pinocchio is
现在你知道匹诺曹是什么样的男孩了
Pinocchio is one of those boys without much sense
匹诺曹是那种没有多少理智的男孩之一
he ended by giving his head a little shake
最后，他微微摇了摇头
and then he told the Fox and the Cat his plans
然后他把他的计划告诉了狐狸和猫
"Let us go: I will come with you"
"我们走吧，我跟你一起去"
and they went to the field of miracles
他们去了奇迹的田野
they walked for half a day and reached a town
他们走了半天，到达了一个小镇
the town was the Trap for Blockheads
这个小镇是 Blockheads 的陷阱
Pinocchio noticed something interesting about this town
匹诺曹注意到这个小镇有一些有趣的地方
everywhere where you looked there were dogs
你看的地方到处都是狗

all the dogs were yawning from hunger
所有的狗都饿得打哈欠
and he saw shorn sheep trembling with cold
他看到剪了毛的羊冻得发抖
even the cockerels were begging for Indian corn
甚至公鸡也在乞求印度玉米
there were large butterflies that could no longer fly
有不能再飞翔的大蝴蝶
because they had sold their beautiful coloured wings
因为他们卖掉了他们美丽的彩色翅膀
there were peacocks that were ashamed to be seen
有些孔雀羞愧地被看到
because they had sold their beautiful coloured tails
因为他们卖掉了他们美丽的彩色尾巴
and pheasants went scratching about in a subdued fashion
野鸡以一种柔和的方式抓挠着
they were mourning for their gold and silver feathers
他们为自己的金银羽毛哀悼
most were beggars and shamefaced creatures
大多数是乞丐和羞愧的生物
but among them some lordly carriage passed
但在他们中间,有一些庄重的马车经过
the carriages contained a Fox, or a thieving Magpie
马车上有一只狐狸,或者一只偷窃的喜鹊
or the carriage seated some other ravenous bird of prey
或者马车上坐着其他一些贪婪的猛禽
"And where is the Field of Miracles?" asked Pinocchio
"奇迹之地在哪里?"
"It is here, not two steps from us"
"它就在这里,离我们不到两步"
They crossed the town and and went over a wall
他们穿过城镇,翻过了一堵墙
and then they came to a solitary field

然后他们来到了一片孤零零的田野
"Here we are," said the Fox to the puppet
"我们到了，"狐狸对木偶说
"Now stoop down and dig with your hands a little hole"
"现在弯下腰，用手挖一个小坑"
"and put your gold pieces into the hole"
"把你的金块放进洞里"
Pinocchio obeyed what the fox had told him
匹诺曹听从了狐狸告诉他的话
He dug a hole and put into it the four gold pieces
他挖了一个洞，把四块金子放进去
and then he filled up the hole with a little earth
然后他用一点泥填满了坑
"Now, then," said the Fox, "go to that canal close to us"
"那么，"狐狸说，"到我们附近的那条运河去吧。
"fetch a bucket of water from the canal"
"从运河里打一桶水"
"water the ground where you have sowed the gold"
"浇灌你播种黄金的土地"
Pinocchio went to the canal without a bucket
匹诺曹没有带桶就去了运河
as he had no bucket, he took off one of his old shoes
由于他没有桶，他脱掉了一只旧鞋
and he filled his shoe with water
他把鞋装满了水
and then he watered the ground over the hole
然后他给洞口的地面浇水
He then asked, "Is there anything else to be done?
然后他问道："还有什么要做的吗？
"you need not do anything else," answered the Fox
"你不需要做任何其他事情，"狐狸回答
"there is no need for us to stay here"

"我们没有必要留在这里"
"you can return in about twenty minutes"
"你大约二十分钟后可以回来"
"and then you will find a shrub in the ground"
"然后你会在地里找到一棵灌木"
"the tree's branches will be loaded with money"
"树枝上必满载钱财"

The poor puppet was beside himself with joy
这个可怜的木偶高兴得在自己身边
he thanked the Fox and the Cat a thousand times
他感谢了狐狸和猫一千次
and he promised them many beautiful presents
他答应给他们许多美丽的礼物
"We wish for no presents," answered the two rascals
"我们不要礼物,"两个流氓回答
"It is enough for us to have taught you how to enrich yourself"
"我们教你如何充实自己就足够了"
"there is nothing worse than seeing others do hard work"
"没有什么比看到别人努力工作更糟糕的了"
"and we are as happy as people out for a holiday"
"我们和外出度假的人一样快乐"
Thus saying, they took leave of Pinocchio
"说着,他们告别了匹诺曹
and they wished him a good harvest
他们祝愿他有好收成
and then they went about their business
然后他们就去做他们的事了

- 136 -

Pinocchio is Robbed of his Money
匹诺曹被抢走了他的钱

The puppet returned to the town
傀儡回到了镇上
and he began to count the minutes one by one
他开始逐个数着时间
and soon he thought he had counted long enough
很快,他觉得自己已经数得够久了
so he took the road leading to the Field of Miracles
于是他走上了通往奇迹之地的路
And he walked along with hurried steps
他迈着匆忙的步伐走着
and his heart beat fast with great excitement
他的心跳得非常兴奋
like a drawing-room clock going very well
就像客厅的时钟运转得很顺利
Meanwhile he was thinking to himself:
与此同时,他心里想:
"what if I don't find a thousand gold pieces?"
"如果我没有找到一千块金币怎么办?"
"what if I find two thousand gold pieces instead?"
"如果我找到两千块金币呢?"
"but what if I don't find two thousand gold pieces?"
"可是,如果我没有找到两千块金币呢?"
"what if I find five thousand gold pieces!"
"如果我找到五千块金币怎么办!"
"what if I find a hundred thousand gold pieces??"
"如果我找到十万块金币怎么办??"
"Oh! what a fine gentleman I should then become!"
"哦!那我该成为一个多么优秀的绅士啊!"
"I could live in a beautiful palace"
"我可以住在美丽的宫殿里"
"and I would have a thousand little wooden horses"

"我就有一千匹小木马"
"a cellar full of currant wine and sweet syrups"
"一个装满醋栗酒和甜糖浆的酒窖"
"and a library quite full of candies and tarts"
"还有一个装满糖果和蛋挞的图书馆"
"and I would have plum-cakes and macaroons"
"我会吃李子蛋糕和马卡龙"
"and I would have biscuits with cream"
"我会吃奶油饼干"
he walked along building castles in the sky
他走在天空中建造城堡
and he build many of these castles in the sky
他在天空中建造了许多这样的城堡
and eventually he arrived at the edge of the field
最终,他来到了田野的边缘
and he stopped to look about for a tree
他停下来四处寻找一棵树
there were other trees in the field
田野里还有其他树木
but they had been there when he had left
但当他离开时,他们一直在那儿
and he saw no money tree in all the field
他在整个田野里没有看到摇钱树
He walked along the field another hundred steps
他沿着田野又走了一百步
but he couldn't find the tree he was looking for
但他找不到他要找的那棵树
he then entered into the field
然后他进入了田野
and he went up to the little hole
他就上到那个小洞里
the hole where he had buried his coins
他埋钱币的洞
and he looked at the hole very carefully

他非常仔细地观察着那个洞
but there was definitely no tree growing there
但那里肯定没有树木
He then became very thoughtful
然后他变得非常沉思
and he forget the rules of society
他忘记了社会的规则
and he didn't care for good manners for a moment
他一时不在乎礼貌
he took his hands out of his pocket
他从口袋里掏出双手
and he gave his head a long scratch
他长长地挠了挠自己的头
At that moment he heard an explosion of laughter
就在这时，他听到了一阵笑声
someone close by was laughing himself silly
附近的人在傻傻地笑自己
he looked up one of the nearby trees
他抬头看了看附近的一棵树
he saw a large Parrot perched on a branch
他看到一只大鹦鹉栖息在树枝上
the parrot brushed the few feathers he had left
鹦鹉拂过他所剩无几的羽毛
Pinocchio asked the parrot in an angry voice;
匹诺曹用愤怒的声音问鹦鹉；
"Why are you here laughing so loud?"
"你为什么在这里笑得这么大声？"
"I am laughing because in brushing my feathers"
"我笑是因为在刷我的羽毛"
"I was just brushing a little under my wings"
"我只是在我的翅膀下刷了一点"
"and while brushing my feathers I tickled myself"
"在刷我的羽毛时，我给自己挠痒痒"
The puppet did not answer the parrot

木偶没有回答鹦鹉

but instead Pinocchio went to the canal
但匹诺曹却去了运河

he filled his old shoe full of water again
他又把旧鞋装满了水

and he proceeded to water the hole once more
他又开始给洞里浇水

While he was busy doing this he heard more laughter
当他忙着做这件事时,他听到了更多的笑声

the laughter was even more impertinent than before
笑声比以前更加无礼

it rang out in the silence of that solitary place
它在那个寂静的地方响起

Pinocchio shouted out even angrier than before
匹诺曹喊道,比以前更愤怒

"Once for all, may I know what you are laughing at?"
"我能知道你在笑什么吗?"

"I am laughing at simpletons," answered the parrot
"我在嘲笑傻瓜,"鹦鹉回答

"simpletons who believe in foolish things
"相信愚蠢事物的傻瓜

"the foolish things that people tell them"
"人们告诉他们的愚蠢事情"

"I laugh at those who let themselves be fooled"
"我嘲笑那些让自己被愚弄的人"

"fooled by those more cunning than they are"
"被那些比他们更狡猾的人愚弄"

"Are you perhaps speaking of me?"
"你也许是在说我吗?"

"Yes, I am speaking of you, poor Pinocchio"
"是的,我说的是你,可怜的匹诺曹"

"you have believed a very foolish thing"
"你相信了一件非常愚蠢的事情"

"you believed that money can be grown in fields"
"你相信钱可以在田里种"
"you thought money can be grown like beans"
"你以为钱可以像豆子一样生长"
"I also believed it once," admitted the parrot
"我也曾经相信过,"鹦鹉承认道
"and today I am suffering for having believed it"
"今天我因为相信了它而受苦"
"but I have learned my lesson from that trick"
"但我从那个伎俩中吸取了教训"
"I turned my efforts to honest work"
"我把精力转向诚实的工作"
"and I have put a few pennies together"
"我把几分钱凑在一起了"
"it is necessary to know how to earn your pennies"
"有必要知道如何赚取你的便士"
"you have to earn them either with your hands"
"你得用双手赚到"
"or you have to earn them with your brains"
"或者你必须用你的大脑来赚取它们"
"I don't understand you," said the puppet
"我不明白你的话,"木偶说
and he was already trembling with fear
他已经吓得浑身发抖
"Have patience!" rejoined the parrot
"要有耐心!"
"I will explain myself better, if you let me"
"如果你允许我的话,我会更好地解释自己。"
"there is something that you must know"
"有件事你必须知道"
"something happened while you were in the town"
"你在镇上的时候出了点事"
"the Fox and the Cat returned to the field"

"狐狸和猫回到了田野"
"they took the money you had buried"
"他们拿走了你埋藏的钱"
"and then they fled from the scene of the crime"
"然后他们逃离了犯罪现场"
"And now he that catches them will be clever"
"现在抓住他们的人会很聪明"

Pinocchio remained with his mouth open
匹诺曹仍然张着嘴

and he chose not to believe the Parrot's words
他选择不相信鹦鹉的话

he began with his hands to dig up the earth
他开始用双手挖土

And he dug deep into the ground
他深深地挖了起来

a rick of straw could have stood in the hole
一堆稻草可能站在洞里

but the money was no longer there
但钱已经不在那里了

He rushed back to the town in a state of desperation
他绝望地赶回镇上

and he went at once to the Courts of Justice
他立即去了法院

and he spoke directly with the judge
他直接与法官交谈

he denounced the two knaves who had robbed him
他谴责了抢劫他的两个小伙子

The judge was a big ape of the gorilla tribe
法官是大猩猩部落的一只大猿

an old ape respectable because of his white beard
一只因白胡子而受人尊敬的老猿

and he was respectable for other reasons
他之所以受人尊敬,还有其他原因

because he had gold spectacles on his nose

因为他的鼻子上戴着金眼镜
although, his spectacles were without glass
虽然，他的眼镜没有眼镜
but he was always obliged to wear them
但他总是不得不戴上它们
on account of an inflammation of the eyes
由于眼睛发炎

Pinocchio told him all about the crime
匹诺曹告诉了他所有关于犯罪的事情
the crime of which he had been the victim of
他曾是该罪行的受害者
He gave him the names and the surnames
他把名字和姓氏都给了他
and he gave all the details of the rascals

他把那些流氓的所有细节都说了出来
and he ended by demanding to have justice
他最后要求伸张正义
The judge listened with great benignity
法官非常善意地听着
he took a lively interest in the story
他对这个故事产生了浓厚的兴趣
he was much touched and moved by what he heard
他被他所听到的深深感动
finally the puppet had nothing further to say
最后，木偶没有什么可说的了
and then the gorilla rang a bell
然后大猩猩响了铃铛
two mastiffs appeared at the door
两只獒犬出现在门口
the dogs were dressed as gendarmes
这些狗打扮成宪兵
The judge then pointed to Pinocchio
法官随后指向匹诺曹
"That poor devil has been robbed"
"那个可怜的魔鬼被抢劫了"
"rascals took four gold pieces from him"
"流氓从他那里拿走了四块金币"
"take him away to prison immediately," he ordered
"马上把他带到监狱里，"他命令道
The puppet was petrified on hearing this
傀儡听到这话吓呆了
it was not at all the judgement he had expected
这根本不是他所期望的判断
and he tried to protest the judge
他试图抗议法官
but the gendarmes stopped his mouth
但宪兵堵住了他的嘴
they didn't want to lose any time

他们不想浪费任何时间
and they carried him off to the prison
他们就把他带到监狱里
And there he remained for four long months
他在那里呆了四个月
and he would have remained there even longer
他会在那里呆得更久
but puppets do sometimes have good fortune too
但木偶有时也确实有好运气
a young King ruled over the Trap for Blockheads
一位年轻的国王统治着 Blockheads 的陷阱
he had won a splendid victory in battle
他在战斗中取得了辉煌的胜利
because of this he ordered great public rejoicings
因此，他下令公众欢呼雀跃
There were illuminations and fireworks
有灯饰和烟花
and there were horse and velocipede races
还有赛马和脚踏车比赛
the King was so happy he released all prisoners
国王非常高兴，他释放了所有囚犯
Pinocchio was very happy at this news
匹诺曹听到这个消息非常高兴
"if they are freed, then so am I"
"如果他们被释放了，那么我也就被释放了"
but the jailor had other orders
但狱卒还有其他命令
"No, not you," said the jailor
"不，不是你，"狱卒说
"because you do not belong to the fortunate class"
"因为你不属于幸运阶层"
"I beg your pardon," replied Pinocchio
"请原谅，"匹诺曹回答
"I am also a criminal," he proudly said

"我也是个罪犯,"他自豪地说
the jailor looked at Pinocchio again
狱卒又看向匹诺曹
"In that case you are perfectly right"
"既然如此,你完全正确"
and he took off his hat
他摘下了帽子
and he bowed to him respectfully
他恭敬地向他鞠了一躬
and he opened the prison doors
他打开了监狱的门
and he let the little puppet escape
他让小傀儡逃走了

Pinocchio Goes back to the Fairy's House
匹诺曹回到仙女之家

You can imagine Pinocchio's joy
你可以想象匹诺曹的喜悦
finally he was free after four months
四个月后,他终于重获自由
but he didn't stop in order to celebrate
但他并没有停下来庆祝
instead, he immediately left the town
相反,他立即离开了小镇
he took the road that led to the Fairy's house
他走了通往仙女家的路
there had been a lot of rain in recent days
最近几天下了很多雨
so the road had become a went boggy and marsh
所以这条路变成了沼泽和沼泽
and Pinocchio sank knee deep into the mud
匹诺曹膝盖深陷在泥泞中

But the puppet was not one to give up
但这个傀儡并不是一个会放弃的人
he was tormented by the desire to see his father
他被见到父亲的愿望所折磨
and he wanted to see his little sister again too
他也想再见到他的妹妹
and he ran through the marsh like a greyhound
他像一只灰狗一样在沼泽地里跑来跑去
and as he ran he was splashed with mud
他跑着跑的时候,浑身是泥
and he was covered from head to foot
他从头到脚都被遮盖
And he said to himself as he went along:
他边走边自言自语道:
"How many misfortunes have happened to me"
"我遭遇了多少不幸"
"But I deserved these misfortunes"

"但我活该这些不幸"
"because I am an obstinate, passionate puppet"
"因为我是一个顽固、热情的傀儡"
"I am always bent upon having my own way"
"我总是一心想走自己的路"
"and I don't listen to those who wish me well"
"我不听那些祝我好的人"
"they have a thousand times more sense than I!"
"他们的理智比我高一千倍!"
"But from now I am determined to change"
"但从现在开始,我决心改变"
"I will become orderly and obedient"
"我必变得有秩序和顺服"
"because I have seen what happened"
"因为我看到了发生的事情"
"disobedient boys do not have an easy life"
"不听话的男孩子不会过得轻松"
"they come to no good and gain nothing"
"他们没有得到好处,也没有得到任何好处"
"And has my papa waited for me?"
"我爸爸等我了吗?"
"Shall I find him at the Fairy's house?"
"我可以在仙女家里找到他吗?"
"it has been so long since I last saw him"
"我上次见到他已经很久了"
"I am dying to embrace him again"
"我渴望再次拥抱他"
"I can't wait to cover him with kisses!"
"我迫不及待地想用吻来覆盖他!"
"And will the Fairy forgive me my bad conduct?"
"仙女会原谅我的不良行为吗?"
"To think of all the kindness I received from her"
"想想我从她那里得到的所有善意"

"oh how lovingly did she care for me"
"哦,她多么爱我"
"that I am now alive I owe to her!"
"我现在还活着,这是我欠她的!"
"could you find a more ungrateful boy"
"你能找到一个更忘恩负义的男孩吗"
"is there a boy with less heart than I have?"
"有没有一个男孩比我心胸慢?"

Whilst he was saying this he stopped suddenly
"说这话的时候,他突然停了下来

he was frightened to death
他被吓死了

and he made four steps backwards
他向后退了四步

What had Pinocchio seen?
匹诺曹看到了什么?

He had seen an immense Serpent
他见过一条巨大的蛇

the snake was stretched across the road
蛇被伸到马路对面

the snake's skin was a grass green colour
蛇的皮肤是草绿色的

and it had red eyes in its head
它的头上有一双红眼睛

and it had a long and pointed tail
它有一条又长又尖的尾巴

and the tail was smoking like a chimney
尾巴像烟囱一样冒着烟

It would be impossible to imagine the puppet's terror
无法想象这个木偶的恐怖
He walked away to a safe distance
他走到一个安全的距离
and he sat on a heap of stones
他坐在一堆石头上
there he waited until the Serpent had finished
他在那里等着，直到蛇说完
soon the Serpent's business should be done
很快，蛇的事情就要完成了
He waited an hour; two hours; three hours
他等了一个小时;两个小时;三个小时
but the Serpent was always there
但蛇一直在那里
even from a distance he could see his fiery eyes

即使从远处,他也能看到他炽热的眼睛
and he could see the column of smoke
他可以看到那根烟柱
the smoke that ascended from the end of his tail
从他尾巴末端升起的烟雾
At last Pinocchio tried to feel courageous
最后,匹诺曹试着鼓起勇气来
and he approached to within a few steps
他走近了几步
he spoke to the Serpent in a little soft voice
他用轻柔的声音对蛇说
"Excuse me, Sir Serpent," he insinuated
"对不起,蛇先生,"他暗示道
"would you be so good as to move a little?"
"你能不能稍微动一下?"
"just a step to the side, if you could"
"如果可以的话,就向旁边迈出一步"
He might as well have spoken to the wall
他还不如对着墙说话
He began again in the same soft voice:
他又用同样柔和的声音开始说:
"please know, Sir Serpent, I am on my way home"
"请知道,蛇先生,我正在回家的路上"
"my father is waiting for me"
"我爸爸在等我"
"and it has been such a long time since I saw him!"
"我已经很久没见到他了!"
"Will you, therefore, allow me to continue?"
"所以,你允许我继续说下去吗?"
He waited for a sign in answer to this request
他等待着对这个请求的回应
but the snake made no answer
但蛇没有回答
up to that moment the serpent had been sprightly

直到那一刻，那条蛇一直活泼
up until then it had been full of life
在那之前，它一直充满生机
but now he became motionless and almost rigid
但现在他变得一动不动，几乎僵硬了
He shut his eyes and his tail ceased smoking
他闭上眼睛，尾巴不再冒烟
"Can he really be dead?" said Pinocchio
"他真的会死吗？"
and he rubbed his hands with delight
他高兴地搓了搓手
He decided to jump over him
他决定跳过他
and then he could reach the other side of the road
然后他就可以到达路的另一边
Pinocchio took a little run up
匹诺曹稍微加快了脚步
and he went to jump over the snake
他就想跳过那条蛇
but suddenly the Serpent raised himself on end
但突然间，蛇站了起来
like a spring set in motion
就像一个发动的弹簧
and the puppet stopped just in time
而木偶及时停了下来
he stopped his feet from jumping
他阻止了脚跳
and he fell to the ground
他就倒在地上
he fell rather awkwardly into the mud
他笨拙地掉进了泥里
his head got stuck in the mud
他的头陷在泥里
and his legs went into the air

他的双腿飞向空中
the Serpent went into convulsions of laughter
蛇大笑起来抽搐起来
it laughed until he broke a blood-vessel
它一直笑着,直到他打破了一根血管
and the snake died from all its laughter
蛇就死于它所有的笑声中
this time the snake really was dead
这一次,蛇真的死了
Pinocchio then set off running again
匹诺曹随后再次出发
he hoped to reach the Fairy's house before dark
他希望能在天黑之前到达仙女的家
but soon he had other problems again
但很快他又遇到了其他问题
he began to suffer so dreadfully from hunger
他开始忍受饥饿的折磨
and he could not bear the hunger any longer
他再也忍受不了饥饿
he jumped into a field by the wayside
他跳进了路边的一块田地里
perhaps there were some grapes he could pick
也许他可以采摘一些葡萄
Oh, if only he had never done it!
哦,要是他从来没有这样做就好了!
He had scarcely reached the grapes
他刚够到葡萄
and then there was a "cracking" sound
然后是"噼啪"的声音
his legs were caught between something
他的双腿被什么东西夹住了
he had stepped into two cutting iron bars
他已经踏入了两根切割铁栅栏
poor Pinocchio became giddy with pain

可怜的匹诺曹因疼痛而头晕目眩
stars of every colour danced before his eyes
各种颜色的星星在他眼前翩翩起舞
The poor puppet had been caught in a trap
这个可怜的傀儡被困在一个陷阱里
it had been put there to capture polecats
它被放在那里是为了捕捉 Polecats

Pinocchio Becomes a Watch-Dog
匹诺曹成为看门狗

Pinocchio began to cry and scream
匹诺曹开始哭泣和尖叫
but his tears and groans were useless
但他的眼泪和呻吟毫无用处
because there was not a house to be seen
因为没有房子可看

nor did living soul pass down the road
Living Soul 也没有在这条路上经过
At last the night had come on
夜幕终于降临了
the trap had cut into his leg
陷阱割伤了他的腿
the pain brought him the point of fainting
疼痛使他昏厥
he was scared from being alone
他害怕独自一人
he didn't like the darkness
他不喜欢黑暗
Just at that moment he saw a Firefly
就在那一刻，他看到了一只萤火虫
He called to the firefly and said:
他叫住萤火虫说：
"Oh, little Firefly, will you have pity on me?"
"哦，小萤火虫，你会可怜我吗？"
"please liberate me from this torture"
"请把我从这种折磨中解救出来"
"Poor boy!" said the Firefly
"可怜的孩子！"
the Firefly stopped and looked at him with compassion
萤火虫停下脚步，怜悯地看着他
"your legs have been caught by those sharp irons"
"你的腿被那些锋利的铁镣夹住了"
"how did you get yourself into this trap?
"你是怎么掉进这个陷阱的？"
"I came into the field to pick grapes"
"我到田里来摘葡萄"
"But where did you plant your grapes?"
"可是你把葡萄种在哪里呢？"
"No, they were not my grapes"

"不，它们不是我的葡萄"

"who taught you to carry off other people's property?"
"谁教你拿走别人的财产？"

"I was so hungry," Pinocchio whimpered
"我好饿，"匹诺曹呜咽着

"Hunger is not a good reason"
"饥饿不是一个好理由"

"we cannot appropriated what does not belong to us"
"我们不能挪用不属于我们的东西"

"That is true, that is true!" said Pinocchio, crying
"这是真的，那是真的！"

"I will never do it again," he promised
"我再也不会这样做了，"他承诺

At this moment their conversation was interrupted
就在这时，他们的谈话被打断了

there was a slight sound of approaching footsteps
传来轻微的脚步声

It was the owner of the field coming on tiptoe
是田地的主人踮起脚尖来了

he wanted to see if he had caught a polecat
他想看看自己是不是抓到了一只 Polecat

the polecat that ate his chickens in the night
夜里吃鸡的 Polecat

but he was surprised by what was in his trap
但他对他的陷阱里的东西感到惊讶

instead of a polecat, a boy had been captured
被捕获的不是 Polecat，而是一个男孩

"Ah, little thief," said the angry peasant,
"啊，小贼，"愤怒的农民说，

"then it is you who carries off my chickens?"
"那么，是你把我的鸡带走了？"

"No, I have not been carrying off your chickens"
"不，我没有带走你的鸡"

"I only came into the field to take two grapes!"
"我进田里只是为了摘两颗葡萄！"
"He who steals grapes can easily steal chicken"
"偷葡萄的人很容易偷鸡"
"Leave it to me to teach you a lesson"
"让我给你一个教训"
"and you won't forget this lesson in a hurry"
"而且你不会匆忙忘记这个教训的"
Opening the trap, he seized the puppet by the collar
打开陷阱，他抓住了人偶的衣领
and he carried him to his house like a young lamb
他就把他像小羊羔一样抱到自己家里
they reached the yard in front of the house
他们来到了房子前面的院子里
and he threw him roughly on the ground
然后粗暴地把他扔在地上
he put his foot on his neck and said to him:
他把脚放在他的脖子上，对他说：
"It is late and I want to go to bed"
"很晚了，我想上床睡觉"
"we will settle our accounts tomorrow"
"我们明天算账"
"the dog who kept guard at night died today"
"那只夜守的狗今天死了"
"you will live in his place from now"
"从今以后，你将住在他的位置上"
"You shall be my watch-dog from now"
"从现在开始，你就是我的看门狗"
he took a great dog collar covered with brass knobs
他拿了一个覆盖着黄铜旋钮的大狗项圈
and he strapped the dog collar around Pinocchio's neck
他把狗项圈绑在匹诺曹的脖子上
it was so tight that he could not pull his head out

它太紧了，他无法把头拉出来
the dog collar was attached to a heavy chain
狗项圈系在一条沉重的链子上
and the heavy chain was fastened to the wall
沉重的链条被固定在墙上
"If it rains tonight you can go into the kennel"
"如果今晚下雨，你可以进狗窝"
"my poor dog had a little bed of straw in there"
"我可怜的狗那里有一张小稻草床"
"remember to keep your ears pricked for robbers"
"记得小心你的耳朵，以防强盗"
"and if you hear robbers, then bark loudly"
"如果你听到强盗的声音，就大声吠叫"
Pinocchio had received his orders for the night
匹诺曹收到了他今晚的命令
and the poor man finally went to bed
可怜的男人终于上床睡觉了

Poor Pinocchio remained lying on the ground
可怜的匹诺曹仍然躺在地上
he felt more dead than he felt alive
他觉得自己死得比觉得自己还活着
the cold, and hunger, and fear had taken all his energy
寒冷、饥饿和恐惧已经耗尽了他所有的精力
From time to time he put his hands angrily to the go collar
他不时愤怒地把手伸向围巾
"It serves me right!" he said to himself
"这对我有好处！"
"I was determined to be a vagabond"
"我决心要成为一个流浪者"
"I wanted to live the life of a good-for-nothing"
"我想过一无是处的生活"
"I used to listen to bad companions"
"我以前听坏伙伴的话"
"and that is why I always meet with misfortunes"
"这就是为什么我总是遇到不幸"
"if only I had been a good little boy"
"如果我是个好孩子就好了"
"then I would not be in the midst of the field"
"这样我就不会在田野中了"
"I wouldn't be here if I had stayed at home"
"如果我呆在家里，我就不会在这里"
"I wouldn't be a watch-dog if I had stayed with my papa"
"如果我和爸爸呆在一起，我就不会成为看门狗了"
"Oh, if only I could be born again!"
"哦，要是我能重生就好了！"
"But now it is too late to change anything"
"但现在改变任何事情都为时已晚"
"the best thing to do now is having patience!"

"现在最好的办法就是要有耐心！"
he was relieved by this little outburst
他因这个小小的爆发而松了一口气
because it had come straight from his heart
因为它是直接发自内心的
and he went into the dog-kennel and fell asleep
他走进狗窝，睡着了

Pinocchio Discovers the Robbers
匹诺曹发现劫匪

He had been sleeping heavily for about two hours
他已经沉睡了大约两个小时
then he was aroused by a strange whispering
然后他被一阵奇怪的耳语惊醒了
the strange voices were coming from the courtyard
奇怪的声音从院子里传来
he put the point of his nose out of the kennel
他把鼻尖伸出狗窝
and he saw four little beasts with dark fur
他看到四只长着深色皮毛的小野兽
they looked like cats making a plan
他们看起来像是制定计划的猫
But they were not cats, they were polecats
但他们不是猫，他们是 polecats
what polecats are are carnivorous little animals
北极猫是肉食性小动物
they are especially greedy for eggs and young chickens
他们特别贪吃鸡蛋和小鸡
One of the polecats came to the opening of the kennel
其中一只北极猫来到了狗窝的门口
he spoke in a low voice, "Good evening, Melampo"
他低声说："晚上好，梅兰波。

"My name is not Melampo," answered the puppet
"我不叫梅兰波，"木偶回答
"Oh! then who are you?" asked the polecat
"哦！那你是谁？"
"I am Pinocchio," answered Pinocchio
"我是匹诺曹，"匹诺曹回答
"And what are you doing here?"
"那你在这里做什么？"
"I am acting as watch-dog," confirmed Pinocchio
"我充当看门狗，"匹诺曹证实道
"Then where is Melampo?" wondered the polecat
"那么梅兰波在哪里？"
"Where is the old dog who lived in this kennel?"
"住在这个狗窝里的那只老狗在哪里？"
"He died this morning," Pinocchio informed
"他今天早上死了，"匹诺曹告诉
"Is he dead? Poor beast! He was so good"
"他死了吗？可怜的野兽！他太棒了"
"but I would say that you were also a good dog"
"但我想说你也是一只好狗"
"I can see it in your face"
"我能从你的脸上看到"
"I beg your pardon, I am not a dog"
"请原谅，我不是狗"
"Not a dog? Then what are you?"
"不是狗吗？那你是什么人？"
"I am a puppet," corrected Pinocchio
"我是个傀儡，"匹诺曹纠正道
"And you are acting as watch-dog?"
"你是在充当看门狗？"
"now you understand the situation"
"现在你明白情况了"
"I have been made to be a watch dog as a punishment"

"我被当成看门狗作为惩罚"
"well, then we shall tell you what the deal is"
"好吧,那我们就告诉你这笔交易是什么。"
"the same deal we had with the deceased Melampo"
"我们和死去的梅兰波做的一样"
"I am sure you will be agree to the deal"
"我相信你会同意这笔交易的"
"What are the conditions of this deal?"
"这笔交易的条件是什么?"
"one night a week we will visit the poultry-yard"
"我们每周都会去家禽场"
"and you will allow us to carry off eight chickens"
"你就允许我们带走八只鸡"
"Of these chickens seven are to be eaten by us"
"这些鸡中有七只要被我们吃掉"
"and we will give one chicken to you"
"我们会给你一只鸡"
"your end of the bargain is very easy"
"你的交易很容易"
"all you have to do is pretend to be asleep"
"你所要做的就是假装睡着"
"and don't get any ideas about barking"
"而且不要对吠叫有任何想法"
"you are not to wake the peasant when we come"
"我们来的时候,你不要吵醒农民"
"Did Melampo act in this manner?" asked Pinocchio
"梅兰波是不是这样做了?"
"that is the deal we had with Melampo"
"这就是我们与 Melampo 的交易"
"and we were always on the best terms with him
"我们总是和他保持着最好的关系
"sleep quietly and let us do our business"
"安静地睡觉,让我们做我们的事"

"and in the morning you will have a beautiful chicken"
"早上你会有一只漂亮的鸡"
"it will be ready plucked for your breakfast tomorrow"
"明天就可以采摘了"
"Have we understood each other clearly?"
"我们清楚地了解彼此吗?"
"Only too clearly!" answered Pinocchio
"太清楚了!"
and he shook his head threateningly
他威胁地摇摇头
as if to say: "You shall hear of this shortly!"
仿佛在说:"你很快就会听到这个消息的!
the four polecats thought that they had a deal
四只 Polecats 认为他们达成了交易
so they continued to the poultry-yard
于是他们继续向家禽场走去
first they opened the gate with their teeth
他们首先用牙齿打开了大门
and then they slipped in one by one
然后他们一个接一个地溜进去
they hadn't been in the chicken-coup for long
他们陷入这场鸡巴政变的时间不长
but then they heard the gate shut behind them
但就在这时,他们听到大门在他们身后关上了
It was Pinocchio who had shut the gate
是匹诺曹关上了大门
and Pinocchio took some extra security measures
匹诺曹采取了一些额外的安全措施
he put a large stone against the gate
他把一块大石头放在门上
this way the polecats couldn't get out again
这样,Polecats 就无法再次脱身
and then Pinocchio began to bark like a dog
然后匹诺曹开始像狗一样吠叫

and he barked exactly like a watch-dog barks
他吠叫得跟看门狗的吠叫一模一样
the peasant heard Pinocchio barking
农民听到匹诺曹的吠叫
he quickly awoke and jumped out of bed
他很快就醒了,从床上跳了起来
with his gun he came to the window
他拿着枪来到窗户前
and from the window he called to Pinocchio
他从窗户呼唤匹诺曹
"What is the matter?" he asked the puppet
"怎么了?"他问木偶
"There are robbers!" answered Pinocchio
"有强盗!"
"Where are they?" he wanted to know
"他们在哪里?"
"they are in the poultry-yard," confirmed Pinocchio
"他们在家禽场里,"匹诺曹确认道
"I will come down directly," said the peasant
"我马上下来,"农夫说
and he came down in a great hurry
他急急地下来了
it would have taken less time to say "Amen"
说"阿们"的时间会少一些
He rushed into the poultry-yard
他冲进了家禽场
and quickly he caught all the polecats
很快他就抓住了所有的 polecats
and then he put the polecats into a sack
然后他把 polecats 装进一个袋子里
he said to them in a tone of great satisfaction:
他用一种非常满意的语气对他们说:
"At last you have fallen into my hands!"

"你终于落入我的手里了!"

"I could punish you, if I wanted to"
"如果我愿意,我可以惩罚你"

"but I am not so cruel," he comforted them
"但我没有那么残忍,"他安慰他们

"I will content myself in other ways"
"我会用其他方式满足自己"

"I will carry you in the morning to the innkeeper"
"早上我会带你去见客栈老板。"

"he will skin and cook you like hares"
"他会像野兔一样剥你皮和煮你"

"and you will be served with a sweet sauce"
"你会得到甜酱"

"It is an honour that you don't deserve"
"这是你不配得到的荣誉"

"you're lucky I am so generous with you"
"你很幸运,我对你这么慷慨"

He then approached Pinocchio and stroked him
然后他走近匹诺曹并抚摸他

"How did you manage to discover the four thieves?"
"你是怎么找到那四个贼的?"

"my faithful Melampo never found out anything!"
"我忠实的梅兰波从来没有发现任何事情!"

The puppet could then have told him the whole story
然后,这个傀儡就可以告诉他整个故事

he could have told him about the treacherous deal
他本可以告诉他这个背信弃义的交易

but he remembered that the dog was dead
但他想起那条狗已经死了

and the puppet thought to himself:
傀儡心想:

"of what use it it accusing the dead?"
"控告死者有什么用呢?"

"The dead are no longer with us"
"死者已不在我们身边"
"it is best to leave the dead in peace!"
"最好让死者安息！"
the peasant went on to ask more questions
农民继续问了更多问题
"were you sleeping when the thieves came?"
"贼来的时候你睡着了吗？"
"I was asleep," answered Pinocchio
"我睡着了，"匹诺曹回答
"but the polecats woke me with their chatter"
"可是那些 Polecats 用它们的喋喋不休把我吵醒了"
"one of the polecats came to the kennel"
"其中一只北极猫来到了狗窝"
he tried to make a terrible deal with me
他试图和我做一个糟糕的交易
"promise not to bark and we'll give you fine chicken"
"保证不吠叫，我们会给你好鸡"
"I was offended by such an underhanded offer"
"我被这样一个卑鄙的提议冒犯了"
"I can admit that I am a naughty puppet"
"我可以承认我是一个顽皮的傀儡"
"but there is one thing I will never be guilty of"
"但有一件事我永远不会有罪"
"I will not make terms with dishonest people!"
"我不会和不诚实的人做协议！"
"and I will not share their dishonest gains"
"我不会分享他们不诚实的收益"
"Well said, my boy!" cried the peasant
"说得好，我的孩子！"
and he patted Pinocchio on the shoulder
他拍了拍匹诺曹的肩膀
"Such sentiments do you great honour, my boy"

"你有这样的感情，我的孩子，你感到非常荣幸。"
"let me show you proof of my gratitude to you"
"让我给你看看我对你的感激之情"
"I will at once set you at liberty"
"我必立刻释放你"
"and you may return home as you please"
"你可以随心所欲地回家"
And he removed the dog-collar from Pinocchio
"他摘下了匹诺曹的狗项圈

Pinocchio Flies to the Seashore
匹诺曹飞向海边

a dog-collar had hung around Pinocchio's neck
匹诺曹的脖子上挂着一个狗项圈
but now Pinocchio had his freedom again
但现在匹诺曹又重获自由
and he wore the humiliating dog-collar no more
他不再戴那令人羞辱的狗项圈
he ran off across the fields
他穿过田野跑开了
and he kept running until he reached the road
他一直跑着，直到他到了路上
the road that led to the Fairy's house
通往仙女家的路
in the woods he could see the Big Oak tree
在树林里，他可以看到大橡树
the Big Oak tree to which he had been hung
他被吊死在那棵大橡树上
Pinocchio looked around in every direction
匹诺曹环顾四周
but he couldn't see his sister's house
但他看不到他姐姐的房子

the house of the beautiful Child with blue hair
美丽的蓝发孩子的房子
Pinocchio was seized with a sad presentiment
匹诺曹被一种悲哀的预感所吸引
he began to run with all the strength he had left
他开始用他所剩无几的力气奔跑
in a few minutes he reached the field
几分钟后,他到达了田野
he was where the little house had once stood
他就是那座小房子曾经矗立的地方
But the little white house was no longer there
但小白房子已经不在那里了
Instead of the house he saw a marble stone
他看到的不是房子,而是一块大理石
on the stone were engraved these sad words:
石头上刻着这些悲伤的文字:
"Here lies the child with the blue hair"
"蓝头发的孩子躺在这里"
"she was abandoned by her little brother Pinocchio"
"她被她的弟弟匹诺曹抛弃了"
"and from the sorrow she succumbed to death"
"她因悲伤而死去"
with difficulty he had read this epitaph
他艰难地读完了这篇墓志铭
I leave you to imagine the puppet's feelings
我让你去想象这个木偶的感受
He fell with his face on the ground
他倒在地上,脸朝下
he covered the tombstone with a thousand kisses
他用一千个吻覆盖了墓碑
and he burst into an agony of tears
他痛苦地流下了眼泪
He cried for all of that night
那一夜他都在哭泣

and when morning came he was still crying
天亮时,他还在哭泣
he cried although he had no tears left
尽管他已经没有眼泪了,但他还是哭了
his lamentations were heart-breaking
他的哀叹令人心碎
and his sobs echoed in the surrounding hills
他的啜泣声在周围的山丘上回荡
And while he was weeping he said:
他一边哭泣,一边说:
"Oh, little Fairy, why did you die?"
"哦,小仙女,你怎么死了?"
"Why did I not die instead of you?"
"为什么我不代替你死?"
"I who am so wicked, whilst you were so good"
"我这么坏,而你却这么好"
"And my papa? Where can he be?"
"那我爸爸呢?他在哪里?
"Oh, little Fairy, tell me where I can find him"
"哦,小仙女,告诉我在哪里可以找到他"
"for I want to remain with him always"
"因为我想永远与他同在"
"and I never want to leave him ever again!"
"我再也不想离开他了!"
"tell me that it is not true that you are dead!"
"告诉我,你死了不是真的!"
"If you really love your little brother, come to life again"
"如果你真的爱你的小弟弟,就再活过来"
"Does it not grieve you to see me alone in the world?"
"你看到我孤身一人在世上,岂不感到悲哀吗?"
"does it not sadden you to see me abandoned by everybody?"

"看到我被大家抛弃，你不是很伤心吗？"
"If assassins come they will hang me from the tree again"
"如果刺客来了，他们会再次将我吊在树上"
"and this time I would die indeed"
"这一次我真的会死"
"What can I do here alone in the world?"
"我一个人在这个世界上能做什么？"
"I have lost you and my papa"
"我失去了你和我的爸爸"
"who will love me and give me food now?"
"现在谁会爱我，给我食物呢？"
"Where shall I go to sleep at night?"
"我晚上到哪儿去睡呢？"
"Who will make me a new jacket?"
"谁来给我做一件新夹克？"
"Oh, it would be better for me to die also!"
"哦，我也死了就好了！"
"not to live would be a hundred times better"
"不活着会好一百倍"
"Yes, I want to die," he concluded
"是的，我想死，"他总结道
And in his despair he tried to tear his hair
在绝望中，他试图扯扯自己的头发
but his hair was made of wood
但他的头发是木头做的
so he could not have the satisfaction
所以他无法获得满足
Just then a large Pigeon flew over his head
就在这时，一只大鸽子从他的头上飞过
the pigeon stopped with distended wings
鸽子停了下来，翅膀张开了
and the pigeon called down from a great height

鸽子从高处叫下来
"Tell me, child, what are you doing there?"
"告诉我,孩子,你在那儿做什么?"
"Don't you see? I am crying!" said Pinocchio
"你没看到吗?我在哭!
and he raised his head towards the voice
他抬起头来,朝那个声音
and he rubbed his eyes with his jacket
他用外套揉了揉眼睛
"Tell me," continued the Pigeon
"告诉我,"鸽子继续说
"do you happen to know a puppet called Pinocchio?"
"你碰巧认识一个叫匹诺曹的木偶吗?"
"Pinocchio? Did you say Pinocchio?" repeated the puppet
"匹诺曹?你说的是匹诺曹吗?
and he quickly jumped to his feet
他很快就跳了起来
"I am Pinocchio!" he exclaimed with hope
"我是匹诺曹!"
At this answer the Pigeon descended rapidly
听到这个回答,鸽子迅速地下降了
He was larger than a turkey
他比火鸡还大
"Do you also know Geppetto?" he asked
"你也认识 Geppetto 吗?"
"Do I know him! He is my poor papa!"
"我认识他吗!他是我可怜的爸爸!
"Has he perhaps spoken to you of me?"
"他也许跟你说过我吗?"
"Will you take me to him?"
"你能带我去见他吗?"
"Is he still alive?"

"他还活着吗？"
"Answer me, for pity's sake"
"看在怜悯的份上，回答我"
"is he still alive??"
"他还活着吗？？"
"I left him three days ago on the seashore"
"我三天前把他丢在了海边"
"What was he doing?" Pinocchio had to know
"他在做什么？"匹诺曹必须知道
"He was building a little boat for himself"
"他正在为自己建造一艘小船"
"he was going to cross the ocean"
"他要穿越大洋"
"that poor man has been going all round the world"
"那个可怜的人已经走遍了全世界"
"he has been looking for you"
"他一直在找你"
"but he had no success in finding you"
"但他没能找到你"
"so now he will go to the distant countries"
"所以现在他要去远方的国度。"
"he will search for you in the New World"
"他要在新世界寻找你"
"How far is it from here to the shore?"
"从这里到岸边有多远？"
"More than six hundred miles"
"超过六百英里"
"Six hundred miles?" echoed Pinocchio
"六百英里？"
"Oh, beautiful Pigeon," pleaded Pinocchio
"哦，美丽的鸽子，"匹诺曹恳求道
"what a fine thing it would be to have your wings!"
"要是有你的翅膀那该多好啊！"

"If you wish to go, I will carry you there"
"如果你愿意去,我就带你去那里"
"How could you carry me there?"
"你怎么能带我到那儿去呢?"
"I can carry you on my back"
"我可以把你背在背上"
"Do you weigh much?"
"你体重多吗?"
"I weigh next to nothing"
"我几乎没称重"
"I am as light as a feather"
"我轻如羽毛"
Pinocchio didn't hesitate for another moment
匹诺曹没有再犹豫片刻
and he jumped at once on the Pigeon's back
他立刻跳到鸽子的背上
he put a leg on each side of the pigeon
他在鸽子的每一侧各放了一条腿
just like men do when they're riding horseback
就像男人骑马时一样
and Pinocchio exclaimed joyfully:
匹诺曹高兴地喊道:
"Gallop, gallop, my little horse"
"驰骋,疾驰,我的小马"
"because I am anxious to arrive quickly!"
"因为我很急着赶到!"
The Pigeon took flight into the air
鸽子飞向空中
and in a few minutes they almost touched the clouds
几分钟后,他们几乎碰到了云层

now the puppet was at an immense height
现在这个傀儡已经达到了一个巨大的高度
and he became more and more curious
他变得越来越好奇
so he looked down to the ground
于是他低头看向地面
but his head spun round in dizziness
可是他的头却晕得转过来
he became ever so frightened of the height
他对这个高度越来越害怕
and he had to save himself from the danger of falling
他必须保护自己免于跌倒的危险
and so held tightly to his feathered steed
就这样紧紧地拴着他的羽毛骏马
They flew through the skies all of that day
他们整天都在天空中飞行
Towards evening the Pigeon said:
傍晚时分，鸽子说：

"I am very thirsty from all this flying!"
"我飞得口渴得要命！"
"And I am very hungry!" agreed Pinocchio
"而且我很饿！"
"Let us stop at that dovecote for a few minutes"
"让我们在那个鸽子前停几分钟"
"and then we will continue our journey"
"然后我们将继续我们的旅程"
"then we may reach the seashore by dawn tomorrow"
"那我们明天黎明前就可以到达海边了。"
They went into a deserted dovecote
他们走进了一座荒凉的鸽子
here they found nothing but a basin full of water
他们在这里只找到一个装满水的盆子
and they found a basket full of vetch
他们发现了一个装满紫云英的篮子
The puppet had never in his life been able to eat vetch
这个木偶这辈子从来没有吃过紫云英
according to him it made him sick
据他说，这让他感到恶心
That evening, however, he ate to repletion
然而，那天晚上，他吃得饱饱的
and he nearly emptied the basket of it
他几乎把篮子里的钱都倒空了
and then he turned to the Pigeon and said to him:
然后他转过身来对鸽子说：
"I never could have believed that vetch was so good!"
"我从来不敢相信紫云英这么好！"
"Be assured, my boy," replied the Pigeon
"放心吧，我的孩子，"鸽子回答
"when hunger is real even vetch becomes delicious"
"当饥饿是真实的时，即使是紫云英也变得美味"
"Hunger knows neither caprice nor greediness"

"饥饿不分任性,也不懂贪婪"
the two quickly finished their little meal
两人很快就吃完了他们的小餐
and they recommenced their journey and flew away
他们重新开始了他们的旅程,飞走了
The following morning they reached the seashore
第二天早上,他们到达了海边
The Pigeon placed Pinocchio on the ground
鸽子将匹诺曹放在地上
the pigeon did not wish to be troubled with thanks
鸽子不想被感谢所困扰
it was indeed a good action he had done
他确实做了一件好事
but he had done it out the goodness of his heart
但他是出于内心的善良而做的
and Pinocchio had no time to lose
匹诺曹没有时间可以浪费了
so he flew quickly away and disappeared
于是他飞快地飞走了,消失了
The shore was crowded with people
岸边挤满了人
the people were looking out to sea
人们望向大海
they shouting and gesticulating at something
他们对着什么东西大喊大叫和打手势
"What has happened?" asked Pinocchio of an old woman
"发生了什么事?"匹诺曹问一位老妇人
"there is a poor father who has lost his son"
"有一个可怜的父亲失去了他的儿子"
"he has gone out to sea in a little boat"
"他坐小船出海了"
"he will search for him on the other side of the water"
"他会在水的另一边寻找他"

"and today the sea is most tempestuous"
"今天海面最狂风暴雨"
"and the little boat is in danger of sinking"
"小船有沉没的危险"
"Where is the little boat?" asked Pinocchio
"那条小船在哪儿?"
"It is out there in a line with my finger"
"它在外面与我的手指成一条直线"
and she pointed to a little boat
她指着一艘小船
and the little boat looked like a little nutshell
小船看起来就像一个小坚果壳
a little nutshell with a very little man in it
一个小小的坚果壳,里面有一个非常小的男人
Pinocchio fixed his eyes on the little nutshell
匹诺曹盯着那小坚果壳
after looking attentively he gave a piercing scream:
他仔细地看了一会儿,发出了一声刺耳的尖叫:
"It is my papa! It is my papa!"
"是我爸爸!这是我爸爸!"
The boat, meanwhile, was being beaten by the fury of the waves
与此同时,这艘船正被狂暴的海浪打败
at one moment it disappeared in the trough of the sea
一瞬间,它消失在海槽中
and in the next moment the boat came to the surface again
下一刻,船又浮出水面
Pinocchio stood on the top of a high rock
匹诺曹站在一块高高的岩石顶上
and he kept calling to his father
他不停地呼唤他的父亲
and he made every kind of signal to him
他向他发出了各种信号

he waved his hands, his handkerchief, and his cap
他挥舞着双手、手帕和帽子
Pinocchio was very far away from him
匹诺曹离他很远
but Geppetto appeared to recognize his son
但 Geppetto 似乎认出了他的儿子
and he also took off his cap and waved it
他又摘下帽子，挥舞着
he tried by gestures to make him understand
他试图用手势让他明白
"I would have returned if it were possible"
"如果可能的话，我会回来的"
"but the sea is most tempestuous"
"但大海是最狂风暴雨的"
"and my oars won't take me to the shores again"
"我的桨不会再带我到岸边去了"
Suddenly a tremendous wave rose out of the sea
突然，一股巨大的海浪从海中升起
and then the the little nutshell disappeared
然后 The Little Nutshell 就消失了
They waited, hoping the boat would come again to the surface
他们等待着，希望船能再次浮出水面
but the little boat was seen no more
但那只小船再也看不到了
the fisherman had assembled at the shore
渔夫在岸边集合
"Poor man!" they said of him, and murmured a prayer
"可怜的人！"他们说起他，喃喃地祈祷着
and then they turned to go home
然后他们转身回家
Just then they heard a desperate cry
就在这时，他们听到了绝望的哭声
looking back, they saw a little boy

回头一看，他们看到了一个小男孩
"I will save my papa," the boy exclaimed
"我会救我爸爸的，"男孩喊道
and he jumped from a rock into the sea
他从一块石头上跳进了海里
as you know Pinocchio was made of wood
如你所知，匹诺曹是用木头做的
so he floated easily on the water
所以他轻松地漂浮在水面上
and he swam as well as a fish
他游得像鱼一样
At one moment they saw him disappear under the water
一会儿，他们看到他消失在水下
he was carried down by the fury of the waves
他被海浪的怒火卷走
and in the next moment he reappeared to the surface of the water
下一刻，他又出现在水面上
he struggled on swimming with a leg or an arm
他用一条腿或一只胳膊游泳很挣扎
but at last they lost sight of him
但最后他们看不见他了
and he was seen no more
他就再也见不到了
and they offered another prayer for the puppet
他们又为木偶祈祷

Pinocchio Finds the Fairy Again
匹诺曹再次找到仙女

Pinocchio wanted to be in time to help his father
匹诺曹想及时帮助他的父亲
so he swam all through the night
所以他整夜游来游去
And what a horrible night it was!
那是一个多么可怕的夜晚！
The rain came down in torrents
雨如暴雨般倾泻而下
it hailed and the thunder was frightful
它冰雹，雷声很可怕
the flashes of lightning made it as light as day
闪电使它像白昼一样轻盈

Towards morning he saw a long strip of land
天快亮时,他看到了一片长长的土地
It was an island in the midst of the sea
那是一座位于海中的岛屿
He tried his utmost to reach the shore
他拼命想上岸
but his efforts were all in vain
但他的努力都是徒劳的
The waves raced and tumbled over each other
海浪相互奔腾和翻滚
and the torrent knocked Pinocchio about
洪流把匹诺曹撞了
it was as if he had been a wisp of straw
他仿佛是一缕稻草
At last, fortunately for him, a billow rolled up
最后,幸运的是,一股巨浪卷起
it rose with such fury that he was lifted up
它怒不可遏,他被举了起来
and finally he was thrown on to the sands
最后他被扔到了沙滩上
the little puppet crashed onto the ground
小傀儡砸在了地上
and all his joints cracked from the impact
他所有的关节都因撞击而破裂
but he comforted himself, saying:
但他安慰自己说:
"This time also I have made a wonderful escape!"
"这一次,我也逃脱了一次美妙的旅程!"
Little by little the sky cleared
渐渐地,天空放晴了
the sun shone out in all his splendour
阳光照耀着他所有的光辉
and the sea became as quiet and smooth as oil
海变得像油一样平静和平静

The puppet put his clothes in the sun to dry
木偶把衣服放在阳光下晾干

and he began to look in every direction
他开始向四面八方张望

somewhere on the water there must be a little boat
水面上的某个地方一定有一艘小船

and in the boat he hoped to see a little man
在船上,他希望能看到一个小个子

he looked out to sea as far as he could see
他望着他能看到的大海

but all he saw was the sky and the sea
但他看到的只是天空和大海

"If I only knew what this island was called!"
"要是我知道这个岛叫什么就好了!"

"If I only knew whether it was inhabited"
"如果我只知道它是否有人居住就好了"

"perhaps civilized people do live here"
"也许这里确实住着文明人"

"people who do not hang boys from trees"
"不把男孩吊在树上的人"

"but whom can I ask if there is nobody?"
"可是,如果没有人,我又能问谁呢?"

Pinocchio didn't like the idea of being all alone
匹诺曹不喜欢独自一人的想法

and now he was alone on a great uninhabited country
现在他独自一人在一个无人居住的大国

the idea of it made him melancholy
这个想法使他感到忧郁

he was just about to to cry
他快要哭了

But at that moment he saw a big fish swimming by
但就在这时,他看到一条大鱼游过

the big fish was only a short distance from the shore
大鱼离岸边不远

the fish was going quietly on its own business
这条鱼正在悄悄地做自己的事情
and it had its head out of the water
它的头露出水面
Not knowing its name, the puppet called to the fish
不知道它的名字,木偶叫来了鱼
he called out in a loud voice to make himself heard:
他大声喊道:
"Eh, Sir Fish, will you permit me a word with you?"
"呃,菲什先生,您能允许我跟您说几句话吗?"
"Two words, if you like," answered the fish
"如果你愿意的话,两个字,"鱼回答
the fish was in fact not a fish at all
事实上,这条鱼根本不是一条鱼
what the fish was was a Dolphin
那条鱼是一只海豚
and you couldn't have found a politer dolphin
而且你不可能找到一只 Polter Dolphin
"Would you be kind enough to tell:"
"你能不能好心地告诉他:"
"is there are villages in this island?"
"这个岛上有村子吗?"
"and might there be something to eat in these villages?"
"那么这些村子里有没有吃的呢?"
"and is there any danger in these villages?"
"那么这些村子里有什么危险吗?"
"might one get eaten in these villages?"
"在这些村子里,一个人会被吃掉吗?"
"there certainly are villages," replied the Dolphin
"肯定有村子,"海豚回答
"Indeed, you will find one village quite close by"
"确实,你会在附近找到一个村庄"

- 183 -

"And what road must I take to go there?"
"那我得走哪条路去呢?"
"You must take that path to your left"
"你必须走你左边的那条路"
"and then you must follow your nose"
"然后你得跟着你的鼻子走"
"Will you tell me another thing?"
"你能再告诉我一件事吗?"
"You swim about the sea all day and night"
"你昼夜在海里游"
"have you by chance met a little boat"
"你偶然遇见了一艘小船"
"a little boat with my papa in it?"
"一艘载着我爸爸的小船?"
"And who is your papa?"
"那你爸爸是谁?"
"He is the best papa in the world"
"他是世界上最好的爸爸"
"but it would be difficult to find a worse son than I am"
"可是,要找到比我更坏的儿子是很困难的。"
The fish regretted to tell him what he feared
鱼后悔告诉他他害怕什么
"you saw the terrible storm we had last night"
"你看到了我们昨晚的可怕风暴"
"the little boat must have gone to the bottom"
"那条小船一定是沉到海底了"
"And my papa?" asked Pinocchio
"那我爸爸呢?"
"He must have been swallowed by the terrible Dog-Fish"
"他一定是被可怕的狗鱼吞下了"
"of late he has been swimming on our waters"

"最近他一直在我们的水域游泳"
"and he has been spreading devastation and ruin"
"他一直在散播破坏和毁灭"
Pinocchio was already beginning to quake with fear
匹诺曹已经开始因恐惧而颤抖
"Is this Dog-Fish very big?" asked Pinocchio
"这个狗鱼很大吗?"
"oh, very big!" replied the Dolphin
"哦,非常大!"
"let me tell you about this fish"
"我来告诉你这条鱼"
"then you can form some idea of his size"
"那你就可以对他的体型有所了解了。"
"he is bigger than a five-storied house"
"他比五层楼还大"
"and his mouth is more enormous than you've ever seen"
"他的嘴比你见过的还要大"
"a railway train could pass down his throat"
"火车可以从他的喉咙里穿过"
"Mercy upon us!" exclaimed the terrified puppet
"可怜我们吧!"
and he put on his clothes with the greatest haste
他急忙穿上衣服
"Good-bye, Sir Fish, and thank you"
"再见,菲什爵士,谢谢你"
"excuse the trouble I have given you"
"对不起,我给你添了麻烦"
"and many thanks for your politeness"
"非常感谢您的礼貌"
He then took the path that had been pointed out to him
然后他走了别人给他指出的路
and he began to walk as fast as he could

他开始尽可能快地走路

he walked so fast, indeed, that he was almost running
他走得真快,真的快跑了

And at the slightest noise he turned to look behind him
他听到最轻微的声音,就转过身来看向身后

he feared that he might see the terrible Dog-Fish
他害怕他会看到可怕的狗鱼

and he imagined a railway train in its mouth
他想象着它嘴里有一列火车

a half-hour walk took him to a little village
步行半小时后,他来到了一个小村庄

the village was The Village of the Industrious Bees
这个村庄是勤劳蜜蜂村

The road was alive with people
路上人山人往来

and they were running here and there
他们到处跑

and they all had to attend to their business
他们都得专心办事

all were at work, all had something to do
所有人都在工作,都有事要做

You could not have found an idler or a vagabond
你不可能找到一个闲人或流浪者

even if you searched for him with a lighted lamp
即使你用点亮的灯寻找他

"Ah!" said that lazy Pinocchio at once
"啊!"

"I see that this village will never suit me!"
"我看这个村子永远不适合我!"

"I wasn't born to work!"
"我不是天生就是为了工作而生的!"

In the meanwhile he was tormented by hunger
与此同时,他被饥饿折磨着

he had eaten nothing for twenty-four hours
他已经二十四小时没吃东西了
he had not even eaten vetch
他甚至没有吃过紫云英
What was poor Pinocchio to do?
可怜的匹诺曹该怎么办？
There were only two ways to obtain food
只有两种方法可以获得食物
he could either get food by asking for a little work
他要么通过要求一点工作来获得食物
or he could get food by way of begging
或者他可以通过乞讨来获得食物
someone might be kind enough to throw him a nickel
有人可能会好心地扔给他一分钱
or they might give him a mouthful of bread
或者他们可能会给他一口面包
generally Pinocchio was ashamed to beg
一般来说，匹诺曹都羞于乞讨
his father had always preached him to be industrious
他的父亲一直教导他要勤奋
he taught him no one had a right to beg
他告诉他，没有人有权乞讨
except the aged and the infirm
除了年老体弱的
The really poor in this world deserve compassion
这个世界上真正的穷人应该得到同情
the really poor in this world require assistance
这个世界上真正的穷人需要帮助
only those who are aged or sick
仅限年老或生病的人
those who are no longer able to earn their own bread
那些不再能够自己挣钱的人
It is the duty of everyone else to work
工作是其他人的责任

and if they don't labour, so much the worse for them
如果他们不劳动,情况就更糟了

let them suffer from their hunger
让他们忍受饥饿

At that moment a man came down the road
就在这时,一个男人从路上走了过来

he was tired and panting for breath
他累了,气喘吁吁

He was dragging two carts full of charcoal
他拖着两辆装满木炭的手推车

Pinocchio judged by his face that he was a kind man
匹诺曹从他的脸上判断他是一个善良的人

so Pinocchio approached the charcoal man
于是匹诺曹走近了那个木炭人

he cast down his eyes with shame
他羞愧地垂下了眼睛

and he said to him in a low voice:
他低声对他说:

"Would you have the charity to give me a nickel?"
"你愿意慈善给我一分钱吗?"

"because, as you can see, I am dying of hunger"
"因为,正如你所看到的,我快饿死了"

"You shall have not only a nickel," said the man
"你不仅要有一枚硬币,"那人说

"I will give you a dime"
"我给你一毛钱"

"but for the dime you must do some work"
"但为了一毛钱,你得干点活"

"help me to drag home these two carts of charcoal"
"帮我把这两车木炭拖回家"

"I am surprised at you!" answered the puppet
"我对你感到惊讶!"

and there was a tone of offense in his voice
他的声音里带着冒犯的语气

"Let me tell you something about myself"
"让我告诉你一些关于我自己的事情"
"I am not accustomed to do the work of a donkey"
"我不习惯做驴的工作"
"I have never drawn a cart!"
"我从来没有拉过车！"
"So much the better for you," answered the man
"对你来说好多了，"那人回答
"my boy, I see how you are dying of hunger"
"我的孩子，我看到你是怎么饿死的"
"eat two fine slices of your pride"
"吃两片你的骄傲"
"and be careful not to get indigestion"
"小心不要消化不良"
A few minutes afterwards a mason passed by
几分钟后，一个泥瓦匠经过
he was carrying a basket of mortar
他提着一篮子迫击炮
"Would you have the charity to give me a nickel?"
"你愿意慈善给我一分钱吗？"
"me, a poor boy who is yawning for want of food"
"我，一个因缺乏食物而打哈欠的穷孩子"
"Willingly," answered the man
"愿意，"那人回答
"Come with me and carry the mortar"
"跟我来，把迫击炮搬来"
"and instead of a nickel I will give you a dime"
"我给你一角钱，而不是一分钱"
"But the mortar is heavy," objected Pinocchio
"可是砂浆很重，"匹诺曹反对道
"and I don't want to tire myself"
"我不想让自己疲惫"
"I see you you don't want to tire yourself"

"我明白你了,你不想累自己"

"then, my boy, go amuse yourself with yawning"
"那么,我的孩子,去打哈欠自娱自乐吧"

In less than half an hour twenty other people went by
不到半小时,又有 20 个人走了过来

and Pinocchio asked charity of them all
匹诺曹向他们所有人请求慈善

but they all gave him the same answer
但他们都给了他同样的答案

"Are you not ashamed to beg, young boy?"
"你乞讨不觉得羞耻吗,小伙子?"

"Instead of idling about, look for a little work"
"与其闲逛,不如找点工作"

"you have to learn to earn your bread"
"你得学会挣钱"

finally a nice little woman walked by
终于,一个漂亮的小女人走过

she was carrying two cans of water
她带着两罐水

Pinocchio asked her for charity too
匹诺曹也向她请求慈善

"Will you let me drink a little of your water?"
"你能让我喝一点你的水吗?"

"because I am burning with thirst"
"因为我口渴难耐"

the little woman was happy to help
小女人很乐意帮忙

"Drink, my boy, if you wish it!"
"喝吧,我的孩子,如果你愿意的话!"

and she set down the two cans
她就放下了两个罐子

Pinocchio drank like a fish
匹诺曹像鱼一样喝水

and as he dried his mouth he mumbled:
他一边擦干嘴巴，一边喃喃自语道：
"I have quenched my thirst"
"我已经解渴了"
"If I could only appease my hunger!"
"要是我能平息我的饥饿就好了！"
The good woman heard Pinocchio's pleas
善良的女人听到了匹诺曹的恳求
and she was only too willing to oblige
她只是太愿意答应了
"help me to carry home these cans of water"
"帮我把这些罐装水带回家"
"and I will give you a fine piece of bread"
"我给你一块好面包"
Pinocchio looked at the cans of water
匹诺曹看着水罐
and he answered neither yes nor no
他既不回答"是"，也不回答"否"
and the good woman added more to the offer
而这位善良的女人又增加了更多的提议
"As well as bread you shall have cauliflower"
"除了面包，你还要有花椰菜"
Pinocchio gave another look at the can
匹诺曹又看了一眼罐头
and he answered neither yes nor no
他既不回答"是"，也不回答"否"
"And after the cauliflower there will be more"
"花椰菜之后还会有更多"
"I will give you a beautiful syrup bonbon"
"我会给你一个漂亮的糖浆糖果"
The temptation of this last dainty was great
这最后的美味诱惑是巨大的
finally Pinocchio could resist no longer

最后，匹诺曹再也无法抗拒了
with an air of decision he said:
他带着坚定的语气说：
"I must have patience!"
"我得有耐心！"
"I will carry the water to your house"
"我会把水运到你家"
The water was too heavy for Pinocchio
水对匹诺曹来说太重了
he could not carry it with his hands
他不能用手拿着它
so he had to carry it on his head
所以他不得不把它戴在头上
Pinocchio did not enjoy doing the work
匹诺曹不喜欢做这项工作
but soon they reached the house
但很快他们就到了房子
and the good little woman offered Pinocchio a seat
那个善良的小女人让匹诺曹坐下
the table had already been laid
桌子已经摆好了
and she placed before him the bread
她把饼放在他面前
and then he got the cauliflower and the bonbon
然后他得到了花椰菜和糖果
Pinocchio did not eat his food, he devoured it
匹诺曹不吃他的食物，他狼吞虎咽地吃
His stomach was like an empty apartment
他的肚子就像一间空公寓
an apartment that had been left uninhabited for months
一间几个月无人居住的公寓
but now his ravenous hunger was somewhat appeased
但现在他贪婪的饥饿在某种程度上得到了缓解

he raised his head to thank his benefactress
他抬起头来感谢他的恩人
then he took a better look at her
然后他仔细地看了看她
he gave a prolonged "Oh!" of astonishment
他惊讶地发出了长时间的"哦！
and he continued staring at her with wide open eyes
他继续睁大眼睛盯着她
his fork was in the air
他的叉子在空中
and his mouth was full of cauliflower
他的嘴里装满了花椰菜
it was as if he had been bewitched
就好像他被施了魔法一样
the good woman was quite amused
这位善良的女人被逗乐了
"What has surprised you so much?"
"什么让你这么惊讶？"
"It is..." answered the puppet
"这是……"回答了傀儡
"it's just that you are like..."
"只是你就像……"
"it's just that you remind me of someone"
"只是你让我想起了某人"
"yes, yes, yes, the same voice"
"是的，是的，是的，同一个声音"
"and you have the same eyes and hair"
"而且你的眼睛和头发都是一样的"
"yes, yes, yes. you also have blue hair"
"是的，是的，是的。你也有蓝头发"
"Oh, little Fairy! tell me that it is you!"
"哦，小仙女！告诉我是你！
"Do not make me cry anymore!"

"不要再让我哭了！"
"If only you knew how much I've cried"
"要是你知道我哭了多少就好了"
"and I have suffered so much"
"我受了这么多苦"
And Pinocchio threw himself at her feet
匹诺曹扑倒在她的脚下
and he embraced the knees of the mysterious little woman
他拥抱了那个神秘的小女人的膝盖
and he began to cry bitterly
他开始痛哭

Pinocchio Promises the Fairy he'll be a Good Boy Again
匹诺曹向仙女承诺他会再次成为一个好孩子

At first the good little woman played innocent
起初,这个善良的小女人装作无辜
she said she was not the little Fairy with blue hair
她说她不是那个蓝头发的小仙女
but Pinocchio could not be tricked
但匹诺曹骗不了
she had continued the comedy long enough
她已经把这喜剧延续得够久了
and so she ended by making herself known
于是她以让自己出名而告终
"You naughty little rogue, Pinocchio"
"你这个顽皮的小流氓,匹诺曹"
"how did you discover who I was?"
"你是怎么发现我是谁的?"
"It was my great affection for you that told me"
"是我对你的深情告诉我的"
"Do you remember when you left me?"
"你还记得你什么时候离开我的时候吗?"
"I was still a child back then"
"那时我还是个孩子"
"and now I have become a woman"
"现在我变成了一个女人"
"a woman almost old enough to be your mamma"
"一个几乎年纪大到可以做妈的女人"
"I am delighted at that"
"我对此感到高兴"
"I will not call you little sister anymore"
"我不会再叫你小妹妹了"
"from now I will call you mamma"

"从现在开始,我就叫妈了"
"all the other boys have a mamma"
"所有其他男孩都有一个妈妈"
"and I have always wished to also have a mamma"
"我一直希望也有一个妈妈"
"But how did you manage to grow so fast?"
"但你是怎么长得这么快的?"
"That is a secret," said the fairy
"那是个秘密,"仙女说
Pinocchio wanted to know, "teach me your secret"
匹诺曹想知道,"教我你的秘密"
"because I would also like to grow"
"因为我也想成长"
"Don't you see how small I am?"
"你没看到我有多小吗?"
"I always remain no bigger than a ninepin"
"我永远都不会比9针大"
"But you cannot grow," replied the Fairy
"可是你不能长大,"仙女回答
"Why can't I grow?" asked Pinocchio
"为什么我不能长?"
"Because puppets never grow"
"因为木偶永远不会长大"
"when they are born they are puppets"
"当他们出生时,他们是傀儡"
"and they live their lives as puppets"
"他们像木偶一样生活"
"and when they die they die as puppets"
"他们死后,就像傀儡一样死去"
Pinocchio game himself a slap
匹诺曹游戏自己一巴掌
"Oh, I am sick of being a puppet!"
"哦,我厌倦了当傀儡!"

"It is time that I became a man"
"现在是我成为一个男人的时候了"
"And you will become a man," promised the fairy
"你会变成男人的,"仙女承诺
"but you must know how to deserve it"
"但你必须知道如何配得上它"
"Is this true?" asked Pinocchio
"这是真的吗?"
"And what can I do to deserve to be a man?"
"我能做些什么才能配得上一个男人?"
"it is a very easy thing to deserve to be a man"
"配得上成为一个男人是一件很容易的事情"
"all you have to do is learn to be a good boy"
"你所要做的就是学会做一个好孩子"
"And you think I am not a good boy?"
"你觉得我不是一个好孩子?"
"You are quite the opposite of a good boy"
"你跟好孩子完全相反"
"Good boys are obedient, and you..."
"好孩子都听话,而你……"
"And I never obey," confessed Pinocchio
"我从不服从,"匹诺曹承认
"Good boys like to learn and to work, and you..."
"好孩子喜欢学习和工作,而你……"
"And I instead lead an idle, vagabond life"
"而我反而过着无所事事、流浪的生活"
"Good boys always speak the truth"
"好孩子总是说真话"
"And I always tell lies," admitted Pinocchio
"而且我总是说谎,"匹诺曹承认
"Good boys go willingly to school"
"好男孩心甘情愿地去上学"
"And school gives me pain all over the body"

"学校让我浑身疼痛"
"But from today I will change my life"
"但从今天开始,我将改变我的生活"
"Do you promise me?" asked the Fairy
"你答应我吗?"
"I promise that I will become a good little boy"
"我保证我会成为一个好孩子"
"and I promise be the consolation of my papa"
"我保证会得到我爸爸的安慰"
"Where is my poor papa at this moment?"
"我可怜的爸爸现在在哪里?"
but the fairy didn't know where his papa was
但仙女不知道他的爸爸在哪里
"Shall I ever have the happiness of seeing him again?"
"我能再见到他吗?"
"will I ever kiss him again?"
"我还能再吻他吗?"
"I think so; indeed, I am sure of it"
"我想是的;事实上,我很确定。
At this answer Pinocchio was delighted
听到这个回答,匹诺曹很高兴
he took the Fairy's hands
他握住了仙女的手
and he began to kiss her hands with great fervour
他开始热情地亲吻她的手
he seemed beside himself with joy
他似乎高兴极了
Then Pinocchio raised his face
然后匹诺曹抬起了脸
and he looked at her lovingly
他深情地看着她
"Tell me, little mamma:"
"告诉我,小妈妈。"

"then it was not true that you were dead?"
"那么你不是真的死了吧？"
"It seems not," said the Fairy, smiling
"好像没有，"仙女微笑着说
"If you only knew the sorrow I felt"
"如果你知道我所感受到的悲哀就好了"
"you can't imagined the tightening of my throat"
"你无法想象我的喉咙会紧绷"
"reading what was on that stone almost broke my heart"
"阅读那块石头上的内容几乎让我心碎"
"I know what it did to you"
"我知道它对你做了什么"
"and that is why I have forgiven you"
"这就是我原谅你的原因"
"I saw it from the sincerity of your grief"
"我从你真诚的悲痛中看出了这一点"
"I saw that you have a good heart"
"我看出你心地善良"
"boys with good hearts are not lost"
"心地善良的男孩不会迷失"
"there is always something to hope for"
"总有一些希望"
"even if they are scamps"
"即使他们是流氓"
"and even if they have got bad habits"
"即使他们有坏习惯"
"there is always hope they change their ways"
"他们总是有希望改变自己的方式"
"That is why I came to look for you here"
"这就是我来这里找你的原因"
"I will be your mamma"
"我会成为你的妈妈"

"Oh, how delightful!" shouted Pinocchio
"哦，多么令人愉快！"
and the little puppet jumped for joy
小木偶高兴得跳了起来
"You must obey me, Pinocchio"
"你必须服从我，匹诺曹"
"and you must do everything that I bid you"
"我吩咐你的一切，你都必须去做。"
"I will willingly obey you"
"我愿意服从你"
"and I will do as I'm told!"
"我会按照我说的去做！"
"Tomorrow you will begin to go to school"
"明天你就要开始上学了"
Pinocchio became at once a little less joyful
匹诺曹立刻变得不那么快乐了
"Then you must choose a trade to follow"
"那么你必须选择一个行业来跟随"
"you most choose a job according to your wishes"
"你最好根据自己的意愿选择工作"
Pinocchio became very grave at this
匹诺曹听到这话变得非常严肃
the Fairy asked him in an angry voice:
仙女用愤怒的声音问他：
"What are you muttering between your teeth?"
"你在咬牙切齿地嘟囔着什么？"
"I was saying..." moaned the puppet in a low voice
"我是说……"低声呻吟着木偶
"it seems to me too late for me to go to school now"
"在我看来，现在去上学太晚了"
"No, sir, it is not too late for you to go to school"
"不，先生，你现在去上学还不晚。"
"Keep it in mind that it is never too late"

"请记住,永远不会太晚"
"we can always learn and instruct ourselves"
"我们总是可以学习和指导自己"
"But I do not wish to follow a trade"
"但我不想跟着做生意"
"Why do you not wish to follow an trade?"
"你为什么不想跟着做生意呢?"
"Because it tires me to work"
"因为工作让我很累"
"My boy," said the Fairy lovingly
"我的孩子,"仙女深情地说
"there are two kinds of people who talk like that"
"有两种人会这样说话"
"there are those that are in prison"
"有些人在监狱里"
"and there are those that are in hospital"
"还有那些在医院的人"
"Let me tell you one thing, Pinocchio;"
"我告诉你一件事,匹诺曹;"
"every man, rich or poor, is obliged work"
"每个人,无论贫富,都有义务工作"
"he has to occupy himself with something"
"他得忙点什么"
"Woe to those who lead slothful lives"
"懒惰的人有祸了"
"Sloth is a dreadful illness"
"懒惰是一种可怕的疾病"
"it must be cured at once, in childhood"
"必须在童年时期立即治愈"
"because it can never be cured once you are old"
"因为一旦你老了,它就永远无法治愈"
Pinocchio was touched by these words
匹诺曹被这些话打动了

lifting his head quickly, he said to the Fairy:
他迅速抬起头,对仙女说:

"I will study and I will work"
"我会学习,我会工作"
"I will do all that you tell me"
"你告诉我的一切,我都会遵行"
"for indeed I have become weary of being a puppet"
"因为我实在厌倦了做个傀儡"
"and I wish at any price to become a boy"
"我不惜一切代价都希望成为一个男孩"
"You promised me that I can become a boy, did you

not?"
"你答应过我,我可以变成个男孩,不是吗?"
"I did promise you that you can become a boy"
"我答应过你,你可以变成个男孩"
"and whether you become a boy now depends upon yourself"
"你现在是不是变成男孩,就看你自己了。"

The Terrible Dog-Fish
可怕的狗鱼

The following day Pinocchio went to school
第二天,匹诺曹去上学了
you can imagine the delight of all the little rogues
你可以想象所有小流氓的喜悦
a puppet had walked into their school!
一个傀儡走进了他们的学校!
They set up a roar of laughter that never ended
他们掀起了一阵永无止境的笑声
They played all sorts of tricks on him
他们对他玩了各种把戏
One boy carried off his cap
一个男孩掀掉了他的帽子
another boy pulled Pinocchio's jacket over him
另一个男孩把匹诺曹的外套拉到他身上
one tried to give him a pair of inky mustachios
一个试图给他一对墨色的小胡子
another boy attempted to tie strings to his feet and hands
另一个男孩试图在他的脚和手上绑绳子
and then he tried to make him dance
然后他试图让他跳舞
For a short time Pinocchio pretended not to care

有那么一会儿,匹诺曹假装不在乎

and he got on as well with school as he could
他尽可能地在学校里相处得很好

but at last he lost all his patience
但最后他失去了所有的耐心

he turned to those who were teasing him most
他转向那些最逗他的人

"Beware, boys!" he warned them
"当心,孩子们!"

"I have not come here to be your buffoon"
"我来这里不是为了做你的小丑"

"I respect others," he said
"我尊重别人,"他说

"and I intend to be respected"
"我打算得到尊重"

"Well said, boaster!" howled the young rascals
"说得好,自夸!"

"You have spoken like a book!"
"你说话像书一样!"

and they convulsed with mad laughter
他们疯狂地笑着抽搐着

there was one boy more impertinent than the others
有一个男孩比其他人更无礼

he tried to seize the puppet by the end of his nose
他试图抓住木偶的鼻尖

But he could not do so quickly enough
但他做得不够快

Pinocchio stuck his leg out from under the table
匹诺曹从桌子底下伸出腿

and he gave him a great kick on his shins
他狠狠地踢了他的小腿

the boy roared in pain
男孩痛苦地咆哮着

"Oh, what hard feet you have!"

"噢,你的脚多硬啊!"
and he rubbed the bruise the puppet had given him
他揉了揉木偶给他留下的瘀伤
"And what elbows you have!" said another
"那你有什么胳膊肘啊!"
"they are even harder than his feet!"
"他们甚至比他的脚还硬!"
this boy had also played rude tricks on him
这个男孩还对他耍了粗鲁的把戏
and he had received a blow in the stomach
他的肚子也受到了打击
But, nevertheless, the kick and the blow acquired sympathy
但是,尽管如此,这一踢和打击还是赢得了同情
and Pinocchio earned the esteem of the boys
匹诺曹赢得了男孩们的尊重
They soon all made friends with him
他们很快就和他交上了朋友
and soon they liked him heartily
很快,他们就衷心地喜欢上了他
And even the master praised him
甚至师父也称赞他
because Pinocchio was attentive in class
因为匹诺曹在课堂上很专心
he was a studious and intelligent student
他是一个好学而聪明的学生
and he was always the first to come to school
他总是第一个来到学校的
and he was always the last to leave when school was over
放学后,他总是最后一个离开的
But he had one fault; he made too many friends
但他有一个缺点;他交了太多朋友
and amongst his friends were several rascals

他的朋友中有几个流氓
these boys were well known for their dislike of study
这些男孩以不喜欢学习而闻名
and they especially loved to cause mischief
他们特别喜欢捣蛋
The master warned him about them every day
师父每天都警告他
even the good Fairy never failed to tell him:
即使是善良的仙女也从来没有忘记告诉他：
"Take care, Pinocchio, with your friends!"
"小心点，匹诺曹，和你的朋友们一起！"
"Those bad school-fellows of yours are trouble"
"你那些坏同学真是麻烦"
"they will make you lose your love of study"
"他们会让你失去对学习的热爱"
"they may even bring upon you some great misfortune"
"他们甚至可能会给你带来一些巨大的不幸"
"There is no fear of that!" answered the puppet
"不用担心！"
and he shrugged his shoulders and touched his forehead
他耸了耸肩，摸了摸自己的额头
"There is so much sense here!"
"这里太有意义了！"

one fine day Pinocchio was on his way to school
一个晴朗的日子，匹诺曹正在上学的路上
and he met several of his usual companions
他遇到了几个他平常的同伴
coming up to him, they asked:
他们走到他面前问道：
"Have you heard the great news?"
"你听说过这个好消息吗？"
"No, I have not heard the great news"
"不，我没有听到这个好消息"
"In the sea near here a Dog-Fish has appeared"
"在这附近的海里，出现了一条狗鱼"
"he is as big as a mountain"
"他像山一样大"
"Is it true?" asked Pinocchio

"这是真的吗？"
"Can it be the same Dog-Fish?"
"会是同一个狗鱼吗？"
"The Dog-Fish that was there when my papa drowned"
"我爸爸溺水时在那儿的狗鱼"
"We are going to the shore to see him"
"我们要去岸边看他"
"Will you come with us?"
"你愿意跟我们一起去吗？"
"No; I am going to school"
"不;我要去上学"
"of what great importance is school?"
"学校有什么重要意义呢？"
"We can go to school tomorrow"
"我们明天可以去上学"
"one lesson more or less doesn't matter"
"一节课或多或少无关紧要"
"we shall always remain the same donkeys"
"我们将永远是一样的驴子"
"But what will the master say?"
"可是，主人会怎么说呢？"
"The master may say what he likes"
"主人想说什么就说什么"
"He is paid to grumble all day"
"他整天抱怨是有报酬的"
"And what will my mamma say?"
"那我妈妈会怎么说呢？"
"Mammas know nothing," answered the bad little boys
"妈妈们什么都不知道，"坏小男孩们回答
"Do you know what I will do?" said Pinocchio
"你知道我该怎么办吗？"
"I have reasons for wishing to see the Dog-Fish"
"我有理由希望看到狗鱼"

- 208 -

"but I will go and see him when school is over"
"不过我放学后会去看他。"

"Poor donkey!" exclaimed one of the boys
"可怜的驴子！"

"Do you suppose a fish of that size will wait your convenience?"
"你觉得这么大的鱼会等你吗？"

"when he is tired of being here he will go another place"
"当他厌倦了在这里时，他会去另一个地方"

"and then it will be too late"
"然后就太晚了"

the Puppet had to think about this
傀儡不得不考虑这个问题

"How long does it take to get to the shore?"
"到岸边需要多长时间？"

"We can be there and back in an hour"
"我们可以在一个小时内到达并返回"

"Then off we go!" shouted Pinocchio
"那我们走吧！"

"and he who runs fastest is the best!"
"跑得最快的就是最好的！"

and the boys rushed off across the fields
男孩们就冲过田野跑了

and Pinocchio was always the first
而匹诺曹总是第一个

he seemed to have wings on his feet
他的脚上似乎长了翅膀

From time to time he turned to jeer at his companions
他时不时地转过来嘲笑他的同伴

they were some distance behind
他们落后了一段距离

he saw them panting for breath

and they were covered with dust
他们被尘土覆盖
and their tongues were hanging out of their mouths
他们的舌头从口中伸出来
and Pinocchio laughed heartily at the sight
匹诺曹看到这一幕，爽朗地笑了起来
The unfortunate boy did not know what was to come
这个不幸的男孩不知道会发生什么
the terrors and horrible disasters that were coming!
即将到来的恐怖和可怕的灾难！

Pinocchio is Arrested by the Gendarmes
匹诺曹被宪兵逮捕

Pinocchio arrived at the shore
匹诺曹到达岸边
and he looked out to sea
他望向大海
but he saw no Dog-Fish
但他没有看到狗鱼
The sea was as smooth as a great crystal mirror
海面像一面巨大的水晶镜子一样光滑
"Where is the Dog-Fish?" he asked
"狗鱼在哪儿？"
and he turned to his companions
他转向他的同伴
all the boys laughed together
所有男孩都一起笑了起来
"He must have gone to have his breakfast"
"他一定是去吃早餐了"
"Or he has thrown himself on to his bed"
"或者他已经倒在床上了"

"yes, he's having a little nap"
"是的,他在小睡一会儿"
and they laughed even louder
他们笑得更大声了
their answers seemed particularly absurd
他们的回答似乎特别荒谬
and their laughter was very silly
他们的笑声非常愚蠢
Pinocchio looked around at his friends
匹诺曹环顾四周,看着他的朋友们
his companions seemed to be making a fool of him
他的同伴们似乎在愚弄他
they had induced him to believe a tale
他们诱使他相信了一个故事
but there was no truth to the tale
但这个故事没有真相
Pinocchio did not take the joke well
匹诺曹没有很好地接受这个笑话
and he spoke angrily with the boys
他和男孩们生气地说话
"And now??" he shouted
"现在呢??"
"you told me a story of the Dog-Fish"
"你给我讲了个狗鱼的故事"
"but what fun did you find in deceiving me?"
"可是你骗我有什么乐趣呢?"
"Oh, it was great fun!" answered the little rascals
"噢,真好玩啊!"
"And in what did this fun consist of?"
"那么这种乐趣包括什么?"
"we made you miss a day of school"
"我们让你错过了一天的学校"
"and we persuaded you to come with us"
"我们说服了你跟我们走"

"Are you not ashamed of your conduct?"
"你不为自己的行为感到羞耻吗？"
"you are always so punctual to school"
"你总是那么准时上学"
"and you are always so diligent in class"
"而且你在课堂上总是那么勤奋"
"Are you not ashamed of studying so hard?"
"你这么努力学习不觉得羞耻吗？"
"so what if I study hard?"
"那么，如果我努力学习呢？"
"what concern is it of yours?"
"你关心什么？"
"It concerns us excessively"
"这让我们非常担忧"
"because it makes us appear in a bad light"
"因为它让我们显得很糟糕"
"Why does it make you appear in a bad light?"
"为什么它会让你显得不好？"
"there are those of us who have no wish to study"
"我们有些人不想学习"
"we have no desire to learn anything"
"我们不想学习任何东西"
"good boys make us seem worse by comparison"
"相比之下，好男孩让我们看起来更糟糕"
"And that is too bad for you"
"这对你来说太糟糕了"
"We, too, have our pride!"
"我们也有我们的骄傲！"
"Then what must I do to please you?"
"那么，我该怎么做才能取悦你呢？"
"You must follow our example"
"你必须以我们为榜样"
"you must hate school like us"

"你一定像我们一样讨厌学校"
"you must rebel in the lessons"
"你必须在课程中反叛"
"and you must disobey the master"
"你必须违背主人"
"those are our three greatest enemies"
"这是我们最大的三个敌人"
"And if I wish to continue my studies?"
"那么,如果我想继续我的学业呢?"
"In that case we will have nothing more to do with you"
"那样的话,我们就和你没有什么关系了"
"and at the first opportunity we will make you pay for it"
"一有机会,我们会让你付钱"
"Really," said the puppet, shaking his head
"真的,"木偶摇着头说
"you make me inclined to laugh"
"你让我很想笑"
"Eh, Pinocchio," shouted the biggest of the boys
"呃,匹诺曹,"男孩中最大的一个喊道
and he confronted Pinocchio directly
他直接与匹诺曹对峙
"None of your superiority works here"
"你的优越性在这里都不起作用"
"don't come here to crow over us"
"不要来这里叫我们"
"if you are not afraid of us, we are not afraid of you"
"如果你不怕我们,我们也不怕你"
"Remember that you are one against seven"
"记住,你是1对7"
"Seven, like the seven deadly sins," said Pinocchio
"七宗罪,就像七宗罪一样,"匹诺曹说

and he shouted with laughter
他大笑着喊道
"Listen to him! He has insulted us all!"
"听他的话！他侮辱了我们所有人！"
"He called us the seven deadly sins!"
"他称我们为七宗罪！"
"Take that to begin with," said one of the boys
"先说吧，"其中一个男孩说
"and keep it for your supper tonight"
"留着留你今晚吃晚饭"
And, so saying, he punched him on the head
"说着，他一拳打在他的头上
But it was a give and take
但这是一个让步
because the puppet immediately returned the blow
因为木偶立即还击
this was no big surprise
这并不奇怪
and the fight quickly got desperate
战斗很快就变得绝望了
it is true that Pinocchio was alone
的确，匹诺曹独自一人
but he defended himself like a hero
但他像英雄一样保护自己
He used his feet, which were of the hardest wood
他用他的脚，那脚是最硬的木头做的
and he kept his enemies at a respectful distance
他与敌人保持着尊重的距离
Wherever his feet touched they left a bruise
他的脚碰到哪里，都会留下瘀伤
The boys became furious with him
男孩们对他大发雷霆
hand to hand they couldn't match the puppet
他们无法与木偶匹匹敌

so they took other weapons into their hands
所以他们拿走了其他武器
the boys loosened their satchels
男孩们松开了他们的书包
and they threw their school-books at him
他们把课本扔向他
grammars, dictionaries, and spelling-books
语法、词典和拼写书
geography books and other scholastic works
地理书籍和其他学术著作
But Pinocchio was quick to react
但匹诺曹很快就反应过来了
and he had sharp eyes for these things
他对这些事情有敏锐的眼睛
he always managed to duck in time
他总是设法及时躲避
so the books passed over his head
于是这些书从他的头上掠过

and instead the books fell into the sea
然而,这些书却掉进了海里
Imagine the astonishment of the fish!
想象一下鱼的惊讶!
they thought the books were something to eat
他们认为这些书是吃的东西
and they all arrived in large shoals of fish
他们都成群结队地来到这里
but they tasted a couple of the pages
但他们品尝了其中的几页
and they quickly spat the paper out again
他们很快又把纸吐了出来
and the fish made wry faces
鱼儿苦笑着
"this isn't food for us at all"
"这根本不是我们的食物"
"we are accustomed to something much better!"
"我们已经习惯了更好的东西!"
The battle meantime had become fiercer than ever
与此同时,战斗变得比以往任何时候都更加激烈
a big crab had come out of the water
一只大螃蟹从水里出来了
and he had climbed slowly up on the shore
他慢慢地爬上了岸
he called out in a hoarse voice
他用嘶哑的声音喊道
it sounded like a trumpet with a bad cold
听起来像是重感冒的小号
"enough of your fighting, you young ruffians"
"受够了你们的战斗,你们这些年轻的恶棍"
"because you are nothing other than ruffians!"
"因为你们不过是地痞流氓!"
"These fights between boys seldom finish well"

"男孩之间的这些打架很少能有好结果"
"Some disaster is sure to happen!"
"肯定会发生一些灾难！"
but the poor crab should have saved himself the trouble
可是这只可怜的螃蟹本来应该省去麻烦的
He might as well have preached to the wind
他不如向风说教
Even that young rascal, Pinocchio, turned around
就连那个年轻的流氓匹诺曹也转过身来
he looked at him mockingly and said rudely:
他嘲讽地看着他，粗鲁地说：
"Hold your tongue, you tiresome crab!"
"住嘴，你这只讨厌的螃蟹！"
"You had better suck some liquorice lozenges"
"你最好吮吸一些甘草锭剂"
"cure that cold in your throat"
"治愈你喉咙里的感冒"
Just then the boys had no more books
就在这时，男孩们没有更多的书了
at least, they had no books of their own
至少，他们没有自己的书
they spied at a little distance Pinocchio's bag
他们在不远处窥探了匹诺曹的包
and they took possession of his things
他们就占了他的财物
Amongst his books there was one bound in card
在他的书中，有一本装订在卡片上的书
It was a Treatise on Arithmetic
这是一篇关于算术的论文
One of the boys seized this volume
其中一个男孩拿走了这本书
and he aimed the book at Pinocchio's head
他把书对准了匹诺曹的头

he threw it at him with all his strength
他用尽全身的力气向他扔去
but the book did not hit the puppet
但这本书并没有击中傀儡
instead the book hit a companion on the head
相反,这本书击中了一个同伴的头
the boy turned as white as a sheet
男孩脸色苍白得像一张床单
"Oh, mother! help, I am dying!"
"哦,妈妈!救命,我快死了!
and he fell his whole length on the sand
他全身都倒在了沙地上
the boys must have thought he was dead
男孩们一定以为他已经死了
and they ran off as fast as their legs could run
他们用腿能跑得最快的速度跑开了
in a few minutes they were out of sight
几分钟后,他们就消失了
But Pinocchio remained with the boy
但匹诺曹仍然和男孩在一起
although he would have rather ran off too
虽然他也宁愿逃跑
because his fear was also great
因为他的恐惧也很大
nevertheless, he ran over to the sea
尽管如此,他还是跑向了大海
and he soaked his handkerchief in the water
他把手帕浸在水里
he ran back to his poor school-fellow
他跑回去找他那可怜的同学
and he began to bathe his forehead
他开始洗额头
he cried bitterly in despair
他绝望地痛哭

and he kept calling him by name
他不停地叫他的名字
and he said many things to him:
他对他说了许多话：
"Eugene! my poor Eugene!"
"尤金！我可怜的尤金！
"Open your eyes and look at me!"
"睁开你的眼睛，看着我！"
"Why do you not answer?"
"你为什么不回答？"
"I did not do it to you"
"我没有对你做"
"it was not I that hurt you so!"
"不是我这么伤你！"
"believe me, it was not me!"
"相信我，那不是我！"
"Open your eyes, Eugene"
"睁开你的眼睛，尤金"
"If you keep your eyes shut I shall die, too"
"如果你闭上眼睛，我也会死"
"Oh! what shall I do?"
"哦！我该怎么办呢？
"how shall I ever return home?"
"我怎么回家呢？"
"How can I ever have the courage to go back to my good mamma?"
"我怎么能有勇气回到我的好妈妈身边呢？"
"What will become of me?"
"我会变成什么样子？"
"Where can I fly to?"
"我可以飞到哪里？"
"had I only gone to school!"
"要是我只去上学就好了！"

"Why did I listen to my companions?"
"我为什么听同伴的话？"
"they have been my ruin"
"他们成了我的毁灭"
"The master said it to me"
"师父对我说的"
"and my mamma repeated it often"
"我妈妈经常重复这句话"
'Beware of bad companions!'
"当心坏伙伴！"
"Oh, dear! what will become of me?"
"噢，亲爱的！我会变成什么样子呢？
And Pinocchio began to cry and sob
匹诺曹开始哭泣
and he struck his head with his fists
他用拳头打他的头
Suddenly he heard the sound of footsteps
突然，他听到了脚步声
He turned and saw two soldiers
他转过身来，看到两个士兵
"What are you doing there?"
"你在那儿做什么？"
"why are you lying on the ground?"
"你为什么躺在地上？"
"I am helping my school-fellow"
"我在帮助我的同学"
"Has he been hurt?"
"他受伤了吗？"
"It seems he has been hurt"
"看来他受了伤"
"Hurt indeed!" said one of them
"确实受伤了！"
and he stooped down to examine Eugene closely

他弯下腰来仔细打量尤金

"This boy has been wounded on the head"
"这个男孩头上受了伤"

"Who wounded him?" they asked Pinocchio
他们问匹诺曹:"谁打伤了他?"

"Not I," stammered the puppet breathlessly
"不是我,"木偶上气不接下气地结结巴巴地说

"If it was not you, who then did it?"
"如果不是你,那是谁干的?"

"Not I," repeated Pinocchio
"不是我,"匹诺曹重复道

"And with what was he wounded?"
"他受了什么伤呢?"

"he was hurt with this book"
"他被这本书伤害了"

And the puppet picked up from the ground his book
"傀儡从地上捡起了他的书

the Treatise on Arithmetic
算术论

and he showed the book to the soldier
他把书拿给士兵看

"And to whom does this belong?"
"那这属于谁呢?"

"It belongs to me," answered Pinocchio, honestly
"它是属于我的,"匹诺曹诚实地回答

"That is enough, nothing more is wanted"
"够了,别无所求"

"Get up and come with us at once"
"快起来跟我们走"

"But I..." Pinocchio tried to object
"可是我......"匹诺曹试图反对

"Come along with us!" they insisted
"跟我们来!"

"But I am innocent" he pleaded
"但我是无辜的,"他恳求道
but they didn't listen. "Come along with us!"
但他们不听。"跟我们来!"
Before they left, the soldiers called a passing fishermen
在他们离开之前,士兵们打电话给一个路过的渔民
"We give you this wounded boy"
"我们把这个受伤的男孩交给你"
"we leave him in your care"
"我们把他交给你照顾"
"Carry him to your house and nurse him"
"把他带到你家,照顾他"
"Tomorrow we will come and see him"
"明天我们会来看他"
They then turned to Pinocchio
然后他们转向匹诺曹
"Forward! and walk quickly"
"前进!快走"
"or it will be the worse for you"
"否则,你就会更糟"
Pinocchio did not need to be told twice
匹诺曹不需要被重复
the puppet set out along the road leading to the village
木偶沿着通往村庄的道路出发
But the poor little Devil hardly knew where he was
可是这个可怜的小魔鬼几乎不知道自己在哪儿
He thought he must be dreaming
他觉得自己一定是在做梦
and what a dreadful dream it was!
那真是个可怕的梦啊!
He saw double and his legs shook
他看到双倍,双腿颤抖
his tongue clung to the roof of his mouth
他的舌头紧贴着他的上颚

and he could not utter a word
他一句话也说不出来
And yet, in the midst of his stupefaction and apathy
然而，在他的愚蠢和冷漠中
his heart was pierced by a cruel thorn
他的心被一根残忍的荆棘刺穿
he knew where he had to walk past
他知道他必须走过哪里
under the windows of the good Fairy's house
在善良仙女家的窗户下
and she was going see him with the soldiers
她要和士兵们一起去见他
He would rather have died
他宁愿死
soon they reached the village
很快他们就到了村子里
a gust of wind blew Pinocchio's cap off his head
一阵风把匹诺曹的帽子吹了下来
"Will you permit me?" said the puppet to the soldiers
"你们能允许我吗？"
"can I go and get my cap?"
"我可以去拿我的帽子吗？"
"Go, then; but be quick about it"
"那么，走吧;但要快点"
The puppet went and picked up his cap
木偶走过去捡起了他的帽子
but he didn't put the cap on his head
但他没有把帽子戴在头上
he put the cap between his teeth
他把帽子夹在牙缝里
and began to run as fast as he could
并开始尽可能快地奔跑
he was running back towards the seashore!
他正向海边跑去！

The soldiers thought it would be difficult to overtake him
士兵们认为很难追上他

so they sent after him a large mastiff
于是他们派了一只大獒犬来追赶他

he had won the first prizes at all the dog races
他在所有的赛狗比赛中都获得了冠军

Pinocchio ran, but the dog ran faster
匹诺曹跑了,但狗跑得更快

The people came to their windows
人们来到他们的窗户前

and they crowded into the street
他们挤到街上

they wanted to see the end of the desperate race
他们想看到这场绝望的比赛结束

Pinocchio Runs the Danger of being Fried in a Pan like a Fish
匹诺曹有像鱼一样在平底锅里煎的危险

the race was not going well for the puppet
傀儡的比赛并不顺利

and Pinocchio thought he had lost
匹诺曹认为他输了

Alidoro, the mastiff, had run swiftly
獒犬阿利多罗跑得很快

and he had nearly caught up with him
他差点就追上了他

the dreadful beast was very close behind him
这只可怕的野兽就在他身后很近

he could hear the panting of the dog
他能听到狗的喘息声

there was not a hand's breadth between them

他们之间没有一手的宽度
he could even feel the dog's hot breath
他甚至能感觉到狗的热气
Fortunately the shore was close
幸运的是，海岸很近
and the sea was but a few steps off
大海离我们只有几步之遥
soon they reached the sands of the beach
很快，他们就到达了海滩的沙滩
they got there almost at the same time
他们几乎同时到达那里
but the puppet made a wonderful leap
但木偶做出了一个美妙的跳跃
a frog could have done no better
一只青蛙再好不过了
and he plunged into the water
他跳进了水里
Alidoro, on the contrary, wished to stop himself
相反，阿利多罗希望阻止自己
but he was carried away by the impetus of the race
但他被比赛的推动冲昏了头脑
he also went into the sea
他也下海去了
The unfortunate dog could not swim
这只不幸的狗不会游泳
but he made great efforts to keep himself afloat
但他付出了巨大的努力来维持自己的生活
and he swam as well as he could with his paws
他用爪子尽可能地游动
but the more he struggled the farther he sank
但他越挣扎，就越沉得越远
and soon his head was under the water
很快他的头就埋在水里了
his head rose above the water for a moment

他的头露出水面一会儿
and his eyes were rolling with terror
他的眼睛惊恐地翻着白眼
and the poor dog barked out:
那条可怜的狗吠叫道：
"I am drowning! I am drowning!"
"我快溺水了！我快淹死了！
"Drown!" shouted Pinocchio from a distance
"淹死了！"匹诺曹从远处喊道
he knew that he was in no more danger
他知道他已经没有危险了
"Help me, dear Pinocchio!"
"帮帮我，亲爱的匹诺曹！"
"Save me from death!"
"救我免于死亡！"
in reality Pinocchio had an excellent heart
实际上，匹诺曹有一颗极好的心
he heard the agonizing cry from the dog
他听到了狗痛苦的哭声
and the puppet was moved with compassion
木偶就被怜悯所感动
he turned to the dog, and said:
他转过身来对狗说：
"I will save you," said Pinocchio
"我会救你的，"匹诺曹说
"but do you promise to give me no further annoyance?"
"可是你答应不给我添麻烦吗？"
"I promise! I promise!" barked the dog
"我保证！我保证！
"Be quick, for pity's sake"
"快点，看在可怜的份上"
"if you delay another half-minute I shall be dead"
"如果你再耽搁半分钟，我就死定了"

Pinocchio hesitated for a moment
匹诺曹犹豫了片刻
but then he remembered what his father had often told him
但随后他想起了他父亲经常告诉他的话
"a good action is never lost"
"一个好的行动永远不会丢失"
he quickly swam over to Alidoro
他迅速游向阿里多罗
and he took hold of his tail with both hands
他用双手抓住自己的尾巴
soon they were on dry land again
很快,他们又回到了陆地上
and Alidoro was safe and sound
阿里多罗安然无恙
The poor dog could not stand
这只可怜的狗无法站立
He had drunk a lot of salt water
他喝了很多盐水
and now he was like a balloon
现在他就像一个气球
The puppet, however, didn't entirely trust him
然而,这个傀儡并不完全信任他
he thought it more prudent to jump again into the water
他认为再次跳入水中更为谨慎
he swam a little distance into the water
他游进了水里一小段距离
and he called out to his friend he had rescued
他向他救出的朋友大声呼喊
"Good-bye, Alidoro; a good journey to you"
"再见了,阿利多罗;祝你旅途愉快"
"and take my compliments to all at home"
"并将我的赞美带给家里的所有人"

"Good-bye, Pinocchio," answered the dog
"再见了,匹诺曹,"狗回答
"a thousand thanks for having saved my life"
"非常感谢你救了我的命"
"You have done me a great service"
"你为我做了很棒的服务"
"and in this world what is given is returned"
"在这个世界上,所给予的都会得到回报"
"If an occasion offers I shall not forget it"
"如果有机会,我不会忘记它"
Pinocchio swam along the shore
匹诺曹沿着岸边游泳
At last he thought he had reached a safe place
最后,他以为自己已经到达了一个安全的地方
so he gave a look along the shore
于是他沿着岸边看了看
he saw amongst the rocks a kind of cave
他在岩石中看到了一种洞穴
from the cave there was a cloud of smoke
山洞里冒出一团烟雾
"In that cave there must be a fire"
"那个山洞里一定有火"
"So much the better," thought Pinocchio
"好多了,"匹诺曹想
"I will go and dry and warm myself"
"我要去擦干暖和自己"
"and then?" Pinocchio wondered
"然后呢?"匹诺曹想知道
"and then we shall see," he concluded
"然后我们就看看,"他总结道
Having taken the resolution he swam landwards
下定决心后,他向陆地游去
he was was about to climb up the rocks

他正要爬上岩石
but he felt something under the water
但他感觉到水下有什么东西
whatever it was rose higher and higher
不管是什么，它都越来越高
and it carried him into the air
它把他带到了空中
He tried to escape from it
他试图逃脱
but it was too late to get away
但已经太晚了
he was extremely surprised when he saw what it was
当他看到那是什么时，他感到非常惊讶
he found himself enclosed in a great net
他发现自己被一张大网包围了
he was with a swarm of fish of every size and shape
他和一群大小不一的鱼在一起
they were flapping and struggling around
他们拍打着翅膀，挣扎着
like a swarm of despairing souls
就像一群绝望的灵魂
At the same moment a fisherman came out of the cave
就在这时，一个渔夫从山洞里出来了
the fisherman was horribly ugly
渔夫长得可怕
and he looked like a sea monster
他看起来就像个海怪
his head was not covered in hair
他的头上没有被头发覆盖
instead he had a thick bush of green grass
相反，他有一丛茂密的绿草
his skin was green and his eyes were green
他的皮肤是绿色的，他的眼睛也是绿色的
and his long beard came down to the ground

他的长胡子掉到了地上
and of course his beard was also green
当然,他的胡子也是绿色的
He had the appearance of an immense lizard
他长得像一只巨大的蜥蜴
a lizard standing on its hind-paws
一只用后爪站立的蜥蜴

the fisherman pulled his net out of the sea
渔夫从海里拉出网
"Thank Heaven!" he exclaimed greatly satisfied
"谢天谢地!"
"Again today I shall have a splendid feast of fish!"
"今天我又要吃一顿丰盛的鱼宴了!"
Pinocchio thought to himself for a moment
匹诺曹心想了一会儿

"What a mercy that I am not a fish!"
"真可怜,我不是一条鱼!"
and he regained a little courage
他又恢复了一点勇气
The netful of fish was carried into the cave
那一网鱼被运进了洞穴
and the cave was dark and smoky
山洞里漆黑的,烟雾缭绕
In the middle of the cave was a large frying-pan
山洞中央有一个大煎锅
and the frying-pan was full of oil
煎锅里装满了油
there was a suffocating smell of mushrooms
有一股令人窒息的蘑菇气味
but the fisherman was very excited
但渔夫非常兴奋
"Now we will see what fish we have taken!"
"现在我们看看我们钓到了什么鱼!"
and he put into the net an enormous hand
他就把一只大手放在网里
his hand had the proportions of a baker's shovel
他的手有面包铲的比例
and he pulled out a handful of fish
他掏出一把鱼
"These fish are good!" he said
"这些鱼很好吃!"
and he smelled the fish complacently
他得意洋洋地闻着鱼的味道
And then he threw the fish into a pan without water
然后他把鱼扔进一个没有水的锅里
He repeated the same operation many times
他多次重复相同的操作
and as he drew out the fish his mouth watered
当他把鱼捞出来时,他的口水流了出来

and the Fisherman chuckled to himself
渔夫自言自语地笑了起来
"What exquisite sardines I've caught!"
"我钓到的沙丁鱼多么精美啊！"
"These mackerel are going to be delicious!"
"这些鲭鱼会很好吃！"
"And these crabs will be excellent!"
"这些螃蟹会很棒！"
"What dear little anchovies they are!"
"它们真是可爱的小凤尾鱼啊！"
The last to remain in the fisher's net was Pinocchio
最后一个留在渔网中的是匹诺曹
his big green eyes opened with astonishment
他那双绿色的大眼睛惊讶地睁开了
"What species of fish is this??"
"这是什么鱼？？"
"Fish of this kind I don't remember to have eaten"
"我不记得吃过这种鱼"
And he looked at him again attentively
他又专心地看着他
and he examined him well all over
他把他浑身都打量得仔细
"I know: he must be a craw-fish"
"我知道，他一定是一条小龙虾"
Pinocchio was mortified at being mistaken for a craw-fish
匹诺曹因为被误认为是小龙虾而感到羞愧
"Do you take me for a craw-fish?"
"你把我当作小龙虾吗？"
"that's no way to treat your guests!"
"那可不是款待你的客人的方式！"
"Let me tell you that I am a puppet"
"让我告诉你，我是一个傀儡"

"A puppet?" replied the fisherman
"一个傀儡？"
"then I must tell you the truth"
"那我必须告诉你真相"
"a puppet is quite a new fish to me"
"木偶对我来说是一条相当新的鱼"
"but that is even better!"
"但那更好！"
"I shall eat you with greater pleasure"
"我会更快乐地吃掉你"
"you can eat me all you want"
"你想吃我就吃我"
"but will you understand that I am not a fish?"
"可是，你能明白我不是一条鱼吗？"
"Do you not hear that I talk?"
"你没听到我说话吗？"
"can you not see that I reason as you do?"
"你难道看不出我跟你一样推理吗？"
"That is quite true," said the fisherman
"这是真的，"渔夫说
"you are indeed a fish with the talent of talking"
"你真是一条有说话天赋的鱼"
"and you are a fish that can reason as I do"
"而你是一条能像我一样推理的鱼"
"I must treat you with appropriate attention"
"我必须适当地照顾你"
"And what would this attention be?"
"那么这种关注会是什么？"
"let me give you a token of my friendship"
"让我给你一个我友谊的信物"
"and let me show my particular regard"
"请允许我表达我特别的敬意"
"I will let you choose how you would like to be

cooked"
"我让你选择你想要的烹饪方式"
"Would you like to be fried in the frying-pan?
"你想在煎锅里煎吗？
"or would you prefer to be stewed with tomato sauce?"
"或者你更喜欢用番茄酱炖？"
"let me tell you the truth," answered Pinocchio
"我实话告诉你，"匹诺曹回答
"if I had to choose, I would like to be set free"
"如果我必须选择，我想被释放"
"You are joking!" laughed the fisherman
"你在开玩笑！"
"why would I lose the opportunity to taste such a rare fish?"
"为什么我会失去品尝如此稀有鱼的机会？"
"I can assure you puppet fish are rare here"
"我可以向你保证，傀儡鱼在这里很少见"
"one does not catch a puppet fish every day"
"不是每天都抓到一条傀儡鱼"
"Let me make the choice for you"
"让我为你做选择"
"you will be with the other fish"
"你会和别的鱼在一起"
"I will fry you in the frying-pan"
"我要在煎锅里煎你"
"and you will be quite satisfied"
"你会很满意的"
"It is always consolation to be fried in company"
"在公司里被煎炸总是令人欣慰的"
At this speech the unhappy Pinocchio began to cry
听到这番话，不高兴的匹诺曹开始哭泣起来
he screamed and implored for mercy
他尖叫着恳求怜悯

"How much better it would have been if I had gone to school!"
"如果我去上学该多好啊！"
"I shouldn't have listened to my companions"
"我不该听我的同伴的话"
"and now I am paying for it"
"现在我正在为此付出代价"
And he wriggled like an eel
他像鳗鱼一样蠕动着
and he made indescribable efforts to slip out
他做出了难以形容的努力，试图溜出去
but he was tight in clutches of the green fisherman
但他紧紧地抓住了那个绿色的渔夫
and all of Pinocchio's efforts were useless
匹诺曹的所有努力都是徒劳的
the fisherman took a long strip of rush
渔夫吃了一大口
and he bound the puppets hands and feet
他把木偶的手和脚绑起来
Poor Pinocchio was tied up like a sausage
可怜的匹诺曹像香肠一样被绑住了
and he threw him into the pan with the other fish
然后他把他和另一条鱼一起扔进锅里
He then fetched a wooden bowl full of flour
然后他拿来一个装满面粉的木碗
and one by one he began to flour each fish
他开始一条一条地给每条鱼撒上面粉
soon all the little fish were ready
很快，所有的小鱼都准备好了
and he threw them into the frying-pan
然后他把它们扔进煎锅里
The first to dance in the boiling oil were the poor whitings
第一个在沸腾的油中跳舞的是可怜的鳕鱼

the crabs were next to follow the dance
螃蟹们紧随其后
and then the sardines came too
然后沙丁鱼也来了
and finally the anchovies were thrown in
最后,凤尾鱼被扔进去
at last it had come to Pinocchio's turn
终于轮到匹诺曹了
he saw the horrible death waiting for him
他看到了等待他的可怕死亡
and you can imagine how frightened he was
你可以想象他有多害怕
he trembled violently and with great effort
他剧烈而费力地颤抖着
and he had neither voice nor breath left for further entreaties
他既没有声音也没有呼吸来继续恳求
But the poor boy implored with his eyes!
但这个可怜的男孩却用他的眼睛恳求!
The green fisherman, however, didn't care the least
然而,这位绿色渔夫一点也不在乎
and he plunged him five or six times in the flour
他又在面粉里扎了五六次
finally he was white from head to foot
最后,他从头到脚都白了
and he looked like a puppet made of plaster
他看起来就像一个石膏做的木偶

Pinocchio Returns to the Fairy's House
匹诺曹回到仙女之家

Pinocchio was dangling over the frying pan
匹诺曹在煎锅上晃来晃去
the fisherman was just about to throw him in
渔夫正要把他扔进去
but then a large dog entered the cave
但随后一只大狗进入了洞穴
the dog had smelled the savoury odour of fried fish
狗闻到了炸鱼的香味
and he had been enticed into the cave
他被引诱进了山洞
"Get out!" shouted the fisherman
"滚出去！"
he was holding the floured puppet in one hand
他一只手拿着那个撒了面粉的木偶
and he threatened the dog with the other hand
他用另一只手威胁那只狗
But the poor dog was as hungry as a wolf
可是这只可怜的狗却饿得像狼一样
and he whined and wagged his tail
他呜地摇着尾巴
if he could have talked he would have said:
如果他能说话，他会说：
"Give me some fish and I will leave you in peace"
"给我一些鱼，我会让你安然无恙"
"Get out, I tell you!" repeated the fisherman
"滚出去，我告诉你！"
and he stretched out his leg to give him a kick
他伸出腿来踢他一脚
But the dog would not stand trifling
但那条狗可不容忍
he was too hungry to be denied the food

他太饿了,不能被拒绝吃

he started growling at the fisherman
他开始对渔夫咆哮

and he showed his terrible teeth
他露出了可怕的牙齿

At that moment a little feeble voice called out
就在这时,一个微弱的声音喊道

"Save me, Alidoro, please!"
"救救我,阿里多罗,求求你了!"

"If you do not save me I shall be fried!"
"如果你不救我,我就会被炸了!"

The dog recognized Pinocchio's voice
狗认出了匹诺曹的声音

all he saw was the floured bundle in the fisherman's hand
他只看到渔夫手中的一捆面粉

that must be where the voice had come from
那一定是声音的来源

So what do you think he did?
那么你认为他做了什么呢?

Alidoro sprung up to the fisherman
阿里多罗跳到渔夫面前

and he seized the bundle in his mouth
他就把那捆东西含在嘴里

he held the bundle gently in his teeth
他用牙齿轻轻地把那捆东西拿着

and he rushed out of the cave again
他又冲出了山洞

and then he was gone like a flash of lightning
然后他就像一道闪电一样消失了

The fisherman was furious
渔夫很生气

the rare puppet fish had been snatched from him
那条稀有的傀儡鱼已经从他那里被抢走了

and he ran after the dog
他追着狗跑
he tried to get his fish back
他试图把他的鱼拿回来
but the fisherman did not run far
但渔夫并没有跑多远
because he had been taken by a fit of coughing
因为他被一阵咳嗽带走了

Alidoro ran almost to the village
阿里多罗几乎跑到了村子里
when he got to the path he stopped
当他走到小路时,他停了下来
he put his friend Pinocchio gently on the ground
他把他的朋友匹诺曹轻轻地放在地上

"How much I have to thank you for!" said the puppet
"我多么感谢你啊!"
"There is no necessity," replied the dog
"没有必要,"狗回答
"You saved me and I have now returned it"
"你救了我,我现在已经还我了"
"You know that we must all help each other in this world"
"你知道我们在这个世界上都必须互相帮助"
Pinocchio was happy to have saved Alidoro
匹诺曹很高兴救了阿利多罗
"But how did you get into the cave?"
"可是你是怎么进山洞的呢?"
"I was lying on the shore more dead than alive"
"我躺在岸上,死的比活的还多"
"then the wind brought to me the smell of fried fish"
"然后风给我带来了炸鱼的香味"
"The smell excited my appetite"
"气味让我胃口大开"
"and I followed my nose"
"我跟着我的鼻子走"
"If I had arrived a second later..."
"如果我晚一秒到达……"
"Do not mention it!" sighed Pinocchio
"别提了!"
he was still trembling with fright
他仍然吓得浑身发抖
"I would be a fried puppet by now"
"我现在会是一个油炸的木偶"
"It makes me shudder just to think of it!"
"光是想想就让我不寒而栗!"
Alidoro laughed a little at the idea
Alidoro 对这个想法微微一笑

but he extended his right paw to the puppet
但他将右爪伸向了木偶
Pinocchio shook his paw heartily
匹诺曹由衷地摇晃着他的爪子
and then they went their separate ways
然后他们就分道扬镳了
The dog took the road home
狗走上了回家的路
and Pinocchio went to a cottage not far off
匹诺曹去了不远处的一间小屋
there was a little old man warming himself in the sun
有一个小老头在阳光下取暖
Pinocchio spoke to the little old man
匹诺曹对小老头说
"Tell me, good man," he started
"告诉我,好人,"他开始说
"do you know anything of a poor boy called Eugene?"
"你知道一个叫尤金的穷孩子吗?"
"he was wounded in the head"
"他的头部受了伤"
"The boy was brought by some fishermen to this cottage"
"这个男孩是一些渔民带到这个小屋的"
"and now I do not know what happened to him"
"现在我不知道他怎么了"
"And now he is dead!" interrupted Pinocchio with great sorrow
"现在他死了!"匹诺曹悲痛地打断了他
"No, he is alive," interrupted the fisherman
"不,他还活着,"渔夫打断了他
"and he has been returned to his home"
"他已经回到了自己的家"
"Is it true?" cried the puppet

"这是真的吗？"
and Pinocchio danced with delight
匹诺曹高兴地跳舞
"Then the wound was not serious?"
"那么伤口不严重吗？"
the little old man answered Pinocchio
小老头回答匹诺曹
"It might have been very serious"
"可能非常严重"
"it could even have been fatal"
"甚至可能是致命的"
"they threw a thick book at his head"
"他们向他的头扔了一本厚书"
"And who threw it at him?"
"谁把它扔向他？"
"One of his school-fellows, by the name of Pinocchio"
"他的一个同学，名叫匹诺曹"
"And who is this Pinocchio?" asked the puppet
"这个匹诺曹是谁？"
and he pretended his ignorance as best he could
他尽可能地假装自己的无知
"They say that he is a bad boy"
"他们说他是个坏孩子"
"a vagabond, a regular good-for-nothing"
"一个流浪汉，一个普通的无用之物"
"Calumnies! all calumnies!"
"诽谤！都是诽谤！"
"Do you know this Pinocchio?"
"你认识这个匹诺曹吗？"
"By sight!" answered the puppet
"凭眼见！"
"And what is your opinion of him?" asked the little man

"那你对他有什么看法呢？"
"He seems to me to be a very good boy"
"在我看来，他是个非常好的孩子"
"he is anxious to learn," added Pinocchio
"他急于学习，"匹诺曹补充道
"and he is obedient and affectionate to his father and family"
"他对父亲和家人很顺从和深情"
the puppet fired off a bunch of lies
傀儡散发出一堆谎言
but then he remembered to touch his nose
但后来他想起了摸自己的鼻子
his nose seemed to have grown by more than a hand
他的鼻子似乎长得不止一只手
Very much alarmed he began to cry:
他非常惊慌，开始喊道：
"Don't believe me, good man"
"别信我，好人"
"what I said were all lies"
"我说的都是谎言"
"I know Pinocchio very well"
"我非常了解匹诺曹"
"and I can assure you that he is a very bad boy"
"我可以向你保证，他是个很坏的孩子。"
"he is disobedient and idle"
"他悖逆，懒惰"
"instead of going to school, he runs off with his companions"
"他没有去上学，而是和他的同伴一起跑了"
He had hardly finished speaking when his nose became shorter
他话还没说完，鼻子就变短了
and finally his nose returned to the old size

最后，他的鼻子又回到了原来的大小
the little old man noticed the boys' colour
小老头注意到了男孩们的肤色
"And why are you all covered with white?"
"为什么你们都浑身都是白色的？"
"I will tell you why," said Pinocchio
"我会告诉你为什么，"匹诺曹说
"Without observing it I rubbed myself against a wall"
"我没有注意到它，我把自己蹭到了墙上"
"little did I know that the wall had been freshly whitewashed"
"我几乎不知道这堵墙刚刚粉刷过"
he was ashamed to confess the truth
他羞于承认真相
in fact he had been floured like a fish
事实上，他已经像鱼一样被撒了面粉
"And what have you done with your jacket?"
"那你把你的夹克弄干了什么？"
"where are your trousers, and your cap?"
"你的裤子和帽子呢？"
"I met some robbers on my journey"
"我在旅途中遇到了一些强盗"
"and they took all my things from me"
"他们就拿走了我所有的东西"
"Good old man, I have a favour to ask"
"老好人家，我有个忙要请。"
"could you perhaps give me some clothes to return home in?"
"你能给我一些衣服回家时穿吗？"
"My boy, I would like to help you"
"我的孩子，我想帮助你"
"but I have nothing but a little sack"
"可是我除了一个小袋子什么都没有"

"it is but a sack in which I keep beans"
"它不过是我装豆子的一个袋子"

"but if you have need of it, take it"
"但如果你需要它,就拿去它"

Pinocchio did not wait to be asked twice
匹诺曹没有等他被问两次

He took the sack at once
他立刻把袋子拿了起来

and he borrowed a pair of scissors
他借了一把剪刀

and he cut a hole at the end of the sack
他在袋子的末端凿了一个洞

at each side, he cut out small holes for his arms
他在每一侧都为他的手臂凿出小孔

and he put the sack on like a shirt
他把麻袋像衬衫一样穿上

And with his new clothing he set off for the village
"于是他带着新衣服向村子里走去

But as he went he did not feel at all comfortable
但当他走的时候,他一点也不舒服

for each step forward he took another step backwards
每向前迈出一步,他就会向后退一步

"How shall I ever present myself to my good little Fairy?"
"我该怎么向我的善良小仙女展示自己呢?"

"What will she say when she sees me?"
"她看到我时会说什么?"

"Will she forgive me this second escapade?"
"她会原谅我这第二次出轨吗?"

"Oh, I am sure that she will not forgive me!"
"哦,我敢肯定她不会原谅我的!"

"And it serves me right, because I am a rascal"
"这对我有好处,因为我是个流氓"

"I am always promising to correct myself"
"我总是承诺要纠正自己"
"but I never keep my word!"
"可是我从来不信守诺言！"
When he reached the village it was night
当他到达村庄时，已经是晚上了
and it had gotten very dark
天色变得非常黑暗
A storm had come in from the shore
一场暴风雨从岸边袭来
and the rain was coming down in torrents
雨如暴雨般倾泻而下
he went straight to the Fairy's house
他径直去了仙女的房子
he was resolved to knock at the door
他决心敲门
But when he was there his courage failed him
但当他到了那里时，他的勇气使他失望了
instead of knocking he ran away some twenty paces
他没有敲门，而是跑了大约二十步
He returned to the door a second time
他第二次回到门口
and he held the door knocker in his hand
他手里拿着门环
trembling, he gave a little knock at the door
他战战兢兢地敲了敲门
He waited and waited for his mother to open the door
他等啊等着妈妈开门
Pinocchio must have waited no less than half an hour
匹诺曹肯定等了不少于半小时
At last a window on the top floor was opened
最后，顶楼的一扇窗户打开了
the house was four stories high
房子有四层楼高

and Pinocchio saw a big Snail
匹诺曹看到了一只大蜗牛

it had a lighted candle on her head to look out
她的头上顶着一根点燃的蜡烛，可以向外看

"Who is there at this hour?"
"这个时候谁在那儿？"

"Is the Fairy at home?" asked the puppet
"仙女在家吗？"

"The Fairy is asleep," answered the snail
"仙女睡着了，"蜗牛回答

"and she must not be awakened"
"她不能被唤醒"

"but who are you?" asked the Snail
"可是你是谁？"

"It is I," answered Pinocchio
"是我，"匹诺曹回答

"Who is I?" asked the Snail
"我是谁？"

"It is I, Pinocchio," answered Pinocchio
"是我，匹诺曹，"匹诺曹回答

"And who is Pinocchio?" asked the Snail
"那匹诺曹是谁？"

"The puppet who lives in the Fairy's house"
"住在仙女家的傀儡"

"Ah, I understand!" said the Snail
"啊，我明白了！"

"Wait for me there"
"在那儿等我"

"I will come down and open the door"
"我下来开门"

"Be quick, for pity's sake"
"快点，看在可怜的份上"

"because I am dying of cold"

"因为我快冻死了"
"My boy, I am a snail"
"我的孩子,我是一只蜗牛"
"and snails are never in a hurry"
"蜗牛从不着急"
An hour passed, and then two
一个小时过去了,然后是两个小时
and the door was still not opened
门还是没开
Pinocchio was wet through and through
匹诺曹全身湿透
and he was trembling from cold and fear
他因寒冷和恐惧而战战兢兢
at last he had the courage to knock again
他终于鼓起勇气再次敲门
this time he knocked louder than before
这一次,他的敲门声比以前更大声
At this second knock a window on the lower story opened
就在这第二次敲门声中,下层的一扇窗户打开了
and the same Snail appeared at the window
同样的蜗牛出现在窗户前
"Beautiful little Snail," cried Pinocchio
"美丽的小蜗牛,"匹诺曹喊道
"I have been waiting for two hours!"
"我已经等了两个小时了!"
"two hours on such a night seems longer than two years"
"在这样的夜晚上两个小时似乎比两年还长"
"Be quick, for pity's sake"
"快点,看在可怜的份上"
"My boy," answered the calm little animal
"我的孩子,"那只平静的小动物回答

"you know that I am a snail"
"你知道我是一只蜗牛"
"and snails are never in a hurry"
"蜗牛从不着急"
And the window was shut again
窗户又关上了
Shortly afterwards midnight struck
不久之后,午夜来了
then one o'clock, then two o'clock
然后是1点钟,然后是2点钟
and the door still remained unopened
门还没开
Pinocchio finally lost all patience
匹诺曹终于失去了所有的耐心
he seized the door knocker in a rage
他一怒之下抓住了门环
he intended bang the door as hard as he could
他打算用尽全力敲门
a blow that would resound through the house
这一击将响彻整个房子
the door knocker was made from iron
门环是铁制的
but suddenly it turned into an eel
但突然间它变成了一条鳗鱼
and the eel slipped out of Pinocchio's hand
鳗鱼从匹诺曹的手中滑落
down the street was a stream of water
街上有一条水流
and the eel disappeared down the stream
鳗鱼就消失在溪流中
Pinocchio was blinded with rage
匹诺曹被愤怒蒙蔽了双眼
"Ah! so that's the way it is?"
"啊!所以是这样的吗?

"then I will kick with all my might"
"那我就用尽全力踢"
Pinocchio took a little run up to the door
匹诺曹跑到门口
and he kicked the door with all his might
他用尽全力踢门
it was indeed a mighty strong kick
这确实是一记有力的踢腿
and his foot went through the door
他的脚穿过了门
Pinocchio tried to pull his foot out
匹诺曹试图把他的脚抽出来
but then he realized his predicament
但后来他意识到了自己的困境
it was as if his foot had been nailed down
他的脚仿佛被钉住了
Think of poor Pinocchio's situation!
想想可怜的匹诺曹的处境吧！
He had to spend the rest of the night on one foot
他不得不用一只脚度过剩下的夜晚
and the other foot was in the air
另一只脚在空中
after many hours daybreak finally came
几个小时后，黎明终于来了
and at last the door was opened
最后，门开了
it had only taken the Snail nine hours
蜗牛只花了九个小时
he had come all the way from the fourth story
他从第四层一路过来
It is evident that her exertions must have been great
显然，她一定付出了巨大的努力
but she was equally confused by Pinocchio
但她同样被匹诺曹迷惑了

"What are you doing with your foot in the door?"
"你用脚进门做什么？"
"It was an accident," answered the puppet
"这是个意外，"木偶回答
"oh beautiful snail, please help me"
"哦，美丽的蜗牛，请帮帮我"
"try and get my foot out the door"
"试着把我的脚伸出门"
"My boy, that is the work of a carpenter""
"我的孩子，那是个木匠的工作。"
"and I have never been a carpenter"
"我从来就不是木匠"
"in that case please get the Fairy for me!"
"既然如此，请帮我把仙女拿来！"
"The Fairy is still asleep"
"仙女还在沉睡"
"and she must not be awakened"
"她不能被唤醒"
"But what can I do with me foot stuck in the door?"
"但是我该怎么办，我的脚卡在门里？"
"there are many ants in this area"
"这片地区蚂蚁多"
"Amuse yourself by counting all the little ants"
"数一数小蚂蚁，自娱自乐"
"Bring me at least something to eat"
"至少给我带点吃的"
"because I am quite exhausted and hungry"
"因为我很累，很饿"
"At once," said the Snail
"马上，"蜗牛说
it was in fact almost as fast as she had said
事实上，这几乎和她说的一样快
after three hours she returned to Pinocchio

三个小时后,她回到了匹诺曹
and on her head was a silver tray
她头上顶着一个银盘
The tray contained a loaf of bread
托盘里装着一条面包
and there was a roast chicken
还有一只烤鸡
and there were four ripe apricots
有四个成熟的杏子
"Here is the breakfast that the Fairy has sent you"
"这是仙女送给你的早餐"
these were all things Pinocchio liked to eat
这些都是匹诺曹喜欢吃的东西
The puppet felt very much comforted at the sight
木偶看到这个景象,感到非常欣慰
But then he began to eat the food
但随后他开始吃这些食物
and he was most disgusted by the taste
他最厌恶的是这种味道
he discovered that the bread was plaster
他发现面包是石膏的
the chicken was made of cardboard
鸡是用纸板做的
and the four apricots were alabaster
四杏是雪花石膏
Poor Pinocchio wanted to cry
可怜的匹诺曹想哭
In his desperation he tried to throw away the tray
在绝望中,他试图扔掉托盘
perhaps it was because of his grief
也许是因为他的悲痛
or it could have been that he was exhausted
或者可能是他已经筋疲力尽了
and the little puppet fainted from the effort

小木偶就因为努力而晕倒了
eventually he regained consciousness
最终他恢复了意识
and he found that he was lying on a sofa
他发现自己躺在沙发上
and the good Fairy was beside him
善良的仙女就在他身边
"I will pardon you once more," the Fairy said
"我会再原谅你一次,"仙女说
"but woe to you if you behave badly a third time!"
"可是,如果你第三次行为不端,那你就有祸了!"
Pinocchio promised and swore that he would study
匹诺曹答应并发誓他会学习
and he swore he would always conduct himself well
他发誓他会永远表现得体
And he kept his word for the remainder of the year
他在那年剩下的时间里信守诺言
Pinocchio got very good grades at school
匹诺曹在学校的成绩非常好
and he had the honour of being the best student
他有幸成为最好的学生
his behaviour in general was very praiseworthy
他的行为总体上非常值得称赞
and the Fairy was very much pleased with him
仙子对他非常满意
"Tomorrow your wish shall be gratified"
"明天你的愿望将得到满足"
"what wish was that?" asked Pinocchio
"那是什么愿望?"
"Tomorrow you shall cease to be a wooden puppet"
"明天你就不再是木偶了"
"and you shall finally become a boy"
"你最终会变成个男孩"
you could not have imagined Pinocchio's joy

你无法想象匹诺曹的喜悦
and Pinocchio was allowed to have a party
匹诺曹被允许举办派对
All his school-fellows were to be invited
他所有的同学都要被邀请
there would be a grand breakfast at the Fairy's house
仙女家将有一顿丰盛的早餐
together they would celebrate the great event
他们将一起庆祝这一重大事件
The Fairy had prepared two hundred cups of coffee and milk
仙子准备了两百杯咖啡和牛奶
and four hundred rolls of bread were cut
又切了四百卷面包
and all the bread was buttered on each side
所有的面包两边都涂了黄油
The day promised to be most happy and delightful
这一天注定会是最快乐和愉快的
but...
但。。。
Unfortunately in the lives of puppets there is always a "but" that spoils everything
不幸的是,在木偶的生活中,总有一个"但是"会破坏一切

The Land of the Boobie Birds
鲸鸟之国

Of course Pinocchio asked the Fairy's permission
匹诺曹当然征得了仙女的同意
"may I go round the town to give out the invitations?"
"我可以到镇上去分发请柬吗？"
and the Fairy said to him:
仙女对他说：
"Go, if you like, you have my permission"
"走吧，如果你愿意，你得我的许可"
"invite your companions for the breakfast tomorrow"
"请你的同伴明天吃早餐"
"but remember to return home before dark"
"但记得在天黑之前回家"
"Have you understood?" she checked
"你明白了吗？"
"I promise to be back in an hour"
"我保证一个小时后回来"
"Take care, Pinocchio!" she cautioned him
"小心点，匹诺曹！"
"Boys are always very ready to promise"
"男孩们总是非常乐于承诺"
"but generally boys struggle to keep their word"
"但一般来说，男孩们都很难信守诺言"
"But I am not like other boys"
"但我和其他男孩不一样"
"When I say a thing, I do it"
"我说一件事，我就去做"
"We shall see if you will keep your promise"
"我们会看看你是否会信守诺言"
"If you are disobedient, so much the worse for you"
"如果你不听话，你就更糟了"

"Why would it be so much the worse for me?"
"为什么对我来说会更糟呢？"
"there are boys who do not listen to the advice"
"有些男孩不听劝告"
"advice from people who know more than them"
"来自比他们更了解的人的建议"
"and they always meet with some misfortune or other"
"他们总是遇到一些不幸或其他事情"
"I have experienced that," said Pinocchio
"我经历过，"匹诺曹说
"but I shall never make that mistake again"
"但我再也不会犯那个错误了。"
"We shall see if that is true"
"我们看看这是不是真的"
and the puppet took leave of his good Fairy
于是木偶离开了他的好仙女
the good Fairy was now like a mamma to him
善良的仙女现在对他来说就像一个妈妈
and he went out of the house singing and dancing
他就唱歌跳舞地走出屋子
In less than an hour all his friends were invited
在不到一个小时的时间里，他所有的朋友都被邀请了
Some accepted at once heartily
有些人立刻由衷地接受了
others at first required some convincing
其他人起初需要一些说服
but then they heard that there would be coffee
但后来他们听说会有咖啡
and the bread was going to be buttered on both sides
面包的两面都涂上了黄油
"We will come also, to do you a pleasure"
"我们也会来，为你们带来快乐"

Now I must tell you that Pinocchio had many friends
现在我必须告诉你,匹诺曹有很多朋友
and there were many boys he went to school with
他和很多男孩一起上学
but there was one boy he especially liked
但有一个男孩他特别喜欢
This boy's name was Romeo
这个男孩叫罗密欧
but he always went by his nickname
但他总是用他的绰号
all the boys called him Candle-wick
所有的男孩都叫他烛芯
because he was so thin, straight and bright
因为他是如此瘦弱、笔直和明亮

like the new wick of a little nightlight
就像小夜灯的新灯芯
Candle-wick was the laziest of the boys
烛芯是男孩中最懒惰的
and he was naughtier than the other boys too
而且他也比其他男孩更顽皮
but Pinocchio was devoted to him
但匹诺曹对他很忠诚
he had gone to Candle-wick's house before the others
他比其他人先去了烛芯的家
but he had not found him
但他没有找到他
He returned a second time, but Candle-wick was not there
他第二次回来了，但烛芯不在那里
He went a third time, but it was in vain
他第三次去了，但徒劳无功
Where could he search for him?
他可以在哪里寻找他？
He looked here, there, and everywhere
他看这里、那里、到处看
and at last he found his friend Candle-wick
最后，他找到了他的朋友烛芯
he was hiding on the porch of a peasant's cottage
他躲在农民小屋的门廊上
"What are you doing there?" asked Pinocchio
"你在那儿做什么？"
"I am waiting for midnight"
"我在等午夜"
"I am going to run away"
"我要逃跑"
"And where are you going?"
"那你要去哪里？"
"I am going to live in another country"

"我要住在另一个国家"
"the most delightful country in the world"
"世界上最令人愉快的国家"
"a real land of sweetmeats!"
"真正的甜食之地！"
"And what is it called?"
"那它叫什么呢？"
"It is called the Land of Boobies"
"它被称为鲣鸟之地"
"Why do you not come, too?"
"你为什么不也来呢？"
"I? No, even if I wanted to!"
"我？不，即使我想！"
"You are wrong, Pinocchio"
"你错了，匹诺曹"
"If you do not come you will repent it"
"如果你不来，你就要悔改"
"Where could you find a better country for boys?"
"你在哪里能找到更适合男孩的国家？"
"There are no schools there"
"那里没有学校"
"there are no masters there"
"那里没有大师"
"and there are no books there"
"而且那里没有书"
"In that delightful land nobody ever studies"
"在那片令人愉快的土地上，没有人学习"
"On Saturday there is never school"
"周六从来没有学校"
"every week consists of six Saturdays"
"每周由六个星期六组成"
"and the remainder of the week are Sundays"
"一周的其余时间是星期天"

"think of all the time there is to play"
"想想所有可以玩的时间"
"the autumn holidays begin on the first of January"
"秋假从 1 月 1 日开始"
"and they finish on the last day of December"
"他们在 12 月的最后一天结束"
"That is the country for me!"
"那是我的国家！"
"That is what all civilized countries should be like!"
"那才是所有文明国家都应该有的样子！"
"But how are the days spent in the Land of Boobies?"
"但是在鲣鸟之地度过的日子是怎样的呢？"
"The days are spent in play and amusement"
"这些日子都花在了玩耍和娱乐中"
"you enjoy yourself from morning till night"
"你从早到晚都享受"
"and when night comes you go to bed"
"当夜幕降临时，你去睡觉"
"and then you recommence the fun the next day"
"然后你第二天再开始玩玩吧"
"What do you think of it?"
"你觉得怎么样？"
"Hum!" said Pinocchio thoughtfully
"哼！"匹诺曹若有所思地说
and he shook his head slightly
他微微摇了摇头
the gesture did seem to say something
这个手势似乎确实在说什么
"That is a life that I also would willingly lead"
"我也愿意过这样的生活"
but he had not accepted the invitation yet
但他还没有接受邀请
"Well, will you go with me?"

"嗯，你愿意跟我一起去吗？"
"Yes or no? Resolve quickly"
"是还是不是？快速解决"
"No, no, no, and no again"
"不，不，不，再不"
"I promised my good Fairy to be good boy"
"我答应过我的好仙女，要做个好孩子"
"and I will keep my word"
"我会信守诺言"
"the sun will soon be setting"
"太阳快要落山了"
"so I must leave you and run away"
"所以我必须离开你逃跑"
"Good-bye, and a pleasant journey to you"
"再见，祝你旅途愉快"
"Where are you rushing off to in such a hurry?"
"你这么匆忙地赶到哪儿去？"
"I am going home," said Pinocchio
"我要回家了，"匹诺曹说
"My good Fairy wishes me to be back before dark"
"我的好仙子祝我在天黑前回来"
"Wait another two minutes"
"再等两分钟"
"It will make me too late"
"这会让我太晚了"
"Only two minutes," Candle-wick pleaded
"只有两分钟，"烛芯恳求道
"And if the Fairy scolds me?"
"如果仙女骂我呢？"
"Let her scold you," he suggested
"让她骂你吧，"他建议道
Candle-wick was quite a persuasive rascal
烛芯是个相当有说服力的流氓

"When she has scolded well she will hold her tongue"
"当她骂得好的时候,她会闭口不言。"
"And what are you going to do?"
"那你打算怎么办?"
"Are you going alone or with companions?"
"你是一个人去还是和同伴一起去?"
"oh don't worry about that Pinocchio"
"哦,别担心那个匹诺曹"
"I will not be alone in the Land of Boobies"
"我不会孤单在鲣鸟之地"
"there will be more than a hundred boys"
"将有一百多个男孩"
"And do you make the journey on foot?"
"你是步行的吗?"
"A coach will pass by shortly"
"马车很快就会经过"
"the carriage will take me to that happy country"
"马车会带我去那个快乐的国度"
"What would I not give for the coach to pass by now!"
"我现在不给什么让马车经过呢!"
"Why do you want the coach to come by so badly?"
"你为什么这么想让教练来?"
"so that I can see you all go together"
"这样我就能看到你们一起去了"
"Stay here a little longer, Pinocchio"
"在这里多待一会儿,匹诺曹"
"stay a little longer and you will see us"
"多待一会儿,你会看到我们"
"No, no, I must go home"
"不,不,我必须回家"
"just wait another two minutes"
"再等两分钟"
"I have already delayed too long"

"我已经耽搁太久了"
"The Fairy will be anxious about me"
"仙女会为我着急"
"Is she afraid that the bats will eat you?"
"她怕蝙蝠吃掉你吗？"
Pinocchio had grown a little curious
匹诺曹变得有点好奇了
"are you certain that there are no schools?"
"你确定没有学校吗？"
"there is not even the shadow of a school"
"甚至没有学校的影子"
"And are there no masters either?"
"那也没有主人吗？"
"the Land of the Boobies is free of masters"
"鲣鸟之地没有主人"
"And no one is ever made to study?"
"没有人被强迫学习吗？"
"Never, never, and never again!"
"永远，永远，永远不要再！"
Pinocchio's mouth watered at the idea
匹诺曹对这个想法垂涎三尺
"What a delightful country!" said Pinocchio
"多么令人愉快的国家啊！"
"I have never been there," said Candle-wick
"我从来没有去过那里，"烛芯说
"but I can imagine it perfectly well"
"但我能想象得非常清楚"
"Why will you not come also?"
"你为什么不也来呢？"
"It is useless to tempt me"
"试探我也没用"
"I made a promise to my good Fairy"
"我向我的好仙女许下了承诺"

"I will become a sensible boy"
"我会成为一个懂事的男孩"
"and I will not break my word"
"我必不食言"
"Good-bye, then," said Candle-wick
"那么，再见了，"烛芯说
"give my compliments to all the boys at school"
"向学校里的所有男孩致意"
"Good-bye, Candle-wick; a pleasant journey to you"
"再见了，烛芯;祝您旅途愉快"
"amuse yourself in this pleasant land"
"在这片宜人的土地上自娱自乐"
"and think sometimes of your friends"
"有时想想你的朋友"
Thus saying, the puppet made two steps to go
说着，傀儡走了两步
but then he stopped halfway in his track
但随后他停在了半路上
and, turning to his friend, he inquired:
然后，他转向他的朋友，问道：
"But are you quite certain about all this?"
"可是你对这一切很确定吗？"
"in that country all the weeks consist of six Saturdays?"
"在那个国家，所有的星期都是六个星期六？"
"and the rest of the week consists of Sundays?"
"那么这周剩下的时间是星期天呢？"
"all the weekdays most certainly consist of six Saturdays"
"所有的工作日肯定都包括6个星期六"
"and the rest of the days are indeed Sundays"
"其余的日子确实是星期天"
"and are you quite sure about the holidays?"
"那么，你对假期很确定吗？"

"the holidays definitely begin on the first of January?"
"假期肯定从 1 月 1 日开始吧？"
"and you're sure the holidays finish on the last day of December?"
"你确定假期在十二月的最后一天结束吗？"
"I am assuredly certain that this is how it is"
"我确信事情就是这样"
"What a delightful country!" repeated Pinocchio
"多么令人愉快的国家啊！"
and he was enchanted by all that he had heard
他被他所听到的一切迷住了
this time Pinocchio spoke more resolute
这一次匹诺曹说话更加坚决了
"This time really good-bye"
"这次真的再见"
"I wish you pleasant journey and life"
"祝您旅途愉快"
"Good-bye, my friend," bowed Candle-wick
"再见了，我的朋友，"烛芯鞠躬道
"When do you start?" inquired Pinocchio
"你什么时候开始？"
"I will be leaving very soon"
"我很快就会离开"
"What a pity that you must leave so soon!"
"你这么快就走了，真可惜啊！"
"I would almost be tempted to wait"
"我几乎想等"
"And the Fairy?" asked Candle-wick
"那仙子呢？"
"It is already late," confirmed Pinocchio
"已经很晚了，"匹诺曹确认道
"I can return home an hour sooner"
"我可以提前一个小时回家"

"or I can return home an hour later"
"或者我可以晚一个小时回家"
"really it will be all the same"
"真的会一样"
"but what if the Fairy scolds you?"
"可是，如果仙女骂你怎么办？"
"I must have patience!"
"我得有耐心！"
"I will let her scold me"
"我就让她骂我"
"When she has scolded well she will hold her tongue"
"当她骂得好的时候，她会闭口不言。"

In the meantime night had come on
与此同时，夜幕降临了
and by now it had gotten quite dark
这时天已经很黑了
Suddenly they saw in the distance a small light moving
突然，他们看到远处有一道小光在移动

they heard a noise of talking
他们听到了一阵谈话声
and there was the sound of a trumpet
又有号角的声音
but the sound was still small and feeble
但声音仍然很小，很微弱
so the sound still resembled the hum of a mosquito
所以那声音仍然像蚊子的嗡嗡声
"Here it is!" shouted Candle-wick, jumping to his feet
"就在这里！"烛芯喊道，跳了起来
"What is it?" asked Pinocchio in a whisper
"什么事？" 匹诺曹低声问道
"It is the carriage coming to take me"
"是马车来接我"
"so will you come, yes or no?"
"所以你会来吗，是还是不是？"
"But is it really true?" asked the puppet
"但这是真的吗？"
"in that country boys are never obliged to study?"
"在那个国家，男孩子从来没有义务学习吗？"
"Never, never, and never again!"
"永远，永远，永远不要再！"
"What a delightful country!"
"多么令人愉快的国家啊！"

Pinocchio Enjoys Six Months of Happiness
匹诺曹享受六个月的快乐

At last the wagon finally arrived
最后,马车终于到了
and it arrived without making the slightest noise
它来了,没有发出丝毫声音
because its wheels were bound with flax and rags
因为它的轮子是用亚麻和破布捆住的
It was drawn by twelve pairs of donkeys
它由十二对驴拉着
all the donkeys were the same size
所有的驴子都是一样大的
but each donkey was a different colour
但每头驴的颜色都不同
Some of the donkeys were gray
一些驴子是灰色的
and some of the donkeys were white
有些驴是白色的
and some donkeys were brindled like pepper and salt
有些驴子像胡椒和盐一样被磨成斑纹
and other donkeys had large stripes of yellow and blue
其他驴子有大片的黄色和蓝色条纹
But there was something most extraordinary about them
但他们身上有一些最不寻常的东西
they were not shod like other beasts of burden
他们不像其他负重的野兽那样穿鞋
on their feet the donkeys had men's boots
驴子的脚上穿着男靴
"And the coachman?" you may ask
"那车夫呢?"
Picture to yourself a little man broader than long
给自己想象一个比长更宽的小男人

flabby and greasy like a lump of butter
像一块黄油一样松弛油腻
with a small round face like an orange
长着橘子一样的小圆脸
a little mouth that was always laughing
一张总是在笑的小嘴
and a soft, caressing voice of a cat
以及猫轻柔、爱抚的声音
All the boys fought for their place in the coach
所有的男孩都为他们在教练中的位置而战
they all wanted to be conducted to the Land of Boobies
他们都想被带到鲣鸟之地
The carriage was, in fact, quite full of boys
事实上,马车上坐满了男孩
and all the boys were between eight and fourteen years
所有男孩的年龄都在 8 到 14 岁之间
the boys were heaped one upon another
男孩们一个接一个地堆在一起
just like herrings are squeezed into a barrel
就像鲱鱼被挤进桶里一样
They were uncomfortable and packed closely together
他们很不舒服,紧紧地挤在一起
and they could hardly breathe
他们几乎无法呼吸
but not one of the boys thought of grumbling
可是,没有一个男孩想起抱怨
they were consoled by the promises of their destination
他们被目的地的承诺所安慰
a place with no books, no schools, and no masters
一个没有书、没有学校、没有硕士的地方
it made them so happy and resigned
这让他们非常高兴并无奈
and they felt neither fatigue nor inconvenience

他们既不感到疲劳，也不感到不便
neither hunger, nor thirst, nor want of sleep
既不饥饿，也不口渴，也不缺睡眠
soon the wagon had reached them
很快，马车就到了他们身边
the little man turned straight to Candle-wick
小个子男人径直转向烛芯
he had a thousand smirks and grimaces
他有一千个傻笑和鬼脸
"Tell me, my fine boy;"
"告诉我，我的好孩子。"
"would you also like to go to the fortunate country?"
"你也想去那个幸运的国家吗？"
"I certainly wish to go"
"我当然想去"
"But I must warn you, my dear child"
"但我必须警告你，我亲爱的孩子"
"there is not a place left in the wagon"
"马车里没有一个地方了"
"You can see for yourself that it is quite full"
"你可以亲眼看到它已经满了"
"No matter," replied Candle-wick
"没关系，"烛芯回答
"I do not need to sit in the wagon"
"我不需要坐在马车里"
"I will sit on the arch of the wheel"
"我将坐在轮子的拱门上"
And with a leap he sat above the wheel
他一跃而起，坐在了方向盘上方
"And you, my love!" said the little man
"还有你，我的爱人！"
and he turned in a flattering manner to Pinocchio
他以一种奉承的方式转向匹诺曹

"what do you intend to do?"
"你打算做什么？"
"Are you coming with us?
"你跟我们一起来吗？"
"or are you going to remain behind?"
"还是你打算留下来？"
"I will remain behind," answered Pinocchio
"我会留下来的，"匹诺曹回答
"I am going home," he answered proudly
"我要回家了，"他自豪地回答
"I intend to study, as all well conducted boys do"
"我打算学习，就像所有有教养的男孩一样"
"Much good may it do you!"
"这对你有很大的好处！"
"Pinocchio!" called out Candle-wick
"匹诺曹！"
"come with us and we shall have such fun"
"跟我们来吧，我们会玩得很开心"
"No, no, and no again!" answered Pinocchio
"不，不，再也不！"
a chorus of hundred voices shouted from the the coach
马车里传来一百个声音的合唱
"Come with us and we shall have so much fun"
"跟我们来吧，我们会玩得很开心"
but the puppet was not at all sure
但这个傀儡一点也不确定
"if I come with you, what will my good Fairy say?"
"如果我跟你走，我的好仙女会怎么说呢？"
and he was beginning to yield
他开始屈服
"Do not trouble your head with melancholy thoughts"
"不要用忧郁的思念搅扰你的脑袋"
"consider only how delightful it will be"

"只考虑那将是多么令人愉快"
"we are going to the Land of the Boobies"
"我们要去鲣鸟之地"
"all day we shall be at liberty to run riot"
"我们整天都可以自由地发动骚乱"
Pinocchio did not answer, but he sighed
匹诺曹没有回答,但他叹了口气
he sighed again, and then sighed for the third time
他又叹了口气,然后第三次叹了口气
finally Pinocchio made up his mind
最后,匹诺曹下定了决心
"Make a little room for me"
"给我腾出一点空间"
"because I would like to come, too"
"因为我也想来"
"The places are all full," replied the little man
"这些地方都满了,"小个子回答
"but, let me show you how welcome you are"
"但是,让我告诉你你是多么受欢迎"
"I will let you have my seat on the box"
"我会让你在包厢上坐下"
"And where will you sit?"
"那你要坐哪儿?"
"Oh, I will go on foot"
"哦,我要步行去"
"No, indeed, I could not allow that"
"不,确实,我不能允许这样。"
"I would rather mount one of these donkeys"
"我宁愿骑一头这样的驴"
so Pinocchio went up the the first donkey
于是匹诺曹骑着第一头驴上了
and he attempted to mount the animal
他试图骑上这只动物

but the little donkey turned on him
但小驴子却背叛了他
and the donkey gave him a great blow in the stomach
驴子狠狠地打了他的肚子
and it rolled him over with his legs in the air
它把他翻了个身,双腿悬空
all the boys had been watching this
所有的男孩子都一直在看着这个
so you can imagine the laughter from the wagon
所以你可以想象马车里的笑声
But the little man did not laugh
但小个子没有笑
He approached the rebellious donkey
他走近那头叛逆的驴子
and at first he pretended to kiss him
起初,他假装亲吻了他
but then he bit off half of his ear
但随后他咬掉了自己的半只耳朵
Pinocchio in the meantime had gotten up from the ground
与此同时,匹诺曹已经从地上爬了起来
he was still very cross with the animal
他仍然对这只动物非常不满
but with a spring he jumped onto him
但是他用弹簧跳到了他身上
and he seated himself on the poor animal's back
他就坐在这只可怜的动物的背上
And he sprang so well that the boys stopped laughing
他跳得如此之好,以至于男孩们都停止了笑声
and they began to shout: "Hurrah, Pinocchio!"
他们开始大喊:"万岁,匹诺曹!
and they clapped their hands and applauded him
他们拍手为他鼓掌
soon the donkeys were galloping down the track

很快，驴子们就在小路上疾驰而下
and the wagon was rattling over the stones
马车在石头上嘎嘎作响
but the puppet thought that he heard a low voice
但木偶认为他听到了一个低沉的声音
"Poor fool! you should have followed your own way"
"可怜的傻瓜！你应该走你自己的路"
"but but you will repent having come!"
"可是，你得后悔来了！"
Pinocchio was a little frightened by what he had heard
匹诺曹被他所听到的事情吓得有点害怕
he looked from side to side to see what it was
他左右看了看，想看看那是什么
he tried to see where these words could have come from
他试图弄清楚这些话可能来自哪里
but regardless of of where he looked he saw nobody
但无论他往哪儿看，他都看不到人
The donkeys galloped and the wagon rattled
驴子飞驰，马车嘎嘎作响
and all the while the boys inside slept
而里面的男孩们一直都在睡觉
Candle-wick snored like a dormouse
烛芯像睡鼠一样打呼噜
and the little man seated himself on the box
小个子坐在箱子上
and he sang songs between his teeth
他用牙齿唱歌
"During the night all sleep"
"在夜间全睡"
"But I sleep never"
"但我从不睡觉"
soon they had gone another mile
很快他们又走了一英里

Pinocchio heard the same little low voice again
匹诺曹又听到了同样低沉的小声音
"Bear it in mind, simpleton!"
"记住了,傻瓜!"
"there are boys who refuse to study"
"有拒绝学习的男孩"
"they turn their backs upon books"
"他们背弃了书本"
"they think they're too good to go to school"
"他们认为自己太优秀了,不能去上学"
"and they don't obey their masters"
"他们不服从他们的主人"
"they pass their time in play and amusement"
"他们在游戏和娱乐中打发时间"
"but sooner or later they come to a bad end"
"但他们迟早会落得个坏下场"
"I know it from my experience"
"我从我的经验中知道"
"and I can tell you how it always ends"
"我可以告诉你它总是如何结束的"
"A day will come when you will weep"
"总有一天你会哭泣"
"you will weep just as I am weeping now"
"你也会哭泣,就像我现在哭泣一样"
"but then it will be too late!"
"但那样就太晚了!"
the words had been whispered very softly
这些话被非常轻柔地低声说了出来
but Pinocchio could be sure of what he had heard
但匹诺曹可以确定他听到了什么
the puppet was more frightened than ever
木偶比以往任何时候都更加害怕
he sprang down from the back of his donkey

他从驴背上跳下来
and he went and took hold of the donkey's mouth
他就去抓住驴子的口
you can imagine Pinocchio's surprise at what he saw
你可以想象匹诺曹对他所看到的感到惊讶
the donkey was crying just like a boy!
驴子像个男孩一样哭泣！
"Eh! Sir Coachman," cried Pinocchio
"呃！马车夫爵士，"匹诺曹叫道
"here is an extraordinary thing!"
"这是一件非同寻常的事情！"
"This donkey is crying"
"这头驴在哭泣"
"Let him cry," said the coachman
"让他哭吧，"马车夫说
"he will laugh when he is a bridegroom"
"他当新郎时会笑"
"But have you by chance taught him to talk?"
"可是你是偶然教他说话的吗？"
"No; but he spent three years with learned dogs"
"不;但他花了三年时间与博学的狗在一起"
"and he learned to mutter a few words"
"他学会了喃喃自语几句"
"Poor beast!" added the coachman
"可怜的畜生！"
"but don't you worry," said the little man
"不过你别担心，"小个子说
"don't let us waste time in seeing a donkey cry"
"不要让我们浪费时间看到驴子哭泣"
"Mount him and let us go on"
"骑上他，我们继续前进"
"the night is cold and the road is long"
"夜寒路漫"

Pinocchio obeyed without another word
匹诺曹一言不发地服从了

In the morning about daybreak they arrived
早上天快亮时,他们到了
they were now safely in the Land of Boobie Birds
他们现在安全地来到了鲣鸟之地
It was a country unlike any other country in the world
这是一个不同于世界上任何其他国家的国家
The population was composed entirely of boys
人口完全由男孩组成
The oldest of the boys were fourteen
男孩中最大的 14 岁
and the youngest were scarcely eight years old
最小的还不到八岁
In the streets there was great merriment
街上一片欢乐

the sight of it was enough to turn anybody's head
看到它足以让任何人转头

There were troops of boys everywhere
到处都是男孩大军

Some were playing with nuts they had found
有些人在玩他们找到的坚果

some were playing games with battledores
有些人正在和 Battledores 玩游戏

lots of boys were playing football
很多男孩都在踢足球

Some rode velocipedes, others wooden horses
有些人骑脚踏车，有些人骑木马

A party of boys were playing hide and seek
一群男孩在玩捉迷藏

a few boys were chasing each other
几个男孩在互相追逐

Some were reciting and singing songs
有些人在背诵和唱歌

others were just leaping into the air
其他人只是跳到空中

Some amused themselves with walking on their hands
有些人以用手走路为乐

others were trundling hoops along the road
其他人则在路上拖拽

and some were strutting about dressed as generals
有些人打扮成将军，昂首阔步地走来走去

they were wearing helmets made from leaves
他们戴着树叶制成的头盔

and they were commanding a squadron of cardboard soldiers
他们指挥着一个纸板士兵中队

Some were laughing and some shouting
有些人在笑，有些人在喊叫

and some were calling out silly things

有些人在喊傻话
others clapped their hands, or whistled
其他人则拍手或吹口哨
some clucked like a hen who has just laid an egg
有些人像刚下蛋的母鸡一样咯咯叫
In every square, canvas theatres had been erected
在每个广场上,都竖立了帆布剧院
and they were crowded with boys all day long
他们整天都挤满了男孩
On the walls of the houses there were inscriptions
房屋的墙壁上有铭文
"Long live the playthings"
"玩具万岁"
"we will have no more schools"
"我们将不再有学校"
"down the toilet with arithmetic"
"Down the toilet with arithmetic"
and similar other fine sentiments were written
并写下了类似的其他美好情感
of course all the slogans were in bad spelling
当然,所有的口号都拼写错误
Pinocchio, Candle-wick and the other boys went to the town
匹诺曹、烛芯和其他男孩去了镇上
they were in the thick of the tumult
他们正处于最激烈的骚乱中
and I need not tell you how fun it was
我不需要告诉你这有多有趣
within minutes they acquainted themselves with everybody
几分钟之内,他们就熟悉了每个人
Where could happier or more contented boys be found?
在哪里可以找到更快乐或更满足的男孩?

the hours, days and weeks passed like lightning
数小时、数天、数周如闪电般过去
time flies when you're having fun
时光荏苒,玩得开心
"Oh, what a delightful life!" said Pinocchio
"噢,多么愉快的生活啊!"
"See, then, was I not right?" replied Candle-wick
"那么,你看,我说得对吗?"
"And to think that you did not want to come!"
"而且你还想着你不想来!"
"imagine you had returned home to your Fairy"
"想象一下你回到了你的仙女身边"
"you wanted to lose your time in studying!"
"你想浪费学习的时间!"
"now you are free from the bother of books"
"现在你摆脱了书的烦恼"
"you must acknowledge that you owe it to me"
"你必须承认你欠我的"
"only friends know how to render such great services"
"只有朋友知道如何提供如此出色的服务"
"It is true, Candle-wick!" confirmed Pinocchio
"这是真的,烛芯!"
"If I am now a happy boy, it is all your doing"
"如果我现在是一个快乐的男孩,那都是你的功劳"
"But do you know what the master used to say?"
"可是你知道主人以前说什么吗?"
"Do not associate with that rascal Candle-wick"
"不要跟那个流氓烛芯来往"
"because he is a bad companion for you"
"因为他对你来说是一个坏伙伴"
"and he will only lead you into mischief!"
"他只会让你恶作剧!"
"Poor master!" replied the other, shaking his head

"可怜的主人！"
"I know only too well that he disliked me"
"我太清楚他不喜欢我了"
"and he amused himself by making my life hard"
"他使我的生活变得艰难，以此自娱自乐。"
"but I am generous, and I forgive him!"
"可是我很慷慨，我原谅他！"
"you are a noble soul!" said Pinocchio
"你是个高尚的灵魂！"
and he embraced his friend affectionately
他深情地拥抱了他的朋友
and he kissed him between the eyes
他亲吻了他的眼睛
This delightful life had gone on for five months
这种愉快的生活已经持续了五个月
The days had been entirely spent in play and amusement
这些日子完全花在了玩耍和娱乐上
not a thought was spent on books or school
没有花在书本或学校上
but one morning Pinocchio awoke to a most disagreeable surprise
但有一天早上，匹诺曹醒来时发现了一个非常令人不快的惊喜
what he saw put him into a very bad humour
他所看到的使他陷入了非常糟糕的幽默

Pinocchio Turns into a Donkey
匹诺曹变成驴子

when Pinocchio awoke he scratched his head
当匹诺曹醒来时,他挠了挠头
when scratching his head he discovered something...
当他挠挠头时,他发现了一些东西……
his ears had grown more than a hand!
他的耳朵已经长得比一只手还多了!
You can imagine his surprise
你可以想象他的惊喜
because he had always had very small ears
因为他的耳朵一直都很小
He went at once in search of a mirror
他立刻去找镜子
he had to have a better look at himself
他必须好好审视一下自己
but he was not able to find any kind of mirror
但他找不到任何一面镜子
so he filled the basin with water
"于是他把盆里装满了水
and he saw a reflection he never wished to see
他看到了他从未想看到的倒影
a magnificent pair of donkey's ears embellished his head!
一双华丽的驴子耳朵点缀着他的头!
think of poor Pinocchio's sorrow, shame and despair!
想想可怜的匹诺曹的悲哀、羞愧和绝望吧!
He began to cry and roar
他开始哭泣和咆哮
and he beat his head against the wall
他把头撞在墙上
but the more he cried the longer his ears grew
但他哭得越多,他的耳朵就越长

and his ears grew, and grew, and grew
他的耳朵长大了，长大了，长大了
and his ears became hairy towards the points
他的耳朵向尖尖方向长了毛
a little Marmot heard Pinocchio's loud cries
小土拨鼠听到了匹诺曹的大声哭泣
Seeing the puppet in such grief she asked earnestly:
看到木偶如此悲痛，她认真地问道：
"What has happened to you, my dear fellow-lodger?"
"你怎么了，我亲爱的同房客？"
"I am ill, my dear little Marmot"
"我病了，我亲爱的小土拨鼠"
"very ill, and my illness frightens me"
"病得很重，我的病使我感到害怕"
"Do you understand counting a pulse?"
"你懂数脉搏吗？"
"A little," sobbed Pinocchio
"一点点，"匹诺曹啜泣着
"Then feel and see if by chance I have got fever"
"然后摸摸，看看我是不是偶然发烧了"
The little Marmot raised her right fore-paw
小土拨鼠举起了她的右前爪
and the little Marmot felt Pinocchio's pulse
小土拨鼠感觉到匹诺曹的脉搏
and she said to him, sighing:
她叹息着对他说：
"My friend, it grieves me very much"
"我的朋友，这让我非常难过"
"but I am obliged to give you bad news!"
"可是我不得不告诉你坏消息！"
"What is it?" asked Pinocchio
"什么事？"
"You have got a very bad fever!"

- 283 -

"你发高烧得很厉害！"

"What fever is it?"
"什么热？"

"you have a case of donkey fever"
"你得了驴热"

"That is a fever that I do not understand"
"那是我不明白的发烧"

but he understood it only too well
但他太明白了

"Then I will explain it to you," said the Marmot
"那我就跟你解释一下，"土拨鼠说

"soon you will no longer be a puppet"
"很快你就不会再是一个傀儡了"

"it won't take longer than two or three hours"
"不会超过两三个小时"

"nor will you be a boy either"
"你也不会是个男孩"

"Then what shall I be?"
"那我该怎么办呢？"

"you will well and truly be a little donkey"
"你一定会真正成为一头小驴"

"a donkey like those that draw the carts"
"像拉车的驴子"

"a donkey that carries cabbages to market"
"一头驮着卷心菜去市场的驴子"

"Oh, how unfortunate I am!" cried Pinocchio
"噢，我真不幸啊！"

and he seized his two ears with his hands
他就用手抓住自己的两只耳朵

and he pulled and tore at his ears furiously
他愤怒地拉扯着自己的耳朵

he pulled as if they had been someone else's ears
他拉扯着它们，仿佛它们是别人的耳朵

"My dear boy," said the Marmot
"我亲爱的孩子，"土拨鼠说
and she did her best to console him
她尽了最大的努力安慰他
"you can do nothing about it"
"你对此无能为力"
"It is your destiny to become a donkey"
"成为驴子是你的命中注定"
"It is written in the decrees of wisdom"
"这话写在智慧的律例上"
"it happens to all boys who are lazy"
"所有懒惰的男孩都会遇到这种情况"
"it happens to the boys that dislike books"
"这发生在不喜欢书的男孩身上"
"it happens to the boys that don't go to schools"
"这种情况发生在不上学的男孩身上"
"and it happens to boys who disobey their masters"
"不服从主人的男孩也会遇到这种情况"
"all boys who pass their time in amusement"
"所有在娱乐中打发时间的男孩"
"all the boys who play games all day"
"所有整天玩游戏的男孩"
"boys who distract themselves with diversions"
"用消遣来分散注意力的男孩"
"the same fate awaits all those boys"
"同样的命运等待着所有这些男孩"
"sooner or later they become little donkeys"
"他们迟早会变成小驴子"
"But is it really so?" asked the puppet, sobbing
"但真的是这样吗？"
"It is indeed only too true!"
"这确实太真实了！"
"And tears are now useless"

"眼泪现在已经没用了"
"You should have thought of it sooner!"
"你应该早点想到的！"
"But it was not my fault; believe me, little Marmot"
"但这不是我的错;相信我，小土拨鼠"
"the fault was all Candle-wick's!"
"错全是烛芯的错！"
"And who is this Candle-wick?"
"这个烛芯是谁？"
"Candle-wick is one of my school-fellows"
"烛芯是我的同学之一"
"I wanted to return home and be obedient"
"我想回家并服从"
"I wished to study and be a good boy"
"我希望学习并成为一个好孩子"
"but Candle-wick convinced me otherwise"
"但烛芯使我不相信"
'Why should you bother yourself by studying?'
"你为什么要费心学习呢？"
'Why should you go to school?'
"你为什么要去上学？"
'Come with us instead to the Land of Boobies Birds'
"跟我们一起去鲣鸟之地"
'there we shall none of us have to learn'
"我们谁也不必在那里学习"
'we will amuse ourselves from morning to night'
"我们从早到晚都自娱自乐"
'and we shall always be merry'
"我们将永远快乐"
"that friend of yours was false"
"你的那个朋友是假的"
"why did you follow his advice?"
"你为什么听从他的建议？"

"Because, my dear little Marmot, I am a puppet"
"因为,我亲爱的小土拨鼠,我是一个傀儡"
"I have no sense and no heart"
"我没有理智,也没有心"
"if I had had a heart I would never have left"
"如果我有一颗心,我永远不会离开"
"I left my good Fairy who loved me like a mamma"
"我离开了像妈妈一样爱我的好仙女"
"the good Fairy who had done so much for me!"
"那个为我做了那么多的好仙女!"
"And I was going to be a puppet no longer"
"我不再是一个傀儡"
"I would by this time have become a little boy"
"到这个时候,我已经长成个小男孩了"
"and I would be like the other boys"
"我会和其他男孩一样"
"But if I meet Candle-wick, woe to him!"
"可是,如果我遇见烛芯,他就有祸了!"
"He shall hear what I think of him!"
"他会听到我对他的看法!"
And he turned to go out
他转身出去了
But then he remembered he had donkey's ears
但后来他想起了他有驴耳朵
of course he was ashamed to show his ears in public
当然,他羞于在公共场合露出自己的耳朵
so what do you think he did?
那么你认为他做了什么呢?
He took a big cotton hat
他戴了一顶大棉帽
and he put the cotton hat on his head
他把棉帽戴在头上
and he pulled the hat well down over his nose

他把帽子拉得很低,遮住了鼻子

He then set out in search of Candle-wick
然后他出发去寻找烛芯

He looked for him in the streets
他在街上找他

and he looked for him in the little theatres
他在小剧院里找他

he looked in every possible place
他找遍了每一个可能的地方

but he could not find him wherever he looked
可是他无论往哪儿都找不到

He inquired for him of everybody he met
他向他遇到的每一个人打听

but no one seemed to have seen him
但似乎没有人看到他

He then went to seek him at his house
然后他去他家找他

and, having reached the door, he knocked
他走到门口,敲了敲门

"Who is there?" asked Candle-wick from within
"谁在那儿?"

"It is I!" answered the puppet
"是我!"

"Wait a moment and I will let you in"
"等一下,我会让你进来的"

After half an hour the door was opened
半小时后,门被打开

now you can imagine Pinocchio's feeling at what he saw
现在你可以想象匹诺曹对他所看到的感受

his friend also had a big cotton hat on his head
他的朋友头上也戴着一顶大棉帽

At the sight of the cap Pinocchio felt almost consoled
看到帽子,匹诺曹几乎感到安慰

and Pinocchio thought to himself:
匹诺曹心想：

"Has my friend got the same illness that I have?"
"我的朋友得了和我一样的病吗？"

"Is he also suffering from donkey fever?"
"他也得了驴热病吗？"

but at first Pinocchio pretended not to have noticed
但起初匹诺曹假装没有注意到

he just casually asked him a question, smiling:
他只是随口问了他一个问题，微笑着：

"How are you, my dear Candle-wick?"
"你好吗，我亲爱的烛芯？"

"as well as a mouse in a Parmesan cheese"
"以及帕尔马干酪中的老鼠"

"Are you saying that seriously?"
"你说的是认真的吗？"

"Why should I tell you a lie?"
"我为什么要对你说谎呢？"

"but why, then, do you wear a cotton hat?"
"可是，你为什么戴一顶棉帽呢？"

"is covers up all of your ears"
"它遮住了你所有的耳朵"

"The doctor ordered me to wear it"
"医生让我戴上它"

"because I have hurt this knee"
"因为我伤到了这个膝盖"

"And you, dear puppet," asked Candle-wick
"还有你呢，亲爱的木偶，"烛芯问道

"why have you pulled that cotton hat passed your nose?"
"你为什么把那顶棉帽从你的鼻子里扯下来？"

"The doctor prescribed it because I have grazed my foot"

"医生开了处方,因为我擦伤了我的脚"
"Oh, poor Pinocchio!" - "Oh, poor Candle-wick!"
"哦,可怜的匹诺曹!" - "哦,可怜的烛芯!"
After these words a long silence followed
"这些话之后,人们沉默了很久
the two friends did nothing but look mockingly at each other
两个朋友什么也没做,只是嘲讽地看着对方
At last the puppet said in a soft voice to his companion:
最后,木偶轻声对他的同伴说:
"Satisfy my curiosity, my dear Candle-wick"
"满足我的好奇心,我亲爱的烛芯"
"have you ever suffered from disease of the ears?"
"你得过耳病吗?"
"I have never suffered from disease of the ears!"
"我从来没有患过耳病!"
"And you, Pinocchio?" asked Candle-wick
"那你呢,匹诺曹?"
"have you ever suffered from disease of the ears?"
"你得过耳病吗?"
"I have never suffered from that disease either"
"我也从来没有患过那种病"
"Only since this morning one of my ears aches"
"只是从今天早上开始,我的一只耳朵就疼"
"my ear is also paining me"
"我的耳朵也让我感到痛苦"
"And which of your ears hurts you?"
"那你的哪只耳朵疼了?"
"Both of my ears happen to hurt"
"我的两只耳朵都疼"
"And what about you?"
"那你呢?"

"Both of my ears happen to hurt too"
"我的两只耳朵也好痛"
"Can we have got the same illness?"
我们会不会得同样的病？
"I fear we might have caught a fever"
"我担心我们可能发烧了"
"Will you do me a kindness, Candle-wick?"
"你能好点我吗，烛芯？"
"Willingly! With all my heart"
"愿意！全心全意"
"Will you let me see your ears?"
"你能让我看看你的耳朵吗？"
"Why would I deny your request?"
"我为什么要拒绝你的请求？"
"But first, my dear Pinocchio, I should like to see yours"
"但首先，我亲爱的匹诺曹，我想看看你的。"
"No: you must do so first"
"不，你必须先这样做"
"No, dear. First you and then I!"
"不，亲爱的。先是你，然后是我！
"Well," said the puppet
"嗯，"木偶说
"let us come to an agreement like good friends"
"让我们像好朋友一样达成协议"
"Let me hear what this agreement is"
"让我听听这个协议是什么"
"We will both take off our hats at the same moment"
"我们俩都会同时脱帽"
"Do you agree to do it?"
"你同意吗？"
"I agree, and you have my word"
"我同意，你有我的话"

And Pinocchio began to count in a loud voice:
匹诺曹开始大声数数：
"One, two, three!" he counted
"一、二、三！"
At "Three!" the two boys took off their hats
"三"时，两个男孩脱下了他们的帽子
and they threw their hats into the air
他们把帽子扔向空中
and you should have seen the scene that followed
你应该已经看到了接下来的场景
it would seem incredible if it were not true
如果不是真的，那似乎是不可思议的
they saw they were both struck by the same misfortune
他们看出他们俩都遭遇了同样的不幸
but they felt neither mortification nor grief
但他们既没有感到羞愧，也没有感到悲伤
instead they began to prick their ungainly ears
相反，他们开始刺他们笨拙的耳朵
and they began to make a thousand antics
他们开始做出一千个滑稽动作
they ended by going into bursts of laughter
他们以阵阵的笑声结束
And they laughed, and laughed, and laughed
他们笑了，笑了，笑了
until they had to hold themselves together
直到他们不得不让自己振作起来

But in the midst of their merriment something happened
但是在他们的欢乐中，发生了一些事情
Candle-wick suddenly stopped laughing and joking
烛芯突然停止了笑声和玩笑
he staggered around and changed colour
他踉踉跄跄地走来走去，脸色变了
"Help, help, Pinocchio!" he cried
"救命，救命，匹诺曹！"
"What is the matter with you?"
"你怎么了？"
"Alas, I cannot any longer stand upright"
"唉，我再也站不起来了"
"Neither can I," exclaimed Pinocchio
"我也不能，"匹诺曹喊道
and he began to totter and cry
他开始蹒跚地哭泣

And whilst they were talking, they both doubled up
在他们说话的时候,他们俩都加倍了
and they began to run round the room on their hands and feet
他们开始用手和脚在房间里跑来跑去
And as they ran, their hands became hoofs
当他们奔跑时,他们的手变成了蹄子
their faces lengthened into muzzles
他们的脸拉长成了嘴巴
and their backs became covered with a light gray hairs
他们的背上覆盖着浅灰色的毛发
and their hair was sprinkled with black
他们的头发上洒满了黑色
But do you know what was the worst moment?
但你知道最糟糕的时刻是什么吗?
one moment was worse than all the others
某一刻比其他所有时刻都糟糕
both of the boys grew donkey tails
两个男孩都长了驴尾巴
the boys were vanquished by shame and sorrow
男孩们被羞耻和悲伤所征服
and they wept and lamented their fate
他们哭泣,哀叹自己的命运
Oh, if they had but been wiser!
哦,要是他们再聪明一点就好了!
but they couldn't lament their fate
但他们不能哀叹自己的命运
because they could only bray like asses
因为他们只能像驴子一样吼叫
and they brayed loudly in chorus: "Hee-haw!"
他们齐声吼叫:"嘿嘿!
Whilst this was going on someone knocked at the door
就在这一切发生的时候,有人敲了敲门
and there was a voice on the outside that said:

外面有一个声音说：
"Open the door! I am the little man"
"开门！我就是那个小个子"
"I am the coachman who brought you to this country"
"我是带你来到这个国家的马车夫"
"Open at once, or it will be the worse for you!"
"马上开门，不然对你来说会更糟！"

Pinocchio gets Trained for the Circus
匹诺曹接受马戏团训练

the door wouldn't open at his command
门不会在他的命令下打开
so the little man gave the door a violent kick
于是小个子猛地踢了一脚门
and the coachman burst into the room
马车夫冲进了房间
he spoke with his usual little laugh:
他用他一贯的笑声说：
"Well done, boys! You brayed well"
"干得好，伙计们！你咆哮得好"
"and I recognized you by your voices"
"我凭你们的声音认出了你们"
"That is why I am here"
"这就是我在这里的原因"
the two little donkeys were quite stupefied
两头小驴子都吓呆了
they stood with their heads down
他们低着头站着
they had their ears lowered
他们的耳朵被压低了
and they had their tails between their legs
他们把尾巴夹在两腿之间

At first the little man stroked and caressed them
起初,小个子男人抚摸和爱抚他们
then he took out a currycomb
然后他拿出一把咖喱梳
and he currycombed the donkeys well
他把驴子梳得好
by this process he had polished them
通过这个过程,他已经对它们进行了抛光
and the two donkeys shone like two mirrors
两头驴像两面镜子一样闪闪发光
he put a halter around their necks
他在他们的脖子上套上了缰绳
and he led them to the market-place
他领他们到集市

he was in hopes of selling them
他希望能卖掉它们

he thought he could get a good profit
他认为他可以获得丰厚的利润

And indeed there were buyers for the donkeys
确实有买驴的人

Candle-wick was bought by a peasant
烛芯被一个农民买下

his donkey had died the previous day
他的驴子在前一天死了

Pinocchio was sold to the director of a company
匹诺曹被卖给了一家公司的董事

they were a company of buffoons and tight-rope dancers
他们是一群小丑和走钢丝的舞者

he bought him so that he might teach him to dance
他买下了他，好教他跳舞

he could dance with the other circus animals
他可以和其他马戏团的动物一起跳舞

And now, my little readers, you understand
现在，我的小读者们，你们明白了

the little man was just a businessman
这个小个子只是一个商人

and it was a profitable business that he led
他领导的是一项有利可图的业务

The wicked little monster with a face of milk and honey
那个长着奶和蜜脸的邪恶小怪物

he made frequent journeys round the world
他经常环游世界

he promised and flattered wherever he went
无论他走到哪里，他都承诺和奉承

and he collected all the idle boys
他把所有无所事事的小伙子都收起来了

and there were many idle boys to collect
还有许多无所事事的男孩要收集

all the boys who had taken a dislike to books
所有不喜欢书的男孩

and all the boys who weren't fond of school
还有所有不喜欢上学的男孩

each time his wagon filled up with these boys
每次他的马车上都装满了这些男孩

and he took them all to the Land of Boobie Birds
他把他们都带到了鲣鸟之地

here they passed their time playing games
他们在这里玩游戏打发时间

and there was uproar and much amusement
一片喧嚣和欢乐

but the same fate awaited all the deluded boys
但同样的命运等待着所有受骗的男孩

too much play and no study turned them into donkeys
太多的游戏和没有研究把他们变成了驴子

then he took possession of them with great delight
然后他非常高兴地占有他们

and he carried them off to the fairs and markets
他把他们带到集市和集市上

And in this way he made heaps of money
通过这种方式，他赚了一大笔钱

What became of Candle-wick I do not know
我不知道烛芯后来怎么样了

but I do know what happened to poor Pinocchio
但我确实知道可怜的匹诺曹发生了什么

from the very first day he endured a very hard life
从第一天起，他就忍受了非常艰苦的生活

Pinocchio was put into his stall
匹诺曹被放进了他的马厩

and his master filled the manger with straw
他的主人用稻草装满了马槽

but Pinocchio didn't like eating straw at all
但匹诺曹根本不喜欢吃稻草
and the little donkey spat the straw out again
小驴又把稻草吐了出来
Then his master, grumbling, filled the manger with hay
然后,他的主人抱怨着,把马槽里装满了干草
but hay did not please Pinocchio either
但干草也没有取悦匹诺曹
"Ah!" exclaimed his master in a passion
"啊!"
"Does not hay please you either?"
"你也不高兴吗?"
"Leave it to me, my fine donkey"
"交给我吧,我的好驴子"
"I see you are full of caprices"
"我看你满脑子都是任性"
"but worry not, I will find a way to cure you!"
"但别担心,我会想办法治好你的!"
And he struck the donkey's legs with his whip
他就用鞭子抽打驴子的腿
Pinocchio began to cry and bray with pain
匹诺曹开始痛苦地哭泣和吼叫
"Hee-haw! I cannot digest straw!"
"嘿嘿!我消化不了稻草!"
"Then eat hay!" said his master
"那就吃干草吧!"
he understood perfectly the asinine dialect
他完全听得懂阿西尼方言
"Hee-haw! hay gives me a pain in my stomach"
"嘿嘿!干草让我肚子疼"
"I see how it is little donkey"
"我明白它是怎么小驴子了"

- 299 -

"you would like to be fed with capons in jelly"
"你想用果冻里的 Capons 喂食"
and he got more and more angry
他越来越生气
and he whipped poor Pinocchio again
他又鞭打了可怜的匹诺曹
the second time Pinocchio held his tongue
匹诺曹第二次闭口不言
and he learned to say nothing more
他学会了什么也不多说
The stable was then shut
马厩随后被关闭
and Pinocchio was left alone
匹诺曹独自一人
He had not eaten for many hours
他已经很多小时没有吃东西了
and he began to yawn from hunger
他开始因饥饿而打哈欠
his yawns seemed as wide as an oven
他的哈欠似乎像烤箱一样宽
but he found nothing else to eat
但他找不到别的吃东西
so he resigned himself to his fate
所以他听天由命
and he gave in and chewed a little hay
他就屈服了，咀嚼了一点干草
he chewed the hay well, because it was dry
他把干草嚼得很好，因为它很干
and he shut his eyes and swallowed it
他闭上眼睛，吞了下去
"This hay is not bad," he said to himself
"这干草还不错，"他对自己说
"but better would have been if I had studied!"
"可是如果我读过书就好了！"

"Instead of hay I could now be eating bread"
"我现在可以吃面包,而不是干草"
"and perhaps I would have been eating fine sausages"
"也许我会吃上好的香肠"
"But I must have patience!"
"但我必须要有耐心!"
The next morning he woke up again
第二天早上,他又醒了
he looked in the manger for a little more hay
他在马槽里寻找更多的干草
but there was no more hay to be found
但已经找不到更多的干草了
for he had eaten all the hay during the night
因为他在夜里把所有的干草都吃光了
Then he took a mouthful of chopped straw
然后他吃了一口切碎的稻草
but he had to acknowledge the horrible taste
但他不得不承认这种可怕的味道
it tasted not in the least like macaroni or pie
它的味道一点也不像通心粉或馅饼
"I hope other naughty boys learn from my lesson"
"我希望其他顽皮的男孩能从我的教训中吸取教训"
"But I must have patience!"
"但我必须要有耐心!"
and the little donkey kept chewing the straw
小驴子不停地咀嚼稻草
"Patience indeed!" shouted his master
"真要有耐心!"
he had come at that moment into the stable
他在那一刻走进了马厩
"but don't get too comfortable, my little donkey"
"但别太舒服,我的小驴子"
"I didn't buy you to give you food and drink"
"我买你不是为了给你吃喝"

"I bought you to make you work"
"我买下你，让你工作"
"I bought you so that you earn me money"
"我买下你，是为了让你赚我钱"
"Up you get, then, at once!"
"那么，你马上起来！"
"you must come with me into the circus"
"你得跟我进马戏团"
"there I will teach you to jump through hoops"
"在那里，我将教你跳过重环"
"you will learn to stand upright on your hind legs"
"您将学会用后腿直立"
"and you will learn to dance waltzes and polkas"
"你将学会跳华尔兹和波尔卡舞"
Poor Pinocchio had to learn all these fine things
可怜的匹诺曹必须学习所有这些美好的东西
and I can't say it was easy to learn
我不能说这很容易学习
it took him three months to learn the tricks
他花了三个月的时间才学会这些技巧
he got many a whipping that nearly took off his skin
他挨了很多鞭子，几乎把他的皮肤都打掉了
At last his master made the announcement
最后，他的主人宣布了这个消息
many coloured placards stuck on the street corners
街角贴着许多彩色标语牌
"Great Full Dress Representation"
"出色的正装代表"
"TONIGHT will Take Place the Usual Feats and Surprises"
"今晚将上演往常的壮举和惊喜"
"Performances Executed by All the Artists and horses"
"所有艺术家和马匹的表演"

"and moreover; The Famous LITTLE DONKEY PINOCCHIO"
"而且;著名的小驴匹诺曹》
"THE STAR OF THE DANCE"
"舞蹈之星"
"the theatre will be brilliantly illuminated"
"剧院将灯火通明"
you can imagine how crammed the theatre was
你可以想象剧院里有多拥挤
The circus was full of children of all ages
马戏团里到处都是各个年龄段的孩子
all came to see the famous little donkey Pinocchio dance
大家都来看著名的小驴匹诺曹舞
the first part of the performance was over
表演的第一部分结束了
the director of the company presented himself to the public
公司董事向公众展示自己
he was dressed in a black coat and white breeches
他穿着一件黑色外套和白色马裤
and big leather boots that came above his knees
还有一双长到膝盖以上的大皮靴
he made a profound bow to the crowd
他向人群深深地鞠了一躬
he began with much solemnity a ridiculous speech:
他以非常严肃的方式开始了一段荒谬的演讲：
"Respectable public, ladies and gentlemen!"
"尊敬的公众，女士们，先生们！"
"it is with great honour and pleasure"
"我感到非常荣幸和高兴"
"I stand here before this distinguished audience"
"我站在这尊贵的观众面前"
"and I present to you the celebrated little donkey"

"我向你介绍那只著名的小驴子"
"the little donkey who has already had the honour"
"已经有荣誉的小驴子"
"the honour of dancing in the presence of His Majesty"
"在陛下面前跳舞的荣幸"
"And, thanking you, I beg of you to help us"
"而且,谢谢你,我恳求你帮助我们"
"help us with your inspiring presence"
"以您鼓舞人心的存在帮助我们"
"and please, esteemed audience, be indulgent to us"
"尊敬的观众们,请宽容我们"

This speech was received with much laughter and applause
这次演讲赢得了许多笑声和掌声

but the applause soon was even louder than before
但掌声很快就比以前更响亮了

the little donkey Pinocchio made his appearance
小驴匹诺曹现身

and he stood in the middle of the circus
他站在马戏团的中央

He was decked out for the occasion
他为这个场合打扮得漂漂亮亮的

He had a new bridle of polished leather
他有一条新的抛光皮革缰绳

and he was wearing brass buckles and studs
他戴着黄铜扣和铆钉

and he had two white camellias in his ears
他的耳朵上有两棵白色的山茶花

His mane was divided and curled
他的鬃毛分裂卷曲

and each curl was tied with bows of coloured ribbon
每个卷发都用彩色丝带蝴蝶结系着

He had a girth of gold and silver round his body
他身上有一条金银腰带

his tail was plaited with amaranth and blue velvet ribbons
他的尾巴上编着苋菜和蓝色天鹅绒丝带
He was, in fact, a little donkey to fall in love with!
事实上,他是一头值得爱上的小驴子!
The director added these few words:
导演补充了这几句话:
"My respectable auditors!"
"我尊敬的审计师!"
"I am not here to tell you falsehoods"
"我不是来告诉你谎言的"
"there were great difficulties I had to overcome"
"我必须克服很多困难"
"I understood and subjugated this mammifer"
"我理解并征服了这只哺乳动物"
"he was grazing at liberty amongst the mountains"
"他在群山中自由地吃草"
"he lived in the plains of the torrid zone"
"他住在 Torrid Zone 的平原上"
"I beg you will observe the wild rolling of his eyes"
"我恳求你观察他疯狂的翻白眼"
"Every means had been tried in vain to tame him"
"想尽一切办法都徒劳无功。"
"I have accustomed him to the life of domestic quadrupeds"
"我已经让他习惯了家养四足动物的生活"
"and I spared him the convincing argument of the whip"
"我饶过了他那鞭子的令人信服的论点。"
"But all my goodness only increased his viciousness"
"但我所有的善良只会增加他的恶毒"
"However, I discovered in his cranium a bony cartilage"

"然而,我在他的头盖骨中发现了一块骨质软骨"
"I had him inspected by the Faculty of Medicine of Paris"
"我让巴黎医学院对他进行了检查"
"I spared no cost for my little donkey's treatment"
"我不惜一切代价为我的小驴子治疗"
"in him the doctors found the regenerating cortex of dance"
"医生在他身上找到了舞蹈的再生皮层"
"For this reason I have not only taught him to dance"
"为此,我不仅教他跳舞"
"but I also taught him to jump through hoops"
"但我也教他跳过重环"
"Admire him, and then pass your opinion on him!"
"佩服他,然后把你的意见转达给他!"
"But before taking my leave of you, permit me this;"
"但在我离开你之前,请允许我这样做。"
"ladies and gentlemen, esteemed members of the crowd"
"女士们,先生们,尊敬的人群"
"I invite you to tomorrow's daily performance"
"我邀请你参加明天的日常表演"
Here the director made another profound bow
"说到这里,导演又深深地鞠了一躬
and, then turning to Pinocchio, he said:
然后,他转向匹诺曹说:
"Courage, Pinocchio! But before you begin:"
"勇气,匹诺曹!但在你开始之前:"
"bow to this distinguished audience"
"向这尊贵的听众鞠躬"
Pinocchio obeyed his master's commands
匹诺曹服从了他主人的命令
and he bent both his knees till they touched the

- 306 -

ground
他弯曲双膝,直到膝盖碰到地面
the director cracked his whip and shouted:
导演抽打着鞭子,喊道:
"At a foot's pace, Pinocchio!"
"以一英尺的速度,匹诺曹!"
Then the little donkey raised himself on his four legs
然后,小驴子用四条腿站了起来
and he began to walk round the theatre
他开始在剧院里走来走去
and the whole time he kept at a foot's pace
他全程保持着一英尺的速度
After a little time the director shouted again:
过了一会儿,导演又喊道:
"Trot!" and Pinocchio, obeyed the order
"小跑!"和匹诺曹服从了命令
and he changed his pace to a trot
他改变了步伐,小跑起来
"Gallop!" and Pinocchio broke into a gallop
""匹诺曹开始疾驰起来
"Full gallop!" and Pinocchio went full gallop
"全速驰骋",匹诺曹全速驰骋
he was running round the circus like a racehorse
他像一匹赛马一样在马戏团里跑来跑去
but then the director fired off a pistol
但随后导演用手枪开火
at full speed he fell to the floor
他全速倒在了地上
and the little donkey pretended to be wounded
小驴子假装受伤
he got up from the ground amidst an outburst of applause
他在一片掌声中从地上站起来
there were shouts and clapping of hands

人们欢呼和拍手

and he naturally raised his head and looked up
他自然而然地抬起头来

and he saw in one of the boxes a beautiful lady
他在其中一个盒子里看到一位美丽的女士

she wore round her neck a thick gold chain
她的脖子上戴着一条粗金链子

and from the chain hung a medallion
链子上挂着一枚奖章

On the medallion was painted the portrait of a puppet
奖章上画着木偶的肖像

"That is my portrait!" realized Pinocchio
"那是我的画像！"

"That lady is the Fairy!" said Pinocchio to himself
"那位女士就是仙女！"

Pinocchio had recognized her immediately
匹诺曹立刻就认出了她

and, overcome with delight, he tried to call her
他高兴极了，试着给她打电话

"Oh, my little Fairy! Oh, my little Fairy!"
"哦，我的小仙女！哦，我的小仙女！

But instead of these words a bray came from his throat
但是，这些话不是从他的喉咙里发出的

a bray so prolonged that all the spectators laughed
这场喧嚣如此漫长，以至于所有观众都笑了起来

and all the children in the theatre especially laughed
剧院里的所有孩子都特别笑了

Then the director gave him a lesson
然后导演给他上了一课

it is not good manners to bray before the public
在公众面前吵闹是不礼貌的

with the handle of his whip he smacked the donkey's nose
他用鞭子的手柄打了驴子的鼻子

The poor little donkey put his tongue out an inch
可怜的小驴子把舌头伸出了一英寸

and he licked his nose for at least five minutes
他舔了至少五分钟的鼻子

he thought perhaps that it would ease the pain
他想也许这样会减轻痛苦

But how he despaired when looking up a second time
但是，当他第二次抬起头来时，他是多么的绝望

he saw that the seat was empty
他看到座位是空的

the good Fairy of his had disappeared!
他的好仙女不见了！

He thought he was going to die
他以为自己快要死了

his eyes filled with tears and he began to weep
他的眼睛里充满了泪水，他开始哭泣

Nobody, however, noticed his tears
然而，没有人注意到他的眼泪

"Courage, Pinocchio!" shouted the director
"勇气，匹诺曹！"

"show the audience how gracefully you can jump through the hoops"
"向观众展示你如何优雅地跳过圈子"

Pinocchio tried two or three times
匹诺曹尝试了两三次

but going through the hoop is not easy for a donkey
但对于驴子来说，穿过铁环并不容易

and he found it easier to go under the hoop
他发现钻进篮筐下更容易

At last he made a leap and went through the hoop
最后，他跳了起来，穿过了篮筐

but his right leg unfortunately caught in the hoop
但他的右腿不幸被篮筐夹住了

and that caused him to fall to the ground

这导致他倒在地上
he was doubled up in a heap on the other side
他在另一边被堆成一堆
When he got up he was lame
当他起来时,他瘸了
only with great difficulty did he return to the stable
他好不容易才回到了马厩
"Bring out Pinocchio!" shouted all the boys
"把匹诺曹带出来!"
"We want the little donkey!" roared the theatre
"我们要那头小驴子!"
they were touched and sorry for the sad accident
他们很感动,并为这场悲惨的事故感到抱歉
But the little donkey was seen no more that evening
但那天晚上再也没有看到那头小驴
The following morning the veterinary paid him a visit
第二天早上,兽医去看望了他
the vets are doctors to the animals
兽医是动物的医生
and he declared that he would remain lame for life
他宣布他将终生瘸腿
The director then said to the stable-boy:
"然后,导演对马厩男孩说:
"What do you suppose I can do with a lame donkey?"
"你觉得我能对一头瘸腿的驴做什么呢?"
"He will eat food without earning it"
"他会吃食物,却不挣"
"Take him to the market and sell him"
"带他去市场卖掉他"
When they reached the market a purchaser was found at once
当他们到达市场时,立即发现了一个买家
He asked the stable-boy:
他问马厩男孩:

"How much do you want for that lame donkey?"
"你要多少钱给那头瘸腿的驴子？"
"Twenty dollars and I'll sell him to you"
"二十美元，我就把他卖给你"
"I will give you two dollars"
"我给你两块钱"
"but don't suppose that I will make use of him"
"可是，别以为我会利用他。"
"I am buying him solely for his skin"
"我买他只是为了他的皮肤"
"I see that his skin is very hard"
"我看到他的皮肤很硬"
"I intend to make a drum with him"
"我打算和他一起做个鼓"
he heard that he was destined to become a drum!
他听说自己注定要成为鼓手！
you can imagine poor Pinocchio's feelings
你可以想象可怜的匹诺曹的心情
the two dollars were handed over
这两块钱被交了
and the man was given his donkey
那人得到了他的驴子
he led the little donkey to the seashore
他牵着小驴子来到海边
he then put a stone round his neck
然后他用石头套在他的脖子上
and he gave him a sudden push into the water
他突然把他推入水中
Pinocchio was weighted down by the stone
匹诺曹被石头压倒了
and he went straight to the bottom of the sea
他径直走到海底
his owner kept tight hold of the cord
他的主人紧紧地抓住了绳子

he sat down quietly on a piece of rock
他静静地坐在一块石头上
and he waited until the little donkey was drowned
他一直等到小驴被淹死
and then he intended to skin him
然后他打算剥他的皮

Pinocchio gets Swallowed by the Dog-Fish
匹诺曹被狗鱼吞下

Pinocchio had been fifty minutes under the water
匹诺曹已经在水下呆了 50 分钟
his purchaser said aloud to himself:
他的买主大声对自己说：
"My little lame donkey must by now be quite drowned"
"我那头瘸腿的小驴现在肯定已经被淹死了"
"I will therefore pull him out of the water"
"所以我要把他从水里拉出来"
"and I will make a fine drum of his skin"
"我要用他的皮肤做一个细鼓"
And he began to haul in the rope
"他开始拉绳子
the rope he had tied to the donkey's leg
他拴在驴腿上的绳子
and he hauled, and hauled, and hauled
他拖着，拖着，拖着
he hauled until at last...
他拖着直到最后……
what do you think appeared above the water?
你觉得水面上出现了什么？
he did not pull a dead donkey to land
他没有拉着一头死驴上岸

instead he saw a living little puppet
相反,他看到了一个活生生的小木偶

and this little puppet was wriggling like an eel!
而这个小木偶像鳗鱼一样扭动着!
the poor man thought he was dreaming
穷人以为他在做梦
and he was struck dumb with astonishment
他惊呆了
he eventually recovered from his stupefaction
他最终从昏迷中恢复过来
and he asked the puppet in a quavering voice:
他用颤抖的声音问木偶:
"where is the little donkey I threw into the sea?"
"我扔进海里的那头小驴子在哪里?"

"I am the little donkey!" said Pinocchio
"我就是那头小驴！"
and Pinocchio laughed at being a puppet again
匹诺曹嘲笑又是个傀儡了
"How can you be the little donkey??"
"你怎么能成为那头小驴子？？"
"I was the little donkey," answered Pinocchio
"我是那头小驴，"匹诺曹回答
"and now I'm a little puppet again"
"现在我又变成了一个小傀儡"
"Ah, a young scamp is what you are!!"
"啊，你就是个年轻的流氓！！"
"Do you dare to make fun of me?"
"你敢取笑我吗？"
"To make fun of you?" asked Pinocchio
"取笑你？"
"Quite the contrary, my dear master?"
"恰恰相反，我亲爱的主人？"
"I am speaking seriously with you"
"我正在认真地与你交谈"
"a short time ago you were a little donkey"
"不久前你还是一头小驴"
"how can you have become a wooden puppet?"
"你怎么能变成木偶呢？"
"being left in the water does not do that to a donkey!"
"留在水里不会对驴子造成这种影响！"
"It must have been the effect of sea water"
"一定是海水的影响"
"The sea causes extraordinary changes"
"大海引发了非凡的变化"
"Beware, puppet, I am not in the mood!"
"当心，傀儡，我没心情！"
"Don't imagine that you can amuse yourself at my

expense"
"别以为你可以以我的代价来自娱自乐"

"Woe to you if I lose patience!"
"如果我失去耐心,你就有祸了!"

"Well, master, do you wish to know the true story?"
"嗯,主人,您想知道真实的故事吗?"

"If you set my leg free I will tell it you"
"如果你让我的腿自由,我就告诉你"

The good man was curious to hear the true story
这位好人很想听听这个真实的故事

and he immediately untied the knot
他立即解开了这个结

Pinocchio was again as free as a bird in the air
匹诺曹又像空中的鸟一样自由

and he commenced to tell his story
他开始讲述他的故事

"You must know that I was once a puppet"
"你要知道,我曾经是个傀儡"

"that is to say, I wasn't always a donkey"
"也就是说,我并不总是一头驴"

"I was on the point of becoming a boy"
"我正要成为一个男孩"

"I would have been like the other boys in the world"
"我会像世界上其他男孩一样"

"but like other boys, I wasn't fond of study"
"但和其他男孩一样,我不喜欢学习"

"and I followed the advice of bad companions"
"我听从了坏伙伴的建议"

"and finally I ran away from home"
"最后我离家出走"

"One fine day when I awoke I found myself changed"
"有一天,当我醒来时,我发现自己变了"

"I had become a donkey with long ears"

"我变成了一头长着长耳朵的驴"
"and I had grown a long tail too"
"而且我也长了一条长长的尾巴"
"What a disgrace it was to me!"
"这对我来说是多么的耻辱啊！"
"even your worst enemy would not inflict it upon you!"
"即使是你最坏的敌人也不会加在你身上！"
"I was taken to the market to be sold"
"我被带到市场被卖"
"and I was bought by an equestrian company"
"我被一家马术公司买下了"
"they wanted to make a famous dancer of me"
"他们想让我成为著名的舞者"
"But one night during a performance I had a bad fall"
"但有一天晚上，在一次演出中，我摔得很重"
"and I was left with two lame legs"
"我只剩下两条瘸腿"
"I was of no use to the circus no more"
"我对马戏团已经没有用处了"
"and again I was taken to the market"
"我又一次被带到市场"
"and at the market you were my purchaser!"
"在集市上，你是我的买主！"
"Only too true," remembered the man
"太对了，"那人回忆道
"And I paid two dollars for you"
"我为你付了两美元"
"And now, who will give me back my good money?"
"那么，谁来把我的好钱还给我呢？"
"And why did you buy me?"
"那你为什么买我呢？"
"You bought me to make a drum of my skin!"
"你买来我，是为了用我的皮肤做一个鼓！"

"Only too true!" said the man
"太对了！"
"And now, where shall I find another skin?"
"那么，我到哪儿去找另一张皮呢？"
"Don't despair, master"
"不要绝望，主人"
"There are many little donkeys in the world!"
"世界上有很多小驴子！"
"Tell me, you impertinent rascal;"
"告诉我，你这个无礼的流氓。"
"does your story end here?"
"你的故事到此结束了吗？"
"No," answered the puppet
"不，"木偶回答
"I have another two words to say"
"我还有两句话要说"
"and then my story shall have finished"
"然后我的故事就结束了"
"you brought me to this place to kill me"
"你带我到这个地方来杀我"
"but then you yielded to a feeling of compassion"
"但后来你屈服于一种同情心"
"and you preferred to tie a stone round my neck
"而且你宁愿在我的脖子上系一块石头"
"and you threw me into the sea"
"你把我扔进海里"
"This humane feeling does you great honour"
"这种人情味让您感到非常荣幸"
"and I shall always be grateful to you"
"我将永远感激你"
"But, nevertheless, dear master, you forgot one thing"
"可是，不管怎样，亲爱的主人，你忘了一件事。"
"you made your calculations without considering the

Fairy!"
"你算计的时候,没有考虑仙女!"
"And who is the Fairy?"
"那仙子是谁?"
"She is my mamma," replied Pinocchio
"她是我的妈妈,"匹诺曹回答
"and she resembles all other good mammas"
"她跟所有其他的好妈妈都像"
"and all good mammas care for their children"
"所有善良的妈妈都会关心她们的孩子"
"mammas who never lose sight of their children""
"从不忘记孩子的妈妈们""
"mammas who help their children lovingly"
"充满爱心地帮助孩子的妈妈们"
"and they love them even when they deserve to be abandoned"
"即使他们应该被抛弃,他们也爱他们"
"my good mamma kept me in her sight"
"我的好妈妈把我放在她的视线里"
"and she saw that I was in danger of drowning"
"她看到我有溺水的危险"
"so she immediately sent an immense shoal of fish"
"所以她立即派出了一大群鱼"
"first they really thought I was a little dead donkey"
"起初他们真的认为我是一头死驴"
"and so they began to eat me in big mouthfuls"
"于是他们开始大口吃我"
"I never knew fish were greedier than boys!"
"我从来不知道鱼比男孩子更贪婪!"
"Some ate my ears and my muzzle"
"有些人吃了我的耳朵和口鼻"
"and other fish my neck and mane"
"和我的脖子和鬃毛上的其他鱼"

"some of them ate the skin of my legs"
"他们中的一些吃了我腿上的皮"
"and others took to eating my fur"
"其他人开始吃我的皮毛"
"Amongst them there was an especially polite little fish"
"其中有一条特别有礼貌的小鱼"
"and he condescended to eat my tail"
"他居高临下地吃我的尾巴"
the purchaser was horrified by what he heard
买方对他所听到的情况感到震惊
"I swear that I will never touch fish again!"
"我发誓我再也不会碰鱼了！"
"imagine opening a mullet and finding a donkey's tail!"
"想象一下打开一条鲻鱼，找到一条驴尾巴！"
"I agree with you," said the puppet, laughing
"我同意你的看法，"木偶笑着说
"However, I must tell you what happened next"
"不过，我必须告诉你接下来发生了什么"
"the fish had finished eating the donkey's hide"
"鱼吃完了驴皮"
"the donkey's hide that had covered me"
"盖住我的驴皮"
"then they naturally reached the bone"
"然后他们自然而然地到达了骨头"
"but it was not bone, but rather wood"
"但那不是骨头，而是木头"
"for, as you see, I am made of the hardest wood"
"因为，正如你所看到的，我是用最坚硬的木头做的。"
"they tried to take a few more bites"
"他们试图多咬几口"
"But they soon discovered I was not for eating"

"但他们很快就发现我不适合吃东西"
"disgusted with such indigestible food, they swam off"
"他们厌恶这种难以消化的食物,游走了"
"and they left without even saying thank you"
"他们甚至没有说声谢谢就走了"
"And now, at last, you have heard my story"
"现在,你终于听到了我的故事"
"and that is why you didn't find a dead donkey"
"所以你才没找到一头死驴"
"and instead you found a living puppet"
"相反,你发现了一个活生生的傀儡"
"I laugh at your story," cried the man in a rage
"我嘲笑你的故事,"男人愤怒地喊道
"I only know that I spent two dollars to buy you"
"我只知道我花了两块钱买你"
"and I will have my money back"
"我会拿回我的钱"
"Shall I tell you what I will do?"
"我告诉你我该怎么办好吗?"
"I will take you back to the market"
"我带你回市场"
"and I will sell you by weight as seasoned wood"
"我就把你当作陈年木头的重量卖给你。"
and the purchaser can light fires with you"
买主可以和你一起点火"
Pinocchio was not too worried about this
匹诺曹对此并不太担心
"Sell me if you like; I am content"
"如果你愿意,就卖给我吧;我很满足"
and he plunged back into the water
然后他又跳进了水里
he swam gaily away from the shore
他欢快地游离了岸边

and he called to his poor owner
他呼唤他可怜的主人
"Good-bye, master, don't forget me"
"再见，主人，别忘了我"
"the wooden puppet you wanted for its skin"
"你想要的皮肤木偶"
"and I hope you get your drum one day"
"我希望你有一天能得到你的鼓"
And he laughed and went on swimming
"他笑着继续游泳
and after a while he turned around again
过了一会儿，他又转过身来
"Good-bye, master," he shouted louder
"再见，主人，"他大声喊道
"and remember me when you need well seasoned wood"
"当你需要好干的木材时，记住我"
"and think of me when you're lighting a fire"
"当你点火时想想我"
soon Pinocchio had swam towards the horizon
很快，匹诺曹就游向了地平线
and now he was scarcely visible from the shore
现在从岸上几乎看不到他
he was a little black speck on the surface of the sea
他是海面上的一个小黑点
from time to time he lifted out of the water
他不时地从水里升起
and he leaped and capered like a happy dolphin
他像一只快乐的海豚一样跳跃和跳跃
Pinocchio was swimming and he knew not whither
匹诺曹在游泳，他不知道在哪儿
he saw in the midst of the sea a rock
他看见海中有一块磐石
the rock seemed to be made of white marble

这块岩石似乎是由白色大理石制成的
and on the summit there stood a beautiful little goat
山顶上站着一只漂亮的小山羊
the goat bleated lovingly to Pinocchio
山羊深情地对匹诺曹咩咩叫
and the goat made signs to him to approach
山羊向他打手势,让他靠近
But the most singular thing was this:
但最奇特的是:
The little goat's hair was not white nor black
小山羊的毛发既不白也不黑
nor was it a mixture of two colours
也不是两种颜色的混合
this is usual with other goats
这是其他山羊的常见情况
but the goat's hair was a very vivid blue
但山羊的毛发是非常鲜艳的蓝色
a vivid blue like the hair of the beautiful Child
鲜艳的蓝色,就像美丽孩子的头发
imagine how rapidly Pinocchio's heart began to beat
想象一下匹诺曹的心脏开始跳动得有多快
He swam with redoubled strength and energy
他以加倍的力量和精力游泳
and in no time at all he was halfway there
他很快就走了一半
but then he saw something came out the water
但随后他看到有什么东西从水里出来
the horrible head of a sea-monster!
海怪的可怕头颅!
His mouth was wide open and cavernous
他的嘴巴张得很大,像海绵一样
there were three rows of enormous teeth
有三排巨大的牙齿
even a picture of if would terrify you

即使是一张 if 的照片也会让你感到恐惧

And do you know what this sea-monster was?
你知道这个海怪是什么吗?

it was none other than that gigantic Dog-Fish
不是别人,正是那条巨大的狗鱼

the Dog-Fish mentioned many times in this story
狗鱼在这个故事中多次被提及

I should tell you the name of this terrible fish
我应该告诉你这条可怕的鱼的名字

Attila of Fish and Fishermen
鱼和渔民的阿提拉

on account of his slaughter and insatiable voracity
因为他的杀戮和贪得无厌的贪婪

think of poor Pinocchio's terror at the sight
想想可怜的匹诺曹看到这一景象时的恐惧

a true sea monster was swimming at him
一只真正的海怪正在向他游来

He tried to avoid the Dog-Fish
他试图避开狗鱼

he tried to swim in other directions
他试图向其他方向游去

he did everything he could to escape
他想尽一切办法逃跑

but that immense wide-open mouth was too big
但那张开的巨大嘴巴太大了

and it was coming with the velocity of an arrow
它以箭的速度来

the beautiful little goat tried to bleat
美丽的小山羊试图咩咩叫

"Be quick, Pinocchio, for pity's sake!"
"快点,匹诺曹,看在可怜的份上!"

And Pinocchio swam desperately with all he could
匹诺曹拼命地游着

his arms, his chest, his legs, and his feet

他的手臂、胸部、腿和脚
"Quick, Pinocchio, the monster is close upon you!"
"快点,匹诺曹,怪物就在你身边了!"
And Pinocchio swam quicker than ever
匹诺曹游得比以往任何时候都快
he flew on with the rapidity of a ball from a gun
他以枪中子弹般的速度继续飞行
He had nearly reached the rock
他几乎已经到了那块岩石上
and he had almost reached the little goat
他几乎已经够到那只小山羊了
and the little goat leaned over towards the sea
小山羊俯身向海边
she stretched out her fore-legs to help him
她伸出前腿来帮助他
perhaps she could get him out of the water
也许她能把他从水里救出来
But all their efforts were too late!
但他们所有的努力都为时已晚!
The monster had overtaken Pinocchio
怪物已经追上了匹诺曹
he drew in a big breath of air and water
他大口吸了一口空气和水
and he sucked in the poor puppet
他吸进了这个可怜的傀儡
like he would have sucked a hen's egg
就像他会吮吸母鸡的蛋一样
and the Dog-Fish swallowed him whole
狗鱼把他整个吞了下去

Pinocchio tumbled through his teeth
匹诺曹从他的牙齿里翻滚
and he tumbled down the Dog-Fish's throat
他顺着狗鱼的喉咙翻滚而下
and finally he landed heavily in his stomach
最后,他重重地落在了他的肚子上
he remained unconscious for a quarter of an hour
他昏迷了一刻钟
but eventually he came to himself again
但最终他又清醒过来了
he could not in the least imagine in what world he was
他根本无法想象自己身处什么世界
All around him there was nothing but darkness
他周围只有黑暗
it was as if he had fallen into a pot of ink

他仿佛掉进了一罐墨水里

He listened, but he could hear no noise
他听着,却听不见任何声音

occasionally great gusts of wind blew in his face
偶尔会有阵阵大风吹在他的脸上

first he could not understand from where it came from
起初,他无法理解它从何而来

but at last he discovered the source
但最后他发现了源头

it came out of the monster's lungs
它从怪物的肺里出来

there is one thing you must know about the Dog-Fish
关于 Dog-Fish,您必须了解一件事

the Dog-Fish suffered very much from asthma
狗鱼患哮喘

when he breathed it was exactly like the north wind
他呼吸的时候,就像北风一样

Pinocchio at first tried to keep up his courage
匹诺曹起初试图保持勇气

but the reality of the situation slowly dawned on him
但现实情况慢慢地出现在他身上

he was really shut up in the body of this sea-monster
他真的被关在这个海怪的身体里

and he began to cry and scream and sob
他开始哭泣、尖叫和抽泣

"Help! help! Oh, how unfortunate I am!"
"救命!帮助!哦,我真不幸啊!"

"Will nobody come to save me?"
"没有人来救我吗?"

from the dark there came a voice
从黑暗中传来了一个声音

the voice sounded like a guitar out of tune
声音听起来像一把走调的吉他

"Who do you think could save you, unhappy wretch?"

"你觉得谁能救你呢，不幸的坏蛋？"

Pinocchio froze with terror at the voice
匹诺曹被这个声音吓得愣住了

"Who is speaking?" asked Pinocchio, finally
"谁在说话？"

"It is I! I am a poor Tunny Fish"
"是我！我是一条可怜的金枪鱼"

"I was swallowed by the Dog-Fish along with you"
"我和你一起被狗鱼吞噬了"

"And what fish are you?"
"那你是什么鱼？"

"I have nothing in common with fish"
"我和鱼没有任何共同之处"

"I am a puppet," added Pinocchio
"我是个傀儡，"匹诺曹补充道

"Then why did you let yourself be swallowed?"
"那你为什么让自己被吞下去呢？"

"I didn't let myself be swallowed"
"我没有让自己被吞噬"

"it was the monster that swallowed me!"
"是那个怪物吞噬了我！"

"And now, what are we to do here in the dark?"
"那么现在，我们在黑暗中该怎么办？"

"there's not much we can do but to resign ourselves"
"我们能做的不多，只能放弃自己"

"and now we wait until the Dog-Fish has digested us"
"现在我们等着狗鱼把我们消化掉"

"But I do not want to be digested!" howled Pinocchio
"但我不想被消化！"

and he began to cry again
他又开始哭泣

"Neither do I want to be digested," added the Tunny Fish

"我也不想被消化，"金枪鱼补充道
"but I am enough of a philosopher to console myself"
"但我是一个哲学家，足以安慰自己"
"when one is born a Tunny Fish life can be made sense of"
"当一个人出生时，一条金枪鱼的生活可以变得有意义"
"it is more dignified to die in the water than in oil"
"死在水里比死在油里更有尊严"
"That is all nonsense!" cried Pinocchio
"那都是胡说八道！"
"It is my opinion," replied the Tunny Fish
"这是我的意见，"金枪鱼回答
"and opinions ought to be respected"
"意见应该得到尊重"
"that is what the political Tunny Fish say"
"这就是政治上的金枪鱼是这么说的"
"To sum it all up, I want to get away from here"
"总而言之，我想离开这里"
"I do want to escape."
"我确实想逃跑。"
"Escape, if you are able!"
"如果你能逃走！"
"Is this Dog-Fish who has swallowed us very big?"
"这个吞噬了我们的狗鱼是不是很大？"
"Big? My boy, you can only imagine"
"大？我的孩子，你只能想象"
"his body is two miles long without counting his tail"
"他的身体有两英里长，不算他的尾巴"
they held this conversation in the dark for some time
他们在黑暗中进行了一段时间的对话
eventually Pinocchio's eyes adjusted to the darkness
最终，匹诺曹的眼睛适应了黑暗
Pinocchio thought that he saw a light a long way off

匹诺曹认为他看到了很远的光
"What is that little light I see in the distance?"
"我在远处看到的那点微弱的光芒是什么？"
"It is most likely some companion in misfortune"
"它很可能是某个不幸的同伴"
"he, like us, is waiting to be digested"
"他和我们一样，正在等待被消化"
"I will go and find him"
"我去找他"
"perhaps it is an old fish that knows his way around"
"也许是一条老鱼，知道自己的路"
"I hope it may be so, with all my heart, dear puppet"
"我全心全意地希望是这样，亲爱的木偶"
"Good-bye, Tunny Fish" - "Good-bye, puppet"
"Good-bye，Tunny Fish" - "再见，傀儡"
"and I wish a good fortune to you"
"祝你好运"
"Where shall we meet again?"
"我们在哪里再见面呢？"
"Who can see such things in the future?"
"以后谁能看到这样的东西？"
"It is better not even to think of it!"
"宁愿也不要想它！"

A Happy Surprise for Pinocchio
给匹诺曹的惊喜

Pinocchio said farewell to his friend the Tunny Fish
匹诺曹告别了他的朋友金枪鱼
and he began to grope his way through the Dog-Fish
他开始在狗鱼中摸索
he took small steps in the direction of the light
他朝着光的方向迈了一小步
the small light shining dimly at a great distance
微弱的光芒在很远的地方昏暗地照耀着
the farther he advanced the brighter became the light
他越往前走，光就越亮
and he walked and walked until at last he reached it
他走啊走，终于到了那儿
and when he reached the light, what did he find?
当他到达光明时，他发现了什么？
I will let you have a thousand and one guesses
我让你有一千零一个猜测
what he found was a little table all prepared
他找到的是一张准备好的小桌子
on the table was a lighted candle in a green bottle
桌上放着一根装在绿色瓶子里的点燃蜡烛
and seated at the table was a little old man
桌边坐着一个小老头
the little old man was eating some live fish
小老头正在吃一些活鱼
and the little live fish were very much alive
小活鱼还活着
some of the little fish even jumped out of his mouth
有的小鱼甚至从他的嘴里跳出来
at this sight Pinocchio was filled with happiness
看到这一景，匹诺曹充满了幸福
he became almost delirious with unexpected joy

他因出乎意料的喜悦而几乎神志不清
He wanted to laugh and cry at the same time
他想同时笑又想哭
he wanted to say a thousand things at once
他想同时说一千句话
but all he managed were a few confused words
但他所做的只是几句令人困惑的话
At last he succeeded in uttering a cry of joy
最后，他成功地发出了一声喜悦的叫声
and he threw his arm around the little old man
他用胳膊搂住了那个小老头
"Oh, my dear papa!" he shouted with joy
"哦，我亲爱的爸爸！"
"I have found you at last!" cried Pinocchio
"我终于找到你了！"
"I will never never never never leave you again"
"我永远不会，永远不会，永远不会再离开你"
the little old man couldn't believe it either
小老头也不敢相信
"are my eyes telling the truth?" he said
"我的眼睛说的是实话吗？"
and he rubbed his eyes to make sure
他揉了揉眼睛，确定一下
"then you are really my dear Pinocchio?"
"那么你真的是我亲爱的匹诺曹吗？"
"Yes, yes, I am Pinocchio, I really am!"
"是的，是的，我是匹诺曹，我真的是！"
"And you have forgiven me, have you not?"
"你已经原谅了我，不是吗？"
"Oh, my dear papa, how good you are!"
"哦，我亲爱的爸爸，你真棒啊！"
"And to think how bad I've been to you"
"想想我对你有多糟糕"

"but if you only knew what I've gone through"
"但如果你知道我所经历的一切就好了"
"all the misfortunes I've had poured on me"
"我所经历的所有不幸都倾倒在我身上"
"and all the other things that have befallen me!"
"还有我所遭遇的所有其他事情！"
"oh think back to the day you sold your jacket"
"哦，回想一下你卖掉夹克的那一天"
"oh you must have been terribly cold"
"哦，你一定很冷"
"but you did it to buy me a spelling book"
"但你这样做是为了给我买一本拼写书"
"so that I could study like the other boys"
"这样我就可以像其他男孩一样学习了"
"but instead I escaped to see the puppet show"
"但我反而逃跑去看木偶戏"
"and the showman wanted to put me on the fire"
"表演者想把我放在火上"
"so that I could roast his mutton for him"
"这样我就可以为他烤羊肉了"
"but then the same showman gave me five gold pieces"
"但后来同一个表演者给了我五块金币"
"he wanted me to give you the gold"
"他要我把金子给你"
"but then I met the Fox and the Cat"
"但后来我遇到了狐狸和猫"
"and they took me to the inn of The Red Craw-Fish"
"他们带我去了红小龙虾的客栈。"
"and at the inn they ate like hungry wolves"
"他们在客栈里吃得像饿狼一样"
"and I left by myself in the middle of the night"
"我半夜独自离开了"
"and I encountered assassins who ran after me"

"我遇到了追赶我的刺客"
"and I ran away from the assassins"
"我就逃离了刺客"
"but the assassins followed me just as fast"
"但刺客们跟着我的速度一样快"
"and I ran away from them as fast as I could"
"我以最快的速度逃离了他们"
"but they always followed me however fast I ran"
"可是我跑得多快,他们总是跟着我。"
"and I kept running to get away from them"
"我一直在逃跑以摆脱他们"
"but eventually they caught me after all"
"但最终他们还是抓住了我"
"and they hung me to a branch of a Big Oak"
"他们把我吊在一棵大橡树的树枝上"
"but then there was the beautiful Child with blue hair"
"但后来有那个美丽的蓝头发的孩子"
"she sent a little carriage to fetch me"
"她派了一辆小马车来接我"
"and the doctors all had a good look at me"
"医生们都仔细地看着我"
"and they immediately made the same diagnosis"
"他们立即做出了同样的诊断"
"If he is not dead, it is a proof that he is still alive"
"如果他没有死,那就证明他还活着"
"and then by chance I told a lie"
"然后我偶然说了一个谎"
"and my nose began to grow and grow and grow"
"我的鼻子开始长大、长大、长大"
"and soon I could no longer get through the door"
"很快我就进不进门了"
"so I went again with the Fox and the Cat"
"所以我又带着狐狸和猫去了"

"and together we buried the four gold pieces"
"我们一起埋葬了这四块金币"
"because one piece of gold I had spent at the inn"
"因为我在客栈花了一块金子"
"and the Parrot began to laugh at me"
"鹦鹉就开始嘲笑我了"
"and there were not two thousand pieces of gold"
"金子还不到两千块"
"there were no pieces of gold at all anymore"
"根本没有金子了"
"so I went to the judge of the town to tell him"
"所以我去找镇上的法官告诉他。"
"he said I had been robbed, and put me in prison"
"他说我被抢了,把我关进了监狱。"
"while escaping I saw a beautiful bunch of grapes"
"逃跑时,我看到了一串漂亮的葡萄"
"but in the field I was caught in a trap"
"但在田野里,我被困在一个陷阱里"
"and the peasant had every right to catch me"
"农民完全有权抓住我"
"he put a dog-collar round my neck"
"他在我的脖子上套上了狗项圈"
"and he made me the guard dog of the poultry-yard"
"他让我成为家禽场的看门狗"
"but he acknowledged my innocence and let me go"
"但他承认我是无辜的,放我走了"
"and the Serpent with the smoking tail began to laugh"
"那条长着冒烟的尾巴的蛇开始大笑"
"but the Serpent laughed until he broke a blood-vessel"
"但蛇却笑了,直到他打破了一条血管"
"and so I returned to the house of the beautiful Child"
"于是我回到了美丽孩子的家里"

"but then the beautiful Child was dead"
"但后来那个美丽的孩子死了"
"and the Pigeon could see that I was crying"
"鸽子看得出我在哭。"
"and the Pigeon said, 'I have seen your father'"
"鸽子说：'我见过你爸爸。'
'he was building a little boat to search of you'
"他在造一艘小船来搜寻你"
"and I said to him, 'Oh! if I also had wings,'"
"我对他说，'哦！如果我也有翅膀就好了。"
"and he said to me, 'Do you want to see your father?'"
"他对我说，'你想见你爸爸吗？'"
"and I said, 'Without doubt I would like to see him!'"
"我说，'毫无疑问，我想见他！'"
"'but who will take me to him?' I asked"
"'可是，谁能带我去见他呢？'我问"
"and he said to me, 'I will take you,'"
"他对我说：'我带你去。'"
"and I said to him, 'How will you take me?'"
"我对他说：'你怎么带我去呢？'"
"and he said to me, 'Get on my back,'"
"他对我说，'趴在我背上。'"
"and so we flew through all that night"
"就这样，我们飞过了那一整夜"
"and then in the morning there were all the fishermen"
"然后早上所有的渔夫都在那里"
"and the fishermen were looking out to sea"
"渔民们望向大海"
"and one said to me, 'There is a poor man in a boat'"
"一个人对我说：'船上有个穷人'"
"he is on the point of being drowned"
"他快要被淹死了"
"and I recognized you at once, even at that distance

"because my heart told me that it was you"
"因为我的心告诉我,那是你"
"and I made signs so that you would return to land"
"我做了一些迹象,好让你回去。"
"I also recognized you," said Geppetto
"我也认得你了,"杰佩托说
"and I would willingly have returned to the shore"
"我愿意回到岸上去"
"but what was I to do so far out at sea?"
"可是,我在这么远的海上该怎么办呢?"
"The sea was tremendously angry that day"
"那天大海非常愤怒"
"and a great wave came over and upset my boat"
"一阵巨浪过来,把我的船搅乱了"
"Then I saw the horrible Dog-Fish"
"然后我看到了可怕的狗鱼"
"and the horrible Dog-Fish saw me too"
"可怕的狗鱼也看到了我"
"and so the horrible Dog-Fish came to me"
"于是,可怕的狗鱼来找我了。"
"and he put out his tongue and swallowed me"
"他就伸出舌头把我吞了下去"
"as if I had been a little apple tart"
"仿佛我是个小苹果馅饼"
"And how long have you been shut up here?"
"你在这里关了多久了?"
"that day must have been nearly two years ago"
"那一天肯定是将近两年前的事了"
"two years, my dear Pinocchio," he said
"两年,我亲爱的匹诺曹,"他说
"those two years seemed like two centuries!"
"那两年好像两个世纪!"

"And how have you managed to live?"
"那你是怎么活下来的？"
"And where did you get the candle?"
"那你从哪里弄来的蜡烛？"
"And from where are the matches for the candle?"
"蜡烛的火柴从哪里来的呢？"
"Stop, and I will tell you everything"
"停下来，我会告诉你一切"
"I was not the only one at sea that day"
"那天在海上的不只有一个人"
"the storm had also upset a merchant vessel"
"风暴还掀翻了一艘商船"
"the sailors of the vessel were all saved"
"船上的水手都得救了"
"but the cargo of the vessel sunk to the bottom"
"但船的货物沉到海底"
"the Dog-Fish had an excellent appetite that day"
"那天狗鱼的胃口非常好"
"after swallowing me he swallowed the vessel"
"吞下我之后，他就吞下了器皿"
"How did he swallow the entire vessel?"
"他是怎么吞下整个容器的？"
"He swallowed the whole boat in one mouthful"
"他一口吞下了整条船"
"the only thing that he spat out was the mast"
"他唯一吐出的就是桅杆"
"it had stuck between his teeth like a fish-bone"
"它像鱼骨头一样卡在他的牙齿之间"
"Fortunately for me, the vessel was fully laden"
"幸运的是，这艘船已经满载了"
"there were preserved meats in tins, biscuit"
"罐头里有腌制肉，饼干"
"and there were bottles of wine and dried raisins"

"还有几瓶酒和葡萄干"
"and I had cheese and coffee and sugar"
"我吃了奶酪、咖啡和糖"
"and with the candles were boxes of matches"
"蜡烛旁边是几盒火柴"
"With this I have been able to live for two years"
"有了这个,我就能活两年了"
"But I have arrived at the end of my resources"
"但我已经到了我资源的尽头"
"there is nothing left in the larder"
"食品储藏室里什么都没有"
"and this candle is the last that remains"
"而这根蜡烛是剩下的最后一根蜡烛"
"And after that what will we do?"
"那之后我们该怎么办?"
"oh my dear boy, Pinocchio," he cried
"哦,我亲爱的孩子,匹诺曹,"他喊道
"After that we shall both remain in the dark"
"在那之后,我们俩都要蒙在鼓里"
"Then, dear little papa there is no time to lose"
"那么,亲爱的小爸爸,没有时间可以浪费了。"
"We must think of a way of escaping"
"我们必须想办法逃脱"
"what way of escaping can we think of?"
"我们能想到什么逃生的方法?"
"We must escape through the mouth of the Dog-Fish"
"我们必须从狗鱼的嘴里逃走"
"we must throw ourselves into the sea and swim away"
"我们必须跳进海里游走"
"You talk well, my dear Pinocchio"
"你说得好,我亲爱的匹诺曹"
"but I don't know how to swim"
"但我不会游泳"

"What does that matter?" replied Pinocchio
"这有什么关系呢？"

"I am a good swimmer," he suggested
"我是个游泳好手，"他建议道

"you can get on my shoulders"
"你可以骑在我的肩膀上"

"and I will carry you safely to shore"
"我会把你安全地带到岸上。"

"All illusions, my boy!" replied Geppetto
"全是幻觉，我的孩子！"

and he shook his head with a melancholy smile
他摇摇头，露出忧郁的笑容

"my dear Pinocchio, you are scarcely a yard high"
"我亲爱的匹诺曹，你还不到一码高"

"how could you swim with me on your shoulders?"
"你怎么能把我扛在肩上游泳呢？"

"Try it and you will see!" replied Pinocchio
"试试看，你就会明白的！"

Without another word Pinocchio took the candle
匹诺曹二话不说，接过蜡烛

"Follow me, and don't be afraid"
"跟从我，不要害怕"

and they walked for some time through the Dog-Fish
他们在狗鱼中走了一会儿

they walked all the way through the stomach
他们一路穿过肚子

and they were where the Dog-Fish's throat began
他们是狗鱼的喉咙开始的地方

and here they thought they should better stop
他们认为他们最好停下来

and they thought about the best moment for escaping
他们想着逃跑的最佳时机

Now, I must tell you that the Dog-Fish was very old

现在，我必须告诉你，狗鱼已经很老了
and he suffered from asthma and heart palpitations
他患有哮喘和心悸
so he was obliged to sleep with his mouth open
所以他不得不张着嘴睡觉
and through his mouth they could see the starry sky
透过他的嘴，他们可以看到星空
and the sea was lit up by beautiful moonlight
大海被美丽的月光照亮
Pinocchio carefully and quietly turned to his father
匹诺曹小心翼翼地、悄悄地转向他的父亲
"This is the moment to escape," he whispered to him
"现在是逃跑的时刻，"他低声对他说
"the Dog-Fish is sleeping like a dormouse"
"狗鱼睡得像只睡鼠"
"the sea is calm, and it is as light as day"
"大海平静，像白昼一样轻盈"
"follow me, dear papa," he told him
"跟我来，亲爱的爸爸，"他对他说
"and in a short time we shall be in safety"
"我们很快就会安全了"
they climbed up the throat of the sea-monster
他们爬上了海怪的喉咙
and soon they reached his immense mouth
很快，它们就到了他巨大的嘴里
so they began to walk on tiptoe down his tongue
于是他们开始蹑手蹑脚地沿着他的舌头走
they were about to make the final leap
他们即将进行最后的飞跃
the puppet turned around to his father
傀儡转过身来看向他的父亲
"Get on my shoulders, dear Papa," he whispered
"坐在我的肩膀上，亲爱的爸爸，"他低声说
"and put your arms tightly around my neck"

"把你的手臂紧紧地搂在我的脖子上"
"I will take care of the rest," he promised
"剩下的我会处理的，"他承诺
soon Geppetto was firmly settled on his son's shoulders
很快，Geppetto 就牢牢地落在了儿子的肩膀上
Pinocchio took a moment to build up courage
匹诺曹花了一点时间鼓起勇气
and then he threw himself into the water
然后他跳进了水里
and began to swim away from the Dog-Fish
并开始游离狗鱼
The sea was as smooth as oil
海面像油一样光滑
the moon shone brilliantly in the sky
月亮在天空中绚丽灿烂
and the Dog-Fish was in deep sleep
狗鱼正在沉睡
even cannons wouldn't have awoken him
即使是大炮也不会唤醒他

Pinocchio at last Ceases to be a Puppet and Becomes a Boy
匹诺曹终于不再是木偶，变成了男孩

Pinocchio was swimming quickly towards the shore
匹诺曹迅速地向岸边游去
Geppetto had his legs on his son's shoulders
Geppetto 的双腿搭在儿子的肩膀上
but Pinocchio discovered his father was trembling
但匹诺曹发现他的父亲在颤抖
he was shivering from cold as if in a fever
他冻得浑身发抖，好像发烧了一样

but cold was not the only cause of his trembling
但寒冷并不是他战战兢兢的唯一原因
Pinocchio thought the cause of the trembling was fear
匹诺曹认为颤抖的原因是恐惧
and the Puppet tried to comfort his father
傀儡试图安慰他的父亲
"Courage, papa! See how well I can swim?"
"勇气,爸爸!看看我游泳多好吗?"
"In a few minutes we shall be safely on shore"
"几分钟后我们就可以安全地上岸了"
but his father had a higher vantage point
但他的父亲有更高的优势
"But where is this blessed shore?"
"可是这片受祝福的海岸在哪里呢?"
and he became even more frightened
他变得更加害怕
and he screwed up his eyes like a tailor
他像裁缝一样瞪大了眼睛
when they thread string through a needle
当他们将绳子穿过针时
"I have been looking in every direction"
"我一直在四面八方寻找"
"and I see nothing but the sky and the sea"
"我只看到天空和大海"
"But I see the shore as well," said the puppet
"但我也看到了岸边,"木偶说
"You must know that I am like a cat"
"你要知道,我就像一只猫"
"I see better by night than by day"
"我晚上比白天看得更清楚"
Poor Pinocchio was making a pretence
可怜的匹诺曹在装模作样
he was trying to show optimism
他试图表现出乐观

but in reality he was beginning to feel discouraged
但实际上,他开始感到灰心丧气

his strength was failing him rapidly
他的力量很快就耗尽了

and he was gasping and panting for breath
他喘着粗气

He could not swim much further anymore
他不能再游得更远了

and the shore was still far off
岸边还很远

He swam until he had no breath left
他一直游到没有呼吸

and then he turned his head to Geppetto
然后他把头转向 Geppetto

"Papa, help me, I am dying!" he said
"爸爸,救救我,我快死了!"

The father and son were on the point of drowning
父子俩濒临溺水

but they heard a voice like an out of tune guitar
但他们听到了一个声音,就像一把走调的吉他

"Who is it that is dying?" said the voice
"是谁在死去?"

"It is I, and my poor father!"
"是我,还有我可怜的爸爸!"

"I know that voice! You are Pinocchio!"
"我认识那个声音!你是匹诺曹!

"Precisely; and you?" asked Pinocchio
"正是;那你呢?

"I am the Tunny Fish," said his prison companion
"我是金枪鱼,"他的狱友说

"we met in the body of the Dog-Fish"
"我们在狗鱼的身体里相遇"

"And how did you manage to escape?"

"那你是怎么逃脱的？"
"I followed your example"
"我效仿了你的榜样"
"You showed me the road"
"你给我指了路"
"and I escaped after you"
"我追着你逃走了"
"Tunny Fish, you have arrived at the right moment!"
"金枪鱼，你来得正是时候！"
"I implore you to help us or we are dead"
"我恳求你帮助我们，否则我们就死定了"
"I will help you willingly with all my heart"
"我会全心全意地帮助你"
"You must, both of you, take hold of my tail"
"你们俩必须抓住我的尾巴"
"leave it to me to guide you
"交给我来指导你
"I will take you both on shore in four minutes"
"我会在四分钟内带你们俩上岸"
I don't need to tell you how happy they were
我不需要告诉你他们有多高兴
Geppetto and Pinocchio accepted the offer at once
Geppetto 和 Pinocchio 立即接受了这个提议
but grabbing the tail was not the most comfortable
但抓住尾巴并不是最舒服的
so they got on the Tunny Fish's back
所以他们上了金枪鱼的背

The Tunny Fish did indeed take only four minutes
金枪鱼确实只花了四分钟
Pinocchio was the first to jump onto the land
匹诺曹是第一个跳上陆地的人
that way he could help his father off the fish
这样他就可以帮助他的父亲摆脱困境
He then turned to his friend the Tunny Fish
然后他转向他的朋友金枪鱼
"My friend, you have saved my papa's life"
"我的朋友，你救了我爸爸的命"
Pinocchio's voice was full of deep emotions
匹诺曹的声音充满了深沉的情感

"I can find no words with which to thank you properly"
"我找不到合适的言语来感谢你"

"Permit me at least to give you a kiss"
"至少允许我给你一个吻"

"it is a sign of my eternal gratitude!"
"这是我永远感激的标志！"

The Tunny put his head out of the water
Tunny 把头探出水面

and Pinocchio knelt on the edge of the shore
匹诺曹跪在岸边

and he kissed him tenderly on the mouth
他温柔地吻了他的嘴

The Tunny Fish was not used to such warm affection
金枪鱼不习惯这种温暖的感情

he felt both very touched, but also ashamed
他既感到非常感动，又感到羞愧

because he had started crying like a small child
因为他开始像个小孩子一样哭泣

and he plunged back into the water and disappeared
他又跳回水里，消失了

By this time the day had dawned
此时天已经亮了

Geppetto had scarcely breath to stand
Geppetto 几乎喘不过气来

"Lean on my arm, dear papa, and let us go"
"靠在我的胳膊上，亲爱的爸爸，我们走吧"

"We will walk very slowly, like the ants"
"我们会像蚂蚁一样走得很慢"

"and when we are tired we can rest by the wayside"
"累了，我们可以在路边休息"

"And where shall we go?" asked Geppetto
"那我们该去哪里呢？"

"let us search for some house or cottage"
"让我们找个房子或小屋吧"
"there they will give us some charity"
"他们会在那里给我们一些慈善"
"perhaps we will receive a mouthful of bread"
"也许我们会得到满满一口的面包"
"and a little straw to serve as a bed"
"还有一根小稻草当床"

Pinocchio and his father hadn't walked very far
匹诺曹和他的父亲还没有走很远

they had seen two villainous-looking individuals
他们看到了两个长相恶毒的人

the Cat and the Fox were at the road begging
猫和狐狸在路上乞讨

but they were scarcely recognizable
但他们几乎无法辨认
the Cat had feigned blindness all her life
这只猫一生都在假装失明
and now she became blind in reality
现在她在现实中变成了盲目
and a similar fate must have met the Fox
而狐狸也一定遭遇了类似的命运
his fur had gotten old and mangy
他的皮毛又旧又乱
one of his sides was paralyzed
他的一侧瘫痪了
and he had not even his tail left
他连尾巴都没剩下
he had fallen in the most squalid of misery
他陷入了最肮脏的痛苦中
and one fine day he was obliged to sell his tail
在一个晴朗的日子里，他不得不卖掉他的尾巴
a travelling peddler bought his beautiful tail
一个旅行的小贩买了他漂亮的尾巴
and now his tail was used for chasing away flies
现在他的尾巴被用来赶苍蝇
"Oh, Pinocchio!" cried the Fox
"哦，匹诺曹！"
"give a little in charity to two poor, infirm people"
"向两个贫穷、体弱的人施舍"
"Infirm people," repeated the Cat
"体弱的人，"猫重复道
"Be gone, impostors!" answered the puppet
"，骗子们！"
"You fooled me once with your tricks"
"你用你的伎俩骗过我一次"
"but you will never catch me again"
"但你再也抓不到我了"

"this time you must believe us, Pinocchio"
"这次你一定要相信我们，匹诺曹"
"we are now poor and unfortunate indeed!"
"我们现在真是穷人和不幸！"
"If you are poor, you deserve it"
"如果你穷，你活该"
and Pinocchio asked them to recollect a proverb
匹诺曹让他们回忆一句谚语
"Stolen money never fructifies"
"赃款永不灭亡"
"Be gone, impostors!" he told them
"，骗子们！"
And Pinocchio and Geppetto went their way in peace
匹诺曹和杰佩托平静地走了
soon they had gone another hundred yards
很快他们又走了一百码
they saw a path going into a field
他们看到一条通往田野的小路
and in the field they saw a nice little hut
在田野里，他们看到了一个漂亮的小木屋
the hut was made from tiles and straw and bricks
小屋是用瓦片、稻草和砖头建造的
"That hut must be inhabited by someone"
"那间小屋一定有人住着"
"Let us go and knock at the door"
"我们去敲门"
so they went and knocked at the door
"于是他们去敲门
from in the hut came a little voice
小屋里传来一个小小的声音
"who is there?" asked the little voice
"谁在那儿？"
Pinocchio answered to the little voice

匹诺曹回答了那个小声音
"We are a poor father and son"
"我们是一对贫穷的父子"
"we are without bread and without a roof"
"我们没有食物,也没有屋顶"
the same little voice spoke again:
同样的小声音又开口了:
"Turn the key and the door will open"
"转动钥匙,门就会打开"
Pinocchio turned the key and the door opened
匹诺曹转动钥匙,门打开了
They went in and looked around
他们进去四处张望
they looked here, there, and everywhere
他们看这里、那里、到处看
but they could see no one in the hut
但他们在小屋里看不到任何人
Pinocchio was much surprised the hut was empty
匹诺曹对小屋空无一人感到非常惊讶
"Oh! where is the master of the house?"
"哦!房子的主人在哪里?"
"Here I am, up here!" said the little voice
"我在这里,在上面!"
The father and son looked up to the ceiling
父子俩抬头望向天花板
and on a beam they saw the talking little Cricket
在一根横梁上,他们看到了会说话的小蟋蟀
"Oh, my dear little Cricket!" said Pinocchio
"哦,我亲爱的小蟋蟀!"
and Pinocchio bowed politely to the little Cricket
匹诺曹礼貌地向小蟋蟀鞠了一躬
"Ah! now you call me your dear little Cricket"
"啊!现在你叫我你亲爱的小蟋蟀"
"But do you remember when we first met?"

"但你还记得我们第一次见面是什么时候吗？"
"you wanted me gone from your house"
"你想让我离开你家"
"and you threw the handle of a hammer at me"
"你把锤柄扔向我"
"You are right, little Cricket! Chase me away also!"
"你说得对，小蟋蟀！也把我赶走！"
"Throw the handle of a hammer at me"
"把锤柄扔向我"
"but please, have pity on my poor papa"
"但是，请可怜我可怜的爸爸"
"I will have pity on both father and son"
"我会怜悯父子俩"
"but I wish to remind you of my ill treatment"
"但我想提醒你我所遭受的虐待"
"the ill treatment I received from you"
"我从你那里受到的虐待"
"but there's a lesson I want you to learn"
"但有一个教训要你学"
"life in this world is not always easy"
"这个世界上的生活并不总是一帆风顺的"
"when possible, we must be courteous to everyone"
"在可能的情况下，我们必须对每个人都有礼貌"
"only so can we expect to receive courtesy"
"只有这样，我们才能期望得到礼遇"
"because we never know when we might be in need"
"因为我们永远不知道什么时候会有需要"
"You are right, little Cricket, you are right"
"你说得对，小蟋蟀，你说得对"
"and I will bear in mind the lesson you have taught me"
"我会记住你教给我的教训"
"But tell me how you managed to buy this beautiful

hut"
"但请告诉我你是怎么买下这个漂亮的小屋的"
"This hut was given to me yesterday"
"这个小屋是昨天给我的"
"the owner of the hut was a goat"
"小屋的主人是一只山羊"
"and she had wool of a beautiful blue colour"
"她有美丽的蓝色羊毛"
Pinocchio grew lively and curious at this news
匹诺曹听到这个消息变得活泼和好奇
"And where has the goat gone?" asked Pinocchio
"那只山羊去哪儿了？"
"I do not know where she has gone"
"我不知道她去哪儿了"
"And when will the goat come back?" asked Pinocchio
"那山羊什么时候回来呢？"
"oh she will never come back, I'm afraid"
"哦，她再也回不来了，恐怕"
"she went away yesterday in great grief"
"她昨天悲痛欲绝地走了"
"her bleating seemed to want to say something"
"她的咩咩声似乎想说些什么"
"Poor Pinocchio! I shall never see him again"
"可怜的匹诺曹！我再也见不到他了。
"by now the Dog-Fish must have devoured him!"
"现在，狗鱼肯定已经把他吃掉了！"
"Did the goat really say that?"
"山羊真的这么说吗？"
"Then it was she, the blue goat"
"然后就是她，那只蓝色的山羊"
"It was my dear little Fairy," exclaimed Pinocchio
"是我亲爱的小仙女，"匹诺曹惊呼道
and he cried and sobbed bitter tears

他哭泣着,流下了苦涩的泪水
When he had cried for some time he dried his eyes
他哭了一会儿,就把眼睛擦干了
and he prepared a comfortable bed of straw for Geppetto
他为 Geppetto 准备了一张舒适的稻草床
Then he asked the Cricket for more help
然后他向蟋蟀寻求更多帮助
"Tell me, little Cricket, please"
"告诉我,小蟋蟀,拜托了"
"where can I find a tumbler of milk"
"我在哪里可以找到一瓶牛奶"
"my poor papa has not eaten all day"
"我可怜的爸爸一整天都没吃东西"
"Three fields from here there lives a gardener"
"从这里到三块田地,住着一个园丁"
"the gardener is called Giangio"
"园丁叫吉吉奥"
"and in his garden he also has cows"
"他的园子里也有奶牛"
"he will let you have the milk you want"
"他会让你得到你想要的奶"
Pinocchio ran all the way to Giangio's house
匹诺曹一路跑到吉安吉奥家
and the gardener asked him:
园丁问他:
"How much milk do you want?"
"你想要多少牛奶?"
"I want a tumblerful," answered Pinocchio
"我想要一个不倒翁,"匹诺曹回答
"A tumbler of milk costs five cents"
"一杯牛奶要 5 美分"
"Begin by giving me the five cents"

"先给我五美分"

"I have not even one cent," replied Pinocchio
"我连一分钱都没有，"匹诺曹回答

and he was grieved from being so penniless
他因为身无分文而感到悲哀

"That is bad, puppet," answered the gardener
"那很糟糕，木偶，"园丁回答

"If you have not one cent, I have not a drop of milk"
"你若没有一分钱，我就没有一滴奶"

"I must have patience!" said Pinocchio
"我得有耐心！"

and he turned to go again
他转身又要走

"Wait a little," said Giangio
"等一下，"Giangio 说

"We can come to an arrangement together"
"我们可以一起达成协议"

"Will you undertake to turn the pumping machine?"
"你愿意转动抽水机吗？"

"What is the pumping machine?"
"抽水机是什么？"

"It is a kind of wooden screw"
"这是一种木螺丝"

"it serves to draw up the water from the cistern"
"它的作用是从蓄水池中抽水"

"and then it waters the vegetables"
"然后它给蔬菜浇水"

"I can try to turn the pumping machine"
"我可以试着转动抽水机"

"great, I need a hundred buckets of water"
"太好了，我需要一百桶水"

"and for the work you'll get a tumbler of milk"
"而且你得买一大杯牛奶"

"we have an agreement," confirmed Pinocchio
"我们有一个协议，"匹诺曹证实
Giangio then led Pinocchio to the kitchen garden
然后，Giangio 带着 Pinocchio 去了厨房花园
and he taught him how to turn the pumping machine
他还教他如何转动抽水机
Pinocchio immediately began to work
匹诺曹立即开始工作
but a hundred buckets of water was a lot of work
但一百桶水是一项艰巨的工作
the perspiration was pouring from his head
汗水从他的头上涌出
Never before had he undergone such fatigue
他以前从来没有经历过这样的疲劳
the gardener came to see Pinocchio's progress
园丁来看匹诺曹的进展
"my little donkey used to do this work"
"我的小驴子以前做这项工作"
"but the poor animal is dying"
"可是这只可怜的动物快要死了"
"Will you take me to see him?" said Pinocchio
"你能带我去见他吗？"
"sure, please come to see my little donkey"
"好的，请来看我的小驴子"
Pinocchio went into the stable
匹诺曹走进了马厩
and he saw a beautiful little donkey
他看到了一头漂亮的小驴
but the donkey was stretched out on the straw
但驴子却在稻草上伸展着
he was worn out from hunger and overwork
他因饥饿和过度劳累而筋疲力尽
Pinocchio was much troubled by what he saw
匹诺曹对他所看到的感到非常困扰

"I am sure I know this little donkey!"
"我确定我认识这头小驴！"
"His face is not new to me"
"他的面孔对我来说并不陌生"
and Pinocchio came closer to the little Donkey
匹诺曹走近了小驴
and he spoke to him in asinine language:
他用卑鄙的语言对他说：
"Who are you?" asked Pinocchio
"你是谁？"
the little donkey opened his dying eyes
小驴子张开了他垂死的眼睛
and he answered in broken words in the same language:
他用同样的语言用断断续续的词回答说：
"I... am... Candle-wick"
"我……烛芯"
And, having again closed his eyes, he died
然后，他再次闭上眼睛，死了
"Oh, poor Candle-wick!" said Pinocchio
"噢，可怜的烛芯！"
and he took a handful of straw
他拿了一把稻草
and he dried a tear rolling down his face
他擦干了一滴从脸上滚落的泪水
the gardener had seen Pinocchio cry
园丁看到匹诺曹哭泣
"Do you grieve for a dead donkey?"
"你为一头死驴而悲伤吗？"
"it was not even your donkey"
"那甚至不是你的驴子"
"imagine how I must feel"
"想象我必须有什么感受"

Pinocchio tried to explain his grief
匹诺曹试图解释他的悲伤
"I must tell you, he was my friend!"
"我必须告诉你,他是我的朋友!"
"Your friend?" wondered the gardener
"你的朋友?"
"yes, one of my school-fellows!"
"是的,我的一个同学!"
"How?" shouted Giangio, laughing loudly
"怎么?" Giangio 大声笑着喊道
"Did you have donkeys for school-fellows?"
"你有没有给同学们买的驴子?"
"I can imagine the wonderful school you went to!"
"我可以想象你去的学校有多棒!"
The puppet felt mortified at these words
"傀儡听到这些话感到羞愧
but Pinocchio did not answer the gardener
但匹诺曹没有回答园丁
he took his warm tumbler of milk
他拿起他那杯热乎乎的牛奶
and he returned back to the hut
他又回到了小屋里
for more than five months he got up at daybreak
五个多月以来,他在黎明时分起床
every morning he turned the pumping machine
每天早上他都会转动抽水机
and each day he earned a tumbler of milk
他每天赚一桶牛奶
the milk was of great benefit to his father
牛奶对他的父亲有很大的好处
because his father was in a bad state of health
因为他的父亲健康状况不佳
but Pinocchio was now satisfied with working
但匹诺曹现在对工作感到满意

during the daytime he still had time
白天他还有时间
so he learned to make baskets of rushes
所以他学会了制作篮子灯心草
and he sold the baskets in the market
他在市场上卖掉了篮子
and the money covered all their expenses
这笔钱支付了他们所有的开支
he also constructed an elegant little wheel-chair
他还制作了一把优雅的小轮椅
and he took his father out in the wheel-chair
他带着他爸爸坐在轮椅上
and his father got to breathe fresh air
他的父亲可以呼吸到新鲜空气
Pinocchio was a hard working boy
匹诺曹是一个勤奋的男孩
and he was ingenious at finding work
他在找工作方面很聪明
he not only succeeded in helping his father
他不仅成功地帮助了他的父亲
but he also managed to save five dollars
但他也设法存了5美元
One morning he said to his father:
一天早上，他对父亲说：
"I am going to the neighbouring market"
"我要去邻近的市场"
"I will buy myself a new jacket"
"我给自己买一件新夹克"
"and I will buy a cap and pair of shoes"
"我要买一顶帽子和一双鞋"
and Pinocchio was in jolly spirits
匹诺曹精神抖擞
"when I return you'll think I'm a gentleman"
"等我回来，你会觉得我是个绅士"

And he began to run merrily and happily along
他开始欢快快乐地奔跑着

All at once he heard himself called by name
突然,他听到有人叫他自己的名字

he turned around and what did he see?
他转过身来,看到了什么?

he saw a Snail crawling out from the hedge
他看到一只蜗牛从树篱里爬出来

"Do you not know me?" asked the Snail
"你不认识我吗?"

"I'm sure I know you," thought Pinocchio
"我确定我认识你,"匹诺曹想

"and yet I don't know from where I know you"
"可是我不知道我从哪里认识你"

"Do you not remember the Snail?"
"你不记得那只蜗牛吗?"

"the Snail who was a lady's-maid"
"那个当过女仆的蜗牛"

"a maid to the Fairy with blue hair"
"蓝发仙女的侍女"

"Do you not remember when you knocked on the door?"
"你不记得你什么时候敲门了吗?"

"and I came downstairs to let you in"
"我下楼让你进来"

"and you had your foot caught in the door"
"你的脚被门夹住了"

"I remember it all," shouted Pinocchio
"我都记得,"匹诺曹喊道

"Tell me quickly, my beautiful little Snail"
"快告诉我,我美丽的小蜗牛"

"where have you left my good Fairy?"
"你把我的好仙女放哪儿了?"

"What is she doing?"
"她在做什么？"
"Has she forgiven me?"
"她原谅我了吗？"
"Does she still remember me?"
"她还记得我吗？"
"Does she still wish me well?"
"她还祝我好吗？"
"Is she far from here?"
"她离这儿远吗？"
"Can I go and see her?"
"我可以去看看她吗？"
these were a lot of questions for a snail
对于蜗牛来说，这些都是很多问题
but she replied in her usual phlegmatic manner
但她以她一贯的冷漠态度回答
"My dear Pinocchio," said the snail
"我亲爱的匹诺曹，"蜗牛说
"the poor Fairy is lying in bed at the hospital!"
"可怜的仙子躺在医院的床上！"
"At the hospital?" cried Pinocchio
"在医院里？"
"It is only too true," confirmed the snail
"这太真实了，"蜗牛确认道
"she has been overtaken by a thousand misfortunes"
"她被一千个不幸所追上"
"she has fallen seriously ill"
"她病得很重"
"she has not even enough to buy herself a mouthful of bread"
"她甚至不够给自己买一口面包"
"Is it really so?" worried Pinocchio
"真的是这样吗？"匹诺曹担心道

"Oh, what sorrow you have given me!"
"噢,你给我带来了多么悲哀啊!"
"Oh, poor Fairy! Poor Fairy! Poor Fairy!"
"哦,可怜的仙女!可怜的仙女!可怜的仙女!
"If I had a million I would run and carry it to her"
"如果我有一百万,我会跑去把它带到她那里"
"but I have only five dollars"
"但我只有五美元"
"I was going to buy a new jacket"
"我本来打算买一件新夹克"
"Take my coins, beautiful Snail"
"拿走我的硬币,美丽的蜗牛"
"and carry the coins at once to my good Fairy"
"马上把硬币带到我的好仙女那里去"
"And your new jacket?" asked the snail
"那你的新夹克呢?"
"What matters my new jacket?"
"我的新夹克有什么关系?"
"I would sell even these rags to help her"
"我甚至愿意卖掉这些破布来帮助她"
"Go, Snail, and be quick"
"走吧,蜗牛,快点"
"return to this place, in two days"
"两天后回到这个地方"
"I hope I can then give you some more money"
"我希望我能给你更多的钱"
"Up to now I worked to help my papa"
"到目前为止,我一直在努力帮助爸爸"
"from today I will work five hours more"
"从今天开始,我将多工作5小时"
"so that I can also help my good mamma"
"这样我也能帮助我的好妈妈"
"Good-bye, Snail," he said

"再见了，蜗牛，"他说

"I shall expect you in two days"
"我两天后就等你了"

at this point the snail did something unusual
这时，蜗牛做了一件不寻常的事情

she didn't move at her usual pace
她没有按照平常的速度移动

she ran like a lizard across hot stones
她像蜥蜴一样在热石头上奔跑

That evening Pinocchio sat up till midnight
那天晚上，匹诺曹一直坐到午夜

and he made not eight baskets of rushes
他不做八筐灯心草

but be made sixteen baskets of rushes that night
但那天晚上被做了十六篮灯心草

Then he went to bed and fell asleep
然后他上床睡觉了

And whilst he slept he thought of the Fairy
他睡着的时候，想起了仙女

he saw the Fairy, smiling and beautiful
他看到了仙女，微笑着，美丽无比

and he dreamt she gave him a kiss
他梦见她给了他一个吻

"Well done, Pinocchio!" said the fairy
"干得好，匹诺曹！"

"I will forgive you for all that is past"
"我会原谅你过去的一切"

"To reward you for your good heart"
"报答你的好心"

"there are boys who minister tenderly to their parents"
"有些男孩温柔地服侍他们的父母"

"they assist them in their misery and infirmities"
"他们帮助他们度过痛苦和虚弱"

"such boys are deserving of great praise and affection"

"这样的男孩值得极大的赞美和爱戴"
"even if they cannot be cited as examples of obedience"
"即使他们不能被列为服从的榜样"
"even if their good behaviour is not always obvious"
"即使他们的良好行为并不总是显而易见的"
"Try and do better in the future and you will be happy"
"在未来尝试并做得更好,你会很快乐"
At this moment his dream ended
就在这时,他的梦想结束了
and Pinocchio opened his eyes and awoke
匹诺曹睁开眼睛醒了
you should have been there for what happened next
你应该在场,看看接下来发生的事情
Pinocchio discovered that he was no longer a wooden puppet
匹诺曹发现自己不再是木偶了
but he had become a real boy instead
但他反而变成了一个真正的男孩
a real boy just like all other boys
就像所有其他男孩一样,一个真正的男孩
Pinocchio glanced around the room
匹诺曹环顾了一下房间
but the straw walls of the hut had disappeared
但小屋的稻草墙已经消失了
now he was in a pretty little room
现在他在一个漂亮的小房间里
Pinocchio jumped out of bed
匹诺曹从床上跳了起来
in the wardrobe he found a new suit of clothes
他在衣柜里发现了一套新衣服
and there was a new cap and pair of boots
还有一顶新帽子和一双靴子
and his new clothes fitted him beautifully
他的新衣服很合身

he naturally put his hands in his pocket
他自然而然地把手插在口袋里
and he pulled out a little ivory purse
"说着，他掏出一个小小的象牙钱包
on on the purse were written these words:
钱包上写着这些话：
"From the Fairy with blue hair"
"来自蓝发仙女"
"I return the five dollars to my dear Pinocchio"
"我把这五美元还给我亲爱的匹诺曹"
"and I thank him for his good heart"
"我感谢他的好心"
He opened the purse to look inside
他打开钱包往里面看
but there were not five dollars in the purse
但钱包里没有五美元
instead there were fifty shining pieces of gold
相反，有五十块闪闪发光的金子
the coins had come fresh from the minting press
这些硬币是从造币厂新鲜出来的
he then went and looked at himself in the mirror
然后他去照镜子里的自己
and he thought he was someone else
他以为自己是别人
because he no longer saw his usual reflection
因为他再也看不到他平常的倒影了
he no longer saw a wooden puppet in the mirror
他再也看不到镜子里的木偶了
he was greeted instead by a different image
相反，迎接他的是一个不同的形象
the image of a bright, intelligent boy
一个聪明、聪明的男孩的形象
he had chestnut hair and blue eyes
他有一头栗色的头发和蓝色的眼睛

and he looked as happy as can be
他看起来非常高兴
as if it were the Easter holidays
仿佛这是复活节假期
Pinocchio felt quite bewildered by it all
匹诺曹对这一切感到相当困惑
he could not tell if he was really awake
他不知道自己是否真的醒着
maybe he was dreaming with his eyes open
也许他是睁着眼睛在做梦
"Where can my papa be?" he exclaimed suddenly
"我爸爸在哪儿?"
and he went into the next room
他走进了隔壁房间
there he found old Geppetto quite well
在那里,他很好地找到了老 Geppetto
he was lively, and in good humour
他很活泼,很幽默
just as he had been formerly
就像他以前一样
He had already resumed his trade of wood-carving
他已经恢复了他的木雕生意
and he was designing a beautiful picture frame
他正在设计一个漂亮的相框
there were leaves flowers and the heads of animals
有叶子、花朵和动物的头
"Satisfy my curiosity, dear papa," said Pinocchio
"满足我的好奇心吧,亲爱的爸爸,"匹诺曹说
and he threw his arms around his neck
他用双臂搂住他的脖子
and he covered him with kisses
他用吻盖住他
"how can this sudden change be accounted for?"
"怎么能解释这种突然的变化呢?"

"it comes from all your good doing," answered Geppetto
"这来自你所有的善行，"杰佩托回答
"how could it come from my good doing?"
"怎么会是我做的好事呢？"
"something happens when naughty boys turn over a new leaf"
"当顽皮的男孩翻开新的一页时，会发生一些事情"
"they bring contentment and happiness to their families"
"他们为家人带来满足和幸福"
"And where has the old wooden Pinocchio hidden himself?"
"那那个老木头匹诺曹藏在哪里了？"
"There he is," answered Geppetto
"他在那儿，"杰佩托回答
and he pointed to a big puppet leaning against a chair
"他指着一个靠在椅子上的大木偶
the Puppet had its head on one side
木偶的头在一边
its arms were dangling at its sides
它的手臂垂在身体两侧
and its legs were crossed and bent
它的腿交叉弯曲
it was really a miracle that it remained standing
它能屹立不倒真是一个奇迹
Pinocchio turned and looked at it
匹诺曹转过身来看了看
and he proclaimed with great complacency:
他非常得意地宣布：
"How ridiculous I was when I was a puppet!"
"当我还是个傀儡的时候，我是多么荒谬啊！"
"And how glad I am that I have become a well-behaved

little boy!"
"我多么高兴,我变成了一个乖巧的小男孩!"

www.ingramcontent.com/pod-product-compliance
Lightning Source LLC
Chambersburg PA
CBHW012000090526
44590CB00026B/3804